W9-BOF-906

3 1611 00104 1802

119986

119986

UB   Useem, Michael.
343   Conscription,
.U83   protest, and
            social conflict.

UNIVERSITY LIBRARY
Governors State University
Park Forest South, Il. 60466

CONSCRIPTION, PROTEST, AND SOCIAL CONFLICT

CONSCRIPTION, PROTEST, AND SOCIAL CONFLICT
The Life and Death of a
Draft Resistance Movement

MICHAEL USEEM

A WILEY-INTERSCIENCE PUBLICATION

JOHN WILEY & SONS,
New York · London · Sydney · Toronto

University Library
GOVERNORS STATE UNIVERSITY

Copyright © 1973, by John Wiley & Sons, Inc.

All rights reserved. Published simultaneously in Canada.

No part of this book may be reproduced by any means, nor transmitted, nor translated into a machine language without the written permission of the publisher.

Library of Congress Cataloging in Publication Data:
Useem, Michael.
   Conscription, protest, and social conflict.

   "A Wiley-Interscience publication."
   Includes bibliographical references.
   1. Military service, Compulsory—United States.
2. Government, Resistance to.   I. Title.

UB343.U83   322.4'4'0973   73-9689
ISBN 0-471-89645-4

Printed in the United States of America

10 9 8 7 6 5 4 3 2 1

UB
343
.U83

FOREWORD

The most remarkable of human enterprises is war. The authorities mobilize a large proportion of their able-bodied male subjects of the age of greatest sexual potency and physical activity as full participants in the core activity of war: finding and destroying the like forces mobilized by an opposing enterprise. The whole population of the country of the war maker is expected to participate in the enterprise. The modern war is the prototypical total institution; it demands full commitment of all people, institutions, and resources of the war-making country.

It has been customary for governments that recognize one another as legitimate and honorable to go through certain ceremonies in undertaking war against each other, to observe certain rules in the conduct of the struggle, and to mark return to peace by the signing of solemn pledges. These rules do not apply to warlike activity against social bodies not considered to have equal and honorable standing. By such nonwars empires are built; if the honorable and legitimate member of the family of nations wins the nonwar, the losing body becomes a colony. If the honorable and legitimate entity loses or does not clearly win, a new member may have been added to the club of honorable nations, capable of giving satisfaction.

Although it may appear that a war-making authority has achieved total participation of its people, institutions, and resources, it is doubtful whether it has ever done so. It may have mobilized such a large number of volunteers that the populace seems to be in full accord with the enterprise. Farmers, workmen, clerks, and students become patriotic heroes, urged on by mothers, sweethearts, fathers, colleagues, priests, actors, and even clowns.

Is participation ever total and are the volunteers as fired by the appropriate sentiments as we would like to believe?

Certainly many devices have been used to get volunteers into the King's Navy. Local authorities have been required to supply a levy to the military. Armed service, in peace or war, has been compulsory in many countries. The United States has compelled men by law to join the armed services a number of times.

Men have resisted participation by various means. Some have bought their way out, letting the military service be done by poorer men. Peasants are said to have cut off the trigger finger (what finger would it be now?). So high was the suspicion of malingering in the Austrian army of World War I that the Brave Soldier Schwejk was told that a friend of his (a Czech, of course) had died simulating tuberculosis. If Woman's Liberation has its way, pregnancy may become one more way of avoiding heroism.

Many men have run away from military service. Some of our finest citizens are descended from the draft evaders of Europe in the days when we did not believe in compulsory military service and rather favored as immigrants people who had defied the foreign potentates, allegiance to whom they had to renounce on becoming American citizens. The tables are now turned; we produce refugees instead of taking them in. In World War I many French Canadians, loyal to neither Britain nor France, ran off to camps in the immense north woods; now, young Americans have run off to an uncertain fate in Canadian cities to escape being drafted in the prolonged nonwar. (It became a war that our President proposed to continue until it could be terminated with honor.)

Useem's book is not the story of individual escape from the great total enterprise but of a collective movement to put a wrench in the gears of the mobilizing mechanism. That movement, like other collective resistances, was dramatic. The day-by-day mobilization of humans to work and play is not dramatic; the periodic mobilizing to taxes, festivals, and wars is more so. Collective refraining from expected participation is highly dramatic. It requires communication to a sensitive audience of potential nonparticipants who become actors in a public drama: strikers, before striking was as institutionalized as the military draft; heretics in the day before "denominations" had become respectable and patriotic; these and many others at various points in history have collectively and dramatically refrained from the expected proper conduct. They have often been hanged or burnt for their resistance.

The collective resisters, or refrainers, are never a random sample. Random samples are an artifact, very difficult to manufacture. Society is a system of skews. Even-handed laws strike unevenly the great variety of estates in a society. Statistics of misery and of the burden that human enterprises put on the various estates and conditions of men have proved poor indicators of who will join collective resistance. Perhaps social scientists will discover indicators from which those who make war can predict who will join up gladly and who will resist. Then there will be the further question of the value of the various estates of man to ongoing society, in war and in peace, and of the costs of the steps taken to mobilize a population totally for various kinds of wars and nonwars, of longer or shorter duration. It is already well known that sometimes a won war destroys the winner.

Useem has given us a good account of one movement to resist the draft, a device of the modern war maker. The dimensions of the problem of collective resistance are well laid out. Let others build on it.

EVERETT C. HUGHES

Boston College
Chestnut Hill, Massachusetts

PREFACE

This is an analysis of an American radical protest movement. The movement initially believed that it had discovered the most vulnerable part of the Vietnam war machine—the conscription of young men who were reluctant to serve. An intoxicating sense of unity in shared purpose and an intense preoccupation with ending the killing in Indochina seemed to characterize its membership. The movement organization called itself the Resistance, and it aimed at crippling military activity by putting prospective conscripts on permanent strike. Members declared that their services were no longer at the disposal of the armed forces. The origins, rise, and abrupt collapse of the Resistance suggest much about the nature of protest politics in the United States.

Sociologists are increasingly turning the methods and theories of their discipline to critical descriptions and interpretations of American society. However, although much of the analysis has dealt with the social class structure, the role of the state, and major social problems, relatively little attention has been directed at the political response of people to inequality, alienation, exploitation, and discrimination. What circumstances are conducive to the translation of private ills into public issues and organized political expression that can challenge the existing order? What organizational forms and political ideologies are likely to appear? How will dominant institutions react to challenges to their hegemony? And what lasting effect can political protest have on American life? I chose to focus on the Resistance as a case in point. It provided an opportunity to explore the social processes that give rise to a protest movement in the American context, the movement's consolidation as a protest organization, and its eventual demise.

Nearly all members of the Resistance had made some overt violation of Selective Service regulations, and the movement was engaged in a program of dubious legality. Any group is cautious about exposing itself to probing outsiders, but the special circumstances of the Resistance greatly heightened the level of suspicion that I, for example, encountered. I was not a draft resister. Several acquaintances had joined the movement, and I had participated in a minor way in a few Resistance actions and had been marginally involved in campus protest activities. But I was clearly an outsider for the Resistance. Some of those approached for interviews initially labeled me as a federal agent masquerading as a disinterested social researcher; others were hostile to me as a representative of the politically and philosophically questionable enterprise of social science (many were acquainted with Herbert Marcuse's critique of modern social science in *One-Dimensional Man*). Yet despite their ambivalence, most resisters gave willingly of their time. I am grateful to them for so openly sharing the experience of their revolt against conscription and the American involvement in Vietnam.

Initial encouragement for this research came from Harrison White, and his guidance throughout the early stages proved to be invaluable. In numerous ways Steven Cavrak helped sharpen the details of the field investigation. I was also fortunate to have had lengthy discussions on the inner life of the Resistance with Michael Ferber, Paul Garver, and Richard Mumma. Myron Glazer, John Helmer, Paul Murray, Clarence Normand, Mary Petersen, Richard Wilsnack, and Zick Rubin contributed useful comments on various portions of the manuscript. Many helpful suggestions and much encouragement came from Eric Valentine and Charles Tilly. A major section of the manuscript benefited from the editorial talents of Peter Cowen. My understanding of the Resistance was greatly enhanced by Barrie Thorne's critical reactions to several versions of the study, as well as numerous discussions throughout the research. I am indebted to Gary Marx for much assistance during the early stages in the field and the late stages of analysis. Appreciation for typing portions of the manuscript goes to Grace Curry, Virginia Goodrich, Emily McCarthy, and Lynn Pease. Naturally those who have offered their assistance bear no responsibility for any shortcomings that remain. A number of small grants from Harvard University supported this research.

MICHAEL USEEM

Harvard University
Cambridge, Massachusetts
May 1973

ACKNOWLEDGMENTS

Permission to reprint the following material is gratefully acknowledged:

Quotation, pp. 10–11: from John Rae, *Conscience and Politics*, Oxford University Press, London, 1970, pp. 83–84.

Quotation, pp. 48–49: from Inge Powell Bell, *CORE and the Strategy of Nonviolence*, Random House, Inc., New York, 1968, pp. 126–127.

Quotation, pp. 83–84: from Patrick Owens, "Who They Were: A Special Report on LI's 428 War Dead," *Newsday*, August 2, 1969, p. 5R. Copyright 1969, Newsday Inc. Reprinted by permission.

Table 3.1: data from Albert D. Klassen, Jr., *Military Service in American Life Since World War II: An Overview*, National Opinion Research Center, University of Chicago, 1966, Tables A-VI.1a and VI.5a.

Table 3.2: data from Walter Y. Oi, "The Economic Cost of the Draft," *American Economic Review*, 57 (May 1967), Table 9. By permission of the American Economic Association.

Table 3.2: data from figure on p. 311 of *Indicators of Trends in the Status of American Women*, by Abbott L. Ferriss, © 1971 by Russell Sage Foundation, New York.

Table 3.7: data from *The Harris Survey Yearbook of Public Opinion, 1970. A Compendium of Current American Attitudes*, Louis Harris and Associates, Inc., 1971, pp. 305, 306.

Footnote, p. 139: from Albert J. Mayer and Thomas Ford Hoult, "Social Stratification and Combat Survival," *Social Forces*, 34 (December 1955), p. 157. By permission of the University of North Carolina Press.

Footnote, p. 141: data from 1968 National Election Survey, Center for Political Studies, University of Michigan, Ann Arbor, Mich., 1972. By permission of Andre Modigliani and the University of Michigan, Center for Political Studies.

Quotation, pp. 171–172: from Barrie Thorne, "Resisting the Draft: An Ethnography of the Draft Resistance Movement," Ph.D. dissertation, Brandeis University, 1971, p. 96.

CONTENTS

TABLES

FIGURES

ONE

Capitalists of America, we will fight against you, not for you!

Newspaper of the Industrial Workers of the World, 1917.

The attempt to overthrow conscription by [resistance] . . . will quickly repeat itself in other countries. I believe this because a challenge of such a kind originates in that attitude to the State and in those ideas of social change which are likely to prompt all progressive movements during the next hundred years.

Chairman of the British No-Conscription Fellowship, 1922.

THE RESISTANCE AS
A PROTEST MOVEMENT

In the early fall of 1967 a handful of committed activists in the Boston area circulated a leaflet announcing a rally for October 16 and declaring that on "that day a few thousand young men across the country will make a complete break with the draft system. . . . From that day on, they will work to disrupt the operation of the Selective Service and the armed forces until the United States withdraws from Vietnam." It concluded: "The Resistance begins on October 16. It will not stop until the war is over." The Boston rally attracted more than 200 young men who were willing to risk five years in prison by burning or turning in their draft credentials. Simultaneous demonstrations were held in New York City, Washington, D.C., Philadelphia, Minneapolis, San Francisco, Los Angeles, Chicago, and dozens of other cities across the country. In all, a thousand draft cards were accumulated for return to the Justice Department, and uncounted hundreds went up in flames.

This event launched a movement that ultimately drew 4000 draft-age men into open revolt against a system that had helped to provide troops for four American wars. But it was more than just a group rejection of the draft. It was also an organized political protest, having a self-justifying ideology, a collective sense of purpose, and a program for action against the government. The movement's aim was to cripple military conscription for the Vietnam War, and its primary tactic was public renunciation of the draft system. Potential draftees were encouraged to avoid registration and induction and to publicly return or destroy the draft cards they were legally bound to carry.

The movement's life was extraordinarily short. Following the October 1967 demonstration, similar events were orchestrated every few months across the country, through the spring of 1968, when the movement began to falter. By the end of that year, draft card collections had ceased altogether in many areas, and a number of Resistance offices had closed. At the same time, however, individuals were refusing induction at a steadily increasing rate, and later events connected with the Vietnam conflict—such as the 1970 invasion of Cambodia by U.S. troops—brought sporadic outbreaks of collective attacks on the draft.

Public occasions for declaring resistance to conscription naturally were the most visible part of the movement, but local organizations used a variety of activities to increase membership and to undermine the war. Their tactics included demonstrations, draft counseling, sanctuaries for deserters and AWOL soldiers, direct action against induction centers and draft boards, establishment of antidraft unions, and educational forums. The movement exhibited little national coordination, except for the designation of the nationwide days for resistance action. Decentralization was always the chief operating principle.

Draft resisters (those who, in conjunction with the movement, took an overt illegal step of noncooperation with the draft) developed intense bonds of mutual solidarity, particularly in the months immediately following the demonstrations of October 1967. For a year they shared social events, internal education projects, communal living, and newsletters, which helped sustain an atmosphere of community approaching blood brotherhood.

The membership was varied in some respects. White, middle-class college students or ex-students comprised the bulk of the draft resistance movement, although there were a certain number of minority and working-class participants. Some had no previous political experience, whereas others came from the civil rights movement, Students for a Democratic Society, and pacifist organizations. Besides those who actually had renounced the draft, Resistance activities enlisted large numbers of people who could not or had not resisted. Women and over-age men even assumed some leadership positions.

In the political context of 1967–1968, the Resistance was not an extraordinary event. Inner-city disorders left 23 dead in Newark and 43 in Detroit in July 1967. Half a million American troops were in Vietnam, U.S. battle deaths were running well in excess of 200 per week, and with the abolition of graduate deferments, the induction of college students appeared to be imminent. In February 1968 the Tet offensive traumatized American domestic politics. There was further shock only months later, when Martin Luther King, Jr., and Robert Kennedy were assassinated. At the same time, two out of every five colleges reported student protest against the Indochina conflict during the 1967–1968 academic year. Student building takeovers in April 1968 ended the academic term at Columbia and offered a preview of the coming year for dozens of other universities.

Although its presence was not exceptional—the time was clearly ripe for protest of this nature—the Resistance did introduce a novel protest strategy: it aimed to instigate a wholesale exodus of eligible youth from the draft pool, thereby stopping the war by depriving the military of its troop supply. A vanguard dramatically launched the campaign by taking such action itself, in the hope that its resistance would snowball, inundating the courts and jails and emptying the manpower reserves.

ANTICONSCRIPTION MOVEMENTS

Hundreds of political movements have fought against compulsory military service (1). One survey of agitation against conscription in Australia during a two-year period (1964–1966) counted more than a dozen organizations centrally concerned with abolition of the draft (Guyatt, 1968). Some movements have fixed on the draft as a means of attacking a disliked war; others have protested against conscription itself. Indeed, anticonscription protest has been a recurrent phenomenon in many societies. The use of direct resistance, however, has been rare. The cost of open confrontation with state authority is an obvious factor inhibiting the formation of draft-resisting groups. Nevertheless, the Resistance is not the only representative of an anticonscription movement formed for the purpose of generating a strike of prospective draftees. Such movements have appeared in the twentieth century in Australia, France, and Great Britain. The Australian Draft Resisters' Union was organized in 1970 to oppose the Vietnam war, the Jeune Résistance (Young Resistance) was formed in France in 1959 in response to the Algerian conflict, and the British No-Conscription Fellowship was initiated in 1914 after England's entry into World War I.

The Australian government announced the reintroduction of compulsory service in 1964, and shortly thereafter ground troops were dispatched to Vietnam. By early 1966 conscripts were added to the front lines of the undeclared war, and within a year they constituted a quarter of the war zone troops. Because draftees tended to receive infantry assignments, their casualty rate was substantially above that of volunteers, at least in the early years of the conflict (Forward, 1968, 126).

There is a long tradition of opposition to conscription in Australia, and proposals to conscript men for fighting abroad in World War I were twice defeated in public referenda (Jauncey, 1935; Inglis, 1968; Robson, 1970). Antagonism toward wartime draft reappeared during the Vietnam period as the war became a divisive domestic issue. A number of organizations launched campaigns against the draft, and although Gallup polls revealed little change of opinion until 1967, subsequent public backing of conscription and the stationing of troops in Vietnam steadily declined (2). Student protest against the war was vigorous, and Australia's lottery-based selective induction policies did not offer special protection to students.

In 1967 the induction system began to lose some of its authority over potential draftees. There were incidents of draft card burning (reportedly inspired in part by similar events in the United States) and isolated public declarations of noncooperation; many deliberately failed to register. One count of individuals openly pledged to resist the draft put the total at less than 10 in 1967 but more than 300 by 1971 (Muntz, 1971). Government statistics show that by the end of 1970 nonregistrants numbered more than 10,000 (3).

It was not until 1970, however, that a new movement formed in Australia for the explicit purpose of inspiring collective defiance of the draft. Several dozen resisters founded the Draft Resisters' Union (DRU) in mid-1970, and within several months its membership had expanded to more than 200. DRU had its roots primarily in the student movement, and its activities included street demonstrations, creation of an underground for resisters choosing to avoid prison, and actions protesting the treatment in the courts and in jail of those who were prosecuted for noncooperation. However, the overarching objective was to instigate massive defection among those eligible for the draft. A DRU advocate argued:

> Non-compliers believe conscription can be smashed by building a movement of non-compliers so large that it will make conscription unworkable. . . . Even a small number can provide the catalyst for a massive movement against conscription. That is what is happening in Australia today. . . . If you are opposed to conscription . . . and Australian actions in the Indo-China war, then the most effective way to express your opposition is through non-compliance with the national service act (Muntz, 1971, 8–9).

Snowballing was the tool for transforming a small but committed group of resisters into the mass movement necessary for undermining conscription (see Hamel-Green, 1971; Johnston, 1971).

Similar developments marked the emergence of the Young Resistance group in France during the Algerian crisis. The armed revolt against French rule in Algeria erupted there in the mid-1950s and was not settled until 1962, when Algeria won its independence. French troop strength in Algeria reached half a million men. Troop call-ups for the war were accompanied by several spontaneous though abortive revolts, and desertion increased apace with domestic controversy and the growing bitterness of the war. When de Gaulle came to power in 1958, about

1000 deserters and noncooperators were already in jail and 2000 more were in exile.

In early 1959 a handful of war resisters representing a broad range of political backgrounds (including pacifist, Catholic radical, trade unionist, and communist) met outside France to found a new vehicle for protest against the Algerian conflict. The members of the new movement, the Young Resistance, were resisters who would give organizational coherence and political expression to the growing tendency among the country's youth to avoid military obligations. The Young Resistance believed that expansion of its numbers could seriously hamper French colonial rule of Algeria. Harsh suppression of domestic dissent during the Algerian period forced much of the movement's work underground, however, and the total number of resisters never reached threatening proportions (it did not exceed four figures). The movement provoked an intense public debate over the war issues, and the controversy was further exacerbated in 1960, when a group of 121 prominent French intellectuals issued a statement endorsing politically motivated draft resistance (Levine, 1962; Verlet, 1967). This type of catalytic action seems to have constituted the movement's main impact.

The most extensively organized of the several movements was the No-Conscription Fellowship, which came into existence shortly after Britain entered the Great War. During the war's early months, voluntary enlistments exceeded the country's manpower needs (4). More than 2.6 million men offered their services between August 1914 and the introduction of conscription in June 1916. However, the stalemating of the war in mid-1915 increased the need for troops at the same time that enlistment rates were falling because of growing disillusionment with the war. In August 1915, Parliament required that men between 15 and 65 comply with a national registration, and an "attest-ment" system was introduced in the fall. Men between 18 and 41 were individually canvassed and invited to pledge their availability if needed. Although this measure identi-fied more than a million men who said they were willing to enter the service, it was less successful than expected. In early 1916 Parliament broke with two centuries of tradi-tion and adopted a compulsory service law, the Military Service Act. Single men between 18 and 41 were liable for induction, and several months later the act was amended to include married men.

Fearing military conscription would lead to industrial conscription, most labor organizations vigorously fought each of the steps taken by the government to introduce compulsory service. On the eve of the passage of the 1916 act, resolutions opposing it were ratified by large margins in the Trade Union Congress (representing 3 million workers), the Miners' Federation, the National Union of Railwaymen, and other associations. A Labour party con-ference passed an antidraft resolution by a vote of more than 4 to 1. However, most of the labor movement did not carry its opposition to the point of advocating resistance, and labor generally offered lukewarm support for the war.

One exception was the Independent Labour party (ILP), a Labour party affiliate which had an estimated 30,000 members in 1914. The ILP's stance against conscription stiffened when the war began, and in mid-1915 the Na-tional Administrative Council of the ILP promised sup-port to any members planning to resist. By November the Council was calling for a full assault on conscription, and Council members pledged their own noncooperation:

> [T]he motive behind the movement to impose such compulsory service can only be for the purpose of ob-taining a powerful reactionary weapon which would continually menace the future industrial and political

> developments of democratic institutions. . . . The
> [Council], therefore, calls upon members of the Party
> to resist to the utmost every attempt to impose Con-
> scription. If, in spite of our efforts, the system is im-
> posed, the members of the [Council] pledge them-
> selves to resist its operations, and, while recognizing
> the right of every individual member to act as his or
> her conscience dictates, the [Council] will do all in
> their power to defend those members who individually
> refuse to submit to such compulsion (quoted in Rae,
> 1970, 83–84).

Through 1915 and early 1916 the ILP energetically
pressed its campaign against the draft through means ranging from public rallies to pamphleteering and lobbying
within the Labour party. The ILP did not adopt noncooperation as a regular strategy and did not impose a requirement of resistance on its membership. However, it did create an atmosphere that helped legitimate direct action
against the manpower levy.

The No-Conscription Fellowship (NCF) drew its initial
leadership and the bulk of its membership from young socialists in the ranks of the ILP. The proposal for the NCF
was first broached in the ILP's official newspaper by
A. Fenner Brockway, its editor. Brockway had been active
in efforts against the war, and in late 1914, desiring a more
effective means of opposition, he published a note calling
for an association of men who anticipated noncooperation
if conscription began. "The response was so immediate,
and the earnestness of the writers so moving, that it at once
became clear that there was a need for a Fellowship in
which the prospective resisters might unite" (Brockway,
1919, 22). Within three months a list of nearly 350 members was published, and a London office was opened. By
early fall of 1915 approximately 5000 members were enrolled in 50 local branches. A national convention was held
in November, and a second national convention the

following April brought together 1500 delegates representing nearly 200 branches and more than 10,000 members. The NCF did not expand beyond this scale. In late 1919, following the conclusion of the war and release of its members from prison, the NCF held a final convention and disbanded (5).

NCF records indicate that nearly 1500 members spent time in prison for violation of the Military Service Act. When called up the NCF member was generally denied classification as a conscientious objector by a civilian review board (some members refused even to apply), and at that point he technically became a serviceman. If he refused to appear for military service, a civil court would direct that he be turned over to the military authorities as a deserter or absentee. Once in military hands the objector then committed some type of disobedience such as refusing a medical examination or declining to don a uniform. A military court-martial followed and the convicted objector was normally assigned to a civilian prison, although a majority spent much of their term in special civilian work camps (several dozen objectors were sentenced to death but these sentences were commuted to lengthy terms). Within a year of the war's end all resisters were released through a series of government decrees. A number of NCF leaders were also fined or sentenced for the distribution of antiwar or anticonscription literature in violation of an act prohibiting such activities during the war.

The No-Conscription Fellowship was initially open to all "men of enlistment age who have decided to refuse to take up arms." However, within several months the NCF established an associate membership category for those who were interested in working with the movement even though they were beyond the state's call. When government conscription and suppression of the movement later sent a number of the original NCF leaders to prison, this auxiliary assumed much of the responsibility for running the organization (in 1917 Bertrand Russell became temporary national chairman; later he also served a sentence for activities on behalf of the NCF).

The primary grounds for NCF membership remained a pledge to resist conscription when called, and there was no additional screening of political beliefs. This policy resulted in a highly diverse membership, as noted by the NCF's chairman:

> Some [NCF members] were followers of Tolstoy, but the greater number were Socialists who believed in the Brotherhood of Man as genuinely as the Christians believed in the Fatherhood of God. Others, who have sometimes been called political objectors, resisted Conscription not so much because they were convinced that all war was morally wrong, or because they believed in any supernatural religious creed; they resisted Conscription because it seemed to them a fatal infringement of human liberty; because they feared that industrial freedom would be menaced by military compulsion; because they believed that the Foreign Policy of this country made Britain worthy of at least some measure of blame for the war; or because they believed that the war had been engineered on both sides by groups of men representing a Capitalist System of Society, against which system they protested (Allen, 1919, 9–10).

The main division was between the religious objectors, primarily Quakers, and the political resisters, predominantly ILP followers. Approximately three-quarters of the members could be identified as socialists of widely divergent persuasions. For example, the NCF assembled information on the "grounds of objection" of nearly 1500 imprisoned resisters for whom it had records. One-fifth were associated with the Society of Friends. The remaining four-fifths represented five socialist parties (Independent

Labour party, British Socialist party, Socialist Labour party, Socialist Party of Great Britain, and Industrial Workers of the World) and included a number of unattached socialists and a few anarchists. Two-thirds of the political resisters were affiliated with the ILP (No-Conscription Fellowship, 1919, 37–38).

Prior to the passage of the Military Service Act in 1916, the only resistance option open was promising to refuse arms—the NCF pledge. In late 1915, when it appeared that the conscription measure would soon be passed, the NCF instructed its members to make their decision to resist more widely known. Individual members and local NCF branches were to publicize their pledges through letters to the local press and their representative in Parliament.

After the draft went into operation, new strategies became available to the NCF. One was to generate induction refusal that was sufficiently widespread to materially impair the conscription system. Another was to stir public opposition to conscription by publicizing the resistance of its members and their subsequent mistreatment in prison. These are not mutually exclusive alternatives, but the NCF stressed the latter course, whereas the American Resistance, some 50 years later, emphasized the former. The NCF, for example, was aware that the size of its membership affected its influence on public opinion; but size was not linked to threatening troop procurement. At one point the NCF even temporarily suspended its policy of open membership. Fearing adverse publicity if "slackers" flocked to the movement after conscription was started, it accepted no new members for a period beginning early in 1916. The public image of the movement was deemed more important than its expansion.

The war's immediacy obscured underlying political tensions in the NCF through 1918. Bitter disputes were not absent, but they were mainly tactical—some felt the movement should concentrate on support for imprisoned resisters and some favored broader antiwar programs; there was disagreement over whether members should be encouraged to be total noncooperators. However, the signing of the armistice and cessation of the draft forced more fundamental issues into the open, since the movement's original purpose was no longer meaningful. Although NCF members underwent personal changes during their affiliation with the movement, much of the original political diversity remained, and this paralyzed attempts to reorient the purpose of the group at war's end.

In 1919 the NCF debated a variety of plans to redirect its energies. The original organizer suggested continuation as "a great missionary body inside the Socialist and Christian movement." Other proposals included a focus on international war resistance, working for the overthrow of capitalism, division into pacifist and anticapitalist wings, and dissolution of the national body, leaving local chapters free to direct their own activities. However, consensus did not crystallize around any single proposal, for reasons singled out by one historian who was personally close to the NCF: "Men had united on one specific issue—resistance to war service and all that it implied—but beyond that unity there were conflicting loyalties, varying views on social affairs, and different religions. To have continued the N. C. F. in its then existing form would have meant one of two things: either it would have become a cockpit for heated altercation on social ideals . . . or it would have consisted of a few people with divided loyalties, and gradually would have petered out" (Graham, 1922, 339).

With the membership in rapid decline, a national convention was called in late 1919. The strongest of the many schemes to save the movement (as a "united anti-militarist organization") was defeated by a margin of 3 to 2. The convention then adopted the recommendations drawn up by the National Committee, which effectively resulted in the movement's dissolution (Kennedy, 1968, 410–424).

In a more detailed consideration of the American Resistance, our primary interest is in the way similar social conditions in the United States during 1967–1968 gave this movement its life and form, and ended it so abruptly. The Resistance was predicated on a set of beliefs sharply critical of the American social order, and it was built by people struggling for social change. But radical protest sentiment not simply a product of the proselytizing of movement organizers. What political atmosphere was necessary to make the strategy of resisting plausible?

In the summer of 1967 diverse groups of people around the country were contemplating an assault on military conscription. Others were outraged over America's conduct and presence in Indochina but saw no avenue for exercising effective protest. Yet six months later both groups were hard at work, building a radical protest movement and sharing ideology and action. What social processes gave this movement its life, community spirit, and radical verve? Why were so many young men willing to sacrifice five years in prison by joining the movement?

An organizing framework is mandatory for approaching these issues. The Resistance could be treated as a *social movement*, since a number of characteristics of social movements in general are found in the Resistance. For instance, social movements typically provide an initiation ritual for introducing new members. In this vein, the Resistance periodically sponsored national days of draft resistance, often conducted in religious settings, which resembled passing ceremonies serving to incorporate neophytes into the fold.

But the Resistance was also a *political protest, antiwar,*

and *anticonscription movement*, and characteristics of each made their appearance (6). *Political protest* movements, which normally operate in hostile political environments, tend to develop defensive organizational structures to protect themselves and their membership, and the Resistance was no exception. As a means of ideological protection, for example, resisters were prone to reduce contact with those who were not part of the movement.

The Resistance shared with other *antiwar* movements the inability to establish the impact (if any) of its action on military policy. Rallies could be held and hundreds of draft cards could be burned. But was the war winding down, and if so, did the Resistance action have anything to do with it? Enthusiasm for resistance actions therefore fluctuated, since the ambiguity of the connection between means and end made it virtually impossible to evaluate the effectiveness of any particular tactic. In the absence of objective criteria, subjective assessments were substituted. Later, as the war showed no signs of waning despite redoubled antiwar efforts, there were pressures to switch strategies, simply in the hope that a new approach would bring more success than the old one. Thus faith in draft resistance as a strategy was bound to be of short duration. Within a year or two, in fact, many rejected resistance in favor of new, often more militant, attacks on the war.

The movement's *anticonscription* strategy accounted for still other divisive factors—such as the tension between those directly affected by conscription and those immune from its reach. Registers tended to be accorded a higher status and a greater role in policy making than members who were not fully endangered.

We have chosen to focus on the Resistance as a protest movement. This allows us to explore various issues in the general process of political protest and the nature of protest movements in American society. The following section sketchs the framework for the study of protest movements that is used in our analysis of the Resistance.

THE PROTEST MOVEMENT: A FRAMEWORK FOR ANALYSIS

The protest movement can be approached by way of two distinct levels of analysis. One is the context in which the movement germinates—distressing social conditions and awareness of them on the part of those immediately affected. The other concerns development of the organized movement itself.

Social Origins

The preconditions generating protest reactions can be divided into two aspects. We distinguish between the actual situation of a segment of the society and the perception and interpretation of it. This distinction is often phrased as the difference between the objective condition and the subjective definition of it.

Structural Deprivation. A central element in the analysis of a social order is the degree to which large groups of people share disadvantaged social circumstances. We ask, for example, whether people are experiencing similar life conditions that can be characterized as deprived (7). Any society is filled with such situations; in the United States the black population finds it harder to secure jobs, housing, medical care, and police protection than the white sector. There is a substantial qualitative difference in the working conditions of blue collar employees and those enjoyed by upper-level executives.

The nature of a group's adversity has an important effect on any political reaction to the condition. For instance, social analysts have identified a variety of distressing situations (not all of them analytically or empirically distinct), including those typically labeled discrimination, alienation, relative and absolute deprivation, status loss, powerlessness, anomie, exploitation, and oppression. Widespread racial discrimination normally leads to a form of protest quite different from that induced by economic exploitation. Similarly, powerlessness in the work place yields protest reactions differing from responses to powerlessness in the local community.

Several elements of the particular adverse circumstances should be examined, and these can be quickly listed.

1. What is the specific character of the conditions?
2. Is the adversity intensifying or diminishing?
3. How is the deprivation being experienced? Is the origin of the problem relatively apparent? Are encounters frequent or rare?
4. Is the adversity felt uniformly throughout the population?
5. If several problems exist simultaneously, what are their interrelationships? In the case of working-class black females, for instance, we should consider the relative salience and interaction of the disadvantages associated with class, race, and sex.

Political Awareness and Action. Adverse conditions are of course felt, but seldom are the social roots fully visible. Some awareness may arise from personal and shared experience; but underlying structural origins are usually extremely complex, and the affected individual does not encounter them directly. Although the threat of conscription during the Vietnam era was oppressive to millions of young men, the origins of the war and the importance of conscription for sustaining it were obscure for most.

At times the disadvantaged are unaware of their relative disadvantage. For instance, Rushing (1970) examined feelings of powerlessness among two groups having significantly different degrees of access to power—farmers and agricultural workers in a western state. The farmers' median annual family income was $10,200, whereas the workers earned $3200. The agricultural workers, half of them Chicanos, were poorly organized; only 10 percent held membership in a union of any kind. On the other hand, 90 percent of the farmers were linked with an organization representing their interests (e.g., the Farm Bureau, Grange, or local cooperatives). Nevertheless, these two groups, which were structurally worlds apart, held nearly identical beliefs on their own political efficacy; they saw themselves as having similar degrees of control over their own economic condition.

As the foregoing discrepancies indicate, several factors must be considered in dealing with political awareness. We must first determine whether the social problem is consciously identified. Then, insofar as privately experienced ills are regarded as common problems, we must examine the accompanying interpretations. For instance, the landlord–tenant relationship may be conceived in terms ranging from the specifics of a localized fight over daily maintenance to a general and irreconcilable conflict of interest affecting all people in the community. Another issue of special relevance to protest movements is the degree and form of anger provoked by the conditions. Interpretations will also cover a broad field—from seeing the problem as an accident of history or as an inevitable by-product of modern technology to blaming a manipulative elite, a racial minority, or a "subversive" element. Finally, proposed solutions will also vary from the advocacy of cynical withdrawal to individual salvation or collective pressure. Of particular interest here are those solutions which point toward political protest by the disadvantaged as the most effective response.

Besides objective conditions, two other sets of factors help create a consciousness disposed toward protest politics. These factors can either improve or obscure an individual's awareness and his ability to act. *Ideological persuasion* may come through the media, schooling, informal influence, and explicit propaganda. There are also *political factors*, such as the role of the state in perpetuating and enforcing dominant ideologies, and the role of protest organizations in articulating a countervailing view of society. Other social elements may also be important, including legal opportunities for expressing dissent, physical proximity (or separation) of the disadvantaged, potential for intragroup communication, and specific events that sharply illustrate the underlying social relations.

Variations in the conditions within the afflicted groups also help determine where the critical awareness is likely to mature first. Thus black consciousness and militancy during the 1960s varied substantially depending on education, economic security, and age (Marx, 1969). And the degree of occupational deprivation among black civil rights activists was correlated with both propensity to join the movement and level of activity within it—the poorest were late in joining, although once inside they became some of the most energetic participants (Pinard, Kirk, and von Eschen, 1969).

Social Organization

The second and more visible aspect of political protest is the movement itself—the rules and processes of organizational foundation and maintenance. Six issues are of particular interest here: (1) formation, (2) protest ideology and strategy, (3) organizational structure, (4) recruitment and socialization, (5) movement demise, and (6) political impact.

Since movements often acquire a semiautonomous life, these components must be understood, in part, as they relate to one another. Nevertheless, not only the movement's existence but many of its specific features, as well, continue to be shaped by underlying social conditions. Therefore, the social environment is an important consideration in any analysis of the movement's organized life.

Formation. Initial crystallization of a protest movement is typically contingent on fairly sudden social changes and on the presence of already politicized persons. Sudden reversals play an important role in transforming despair into active political opposition (as Davies, 1962, 1969, and many others have argued), especially if the vital interests of large numbers of the disadvantaged are directly affected —as in the area of economic livelihood. In this context, the presence of people with prior protest movement experience is particularly important. Such individuals help to articulate grievances and to devise appropriate movement responses. For instance, as the farmers' movement spread in Saskatchewan during the 1920s and 1930s, emergence of a socialist critique of the farmers' adverse conditions was heavily influenced by the energetic presence of a preradicalized minority. Some had acquired leftwing politics from experiences prior to settling in the region. Others had developed their ideas in the course of years of work with early local leftist parties (Lipset, 1968, Ch. 4).

Protest Ideology and Strategy. A protest movement is based on a critique of the existing social order and a strategy for changing it. Although the cause for protest, the proposed solutions, and the strategies for achieving them are clearly connected, the relations are loose. Ambiguities in most political situations prevent direct derivation of tactics from broadly conceived goals, and a variety of political programs may seem to be appropriate for achieving the same end. During the 1960s, for example, a relative consensus prevailed among the civil rights organizations on the main source of the problems facing black America— pervasive, persistent white racism. But strategies and objectives ranged from integration to militant black separatism and socialist revolution.

Ideology and strategy often undergo significant reformulation as the movement gains experience, changes its organizational form (and its membership rolls), acquires political sophistication about its political environment, confronts changed conditions among its constituency, and suffers frustrating reversals or outright repression. Hopper (1950), Zald and Ash (1966), and Tucker (1967) discuss some of these factors.

Organizational Structure. A movement must establish organizational boundaries that specify such membership requisites as political views, demonstrated commitment, political action, and ascriptive identification with the stigmatized group. Again, movements may alter such criteria over time. For instance, following a period of growth, integrated ethnic minority movements frequently move to exclude those not clearly belonging to the ethnic minority.

Many topics central to the analysis of all organizations can be studied in the protest movement as well: decision-making structure, mechanisms for social control, maintenance of affiliation and commitment, degree of fragmentation, and interaction of movement values and organizational structure.

For protest movements, the problem of sustaining membership commitment is particularly acute, and it is a focus of discussion among both social analysts (e.g., Bittner, 1963) and movements themselves. Movement involvement offers intrinsic attractions such as political struggle and solidarity, but the costs are often severe to those who are deeply committed. Complete failure after prolonged effort is not unusual, and salaries earned hardly compensate for foregone income and career opportunities. Physical security, too, may be threatened in especially volatile situations. To ensure movement survival, such liabilities must be counterbalanced by mechanisms that continuously reinforce commitment.

Recruitment and Socialization. The factors of recruitment and socialization deserve special attention when movements are expanding. One strategic option frequently selected by protest movements—most often by small or young ones—is to increase political strength through encouraging a growth in membership and support among the disadvantaged. Since political influence is roughly proportional to a movement's size and backing, it is especially important to build a constituency. To this end, any movement must consider how to reach new members. It needs to determine the relative significance of such recruitment techniques as impersonal appeals, attempts to enlist preexisting and newly created personal contacts, agitation around grievances, work within other political organizations and movements, establishment of front groups, and use of exemplary actions (such as the demand by an underground leftist organization in Latin America that a large corporation distribute food and blankets to the poor as ransom for release of a kidnapped official).

Once new people are attracted to the cause, the movement faces a standard problem of incorporating new members. The degree of socialization that is needed depends on each newcomer's level of awareness, the admission criteria, and the character of the organization itself.

Demise. Protest movements are mortal, probably more so than most organizations, and several features of their collapse are of interest. Primary concern is with the social roots of the demise. Many factors, including nearly all those already named, may play a role—alleviation of the distressing conditions that inspired the movement, unwise selection of strategic options, repeated failures, severe suppression, excessively broad membership criteria, inadequate socialization and internal social control, ideological evolution within the movement such that its members no longer consider it a valid political expression, and, of course, successful implementation of its program. A second consideration is the destination of those composing the movement during its declining phase. Do they migrate to new protest causes or return to less intensely political lives, perhaps withdrawing from politics altogether? Do the social bonds forged within the movement outlast the organizational structure?

Another aspect to be examined is the decay process. Characteristic symptoms include plummeting membership rolls, increased sectarianism, loss of confidence and optimism, and attempts to reorient the movement's objectives and style. For instance, the populist Townsend Movement, formed during the Great Depression, survived the return of prosperity and the loss of most of its membership by replacing its original economic goals with emphasis on its associational benefits (Messinger, 1955).

Political Impact. Although crucial for understanding social change, political impact is an area that is relatively immune to analysis. The movement is a product of its social conditions, but it is usually unclear whether changed conditions are in turn produced by movement action. The ambiguity of evidence, which confronts movement activists and analysts alike, is intrinsic in the situation. Protest movements normally select immodest goals—an end to economic oppression, revamping of the nation's welfare system, full racial equality. Also, the social forces that create a particular movement tend to generate competing movements at the same time, as well as effecting change through less visible means. Thus it is difficult to isolate the impact of any specific movement activity.

In fact, this problem can lead to falsely based pessimism or optimism within the movement. Continued escalation of the Vietnam War despite strenuous protest discouraged some antiwar activists, even though careful analysis may indicate that such protest actually slowed the pace of American involvement. Conversely, withdrawal of U.S. troops from Indochina on the heels of similar activities might have inspired a sense of efficacy in the antiwar cause where none was justified, the apparent connection being essentially spurious. On the other hand, protests frequently establish more limited goals, making assessment easier. Typical examples include attempts to expand an organization's scale, radicalization and mobilization of specific segments of the discontented, and fights for small gains on particular grievances.

There are also unintended effects of movement activity, including massive repression, creation of rival protests and countermovements, achievement of reform where radical transformation had been sought, escalation of the protest target's tolerance for and use of violence, and infusion of protest rhetoric into the culture at large.

This framework should serve as a guide for analyzing the origins and life history of the Resistance. However, it must be seen as a heuristic tool, alerting us to important themes in the rise and decline of the movement.

The analytic framework described, data limitations, and especially problematic themes in this protest episode, jointly produced the following coverage. Initial attention is directed at the historical and social antecedents of the Resistance. Here we focus on higher education, the radical student movement, military conscription during the Vietnam period, and early efforts to create a resistance-type attack on the Vietnam War. The relationships of young men to their college environment, to the government by way of the draft, and to the New Left eventually culminated in the revolt of the resisters (Chapters Two and Three). We then turn to the strategic justification for the formation of the Resistance and its anticipated political thrust (Chapter Four). This is followed by a discussion of the movement's political and social consolidation (Chapters Five and Six). Here we deal with such issues as how those new to leftist action became socialized into the radical ideology on which the Resistance was based, and how internal loyalties developed. In the last chapter, we assess the movement's collapse two years after its founding. We shall ask why the Resistance was unable to initiate the nationwide strike among prospective conscripts that had been considered to be essential when the group was formed. Finally, we attempt to learn what forces inhibited attempts to revise the core strategy of the Resistance.

NOTES

1. For one survey, see Prasad and Smythe (1968).

2. Gallup survey results are summarized in Melbourne Draft Resisters' Union (1971, 84–85).

3. The government figures are reported in Melbourne Draft Resisters' Union (1971, 78–80).

4. This discussion of conscription and the No-Conscription Fellowship relies heavily on Graham (1922), Hayes (1949), Boulton (1967), Kennedy (1968), and Rae (1970).

5. The membership figures for February 1915 (350) and October 1915 (5000) are from Kennedy (1968, 65, 80); the April 1916 figure (10,000 members) is from Boulton (1967). The NCF claimed a strength near 15,000 at this point but Rae (1970, 11) argues that this number reflects "tactical exaggeration." The NCF newsletter, the *Tribunal*, apparently reached a weekly circulation near 100,000 (Graham 1922, 191).

6. A *social movement* can be defined as an association of people united around a common desire to change a social condition. The change cannot be readily achieved within existing institutional channels, such as through a church, a government agency, a school, or a political party. A *protest movement* is a social movement that is explicitly concerned with altering the condition of a significant socially, politically, or economically disadvantaged sector of a society. It is also a social movement that exercises political strategies to create these changes; it is chiefly concerned with enhancing the power of the disadvantaged group relative to other sectors and institutions in the society; it seeks changes that would improve the collective welfare of the disadvantaged sector and not simply provide individual benefits to the movement and its members. *Antiwar* and *anticonscription* movements are protest movements that are specifically oriented around ending a war or compulsory military service.

7. There has been considerable debate over the issue of establishing a baseline appropriate for defining structural disadvantage. Representative positions include those of Dahrendorf (1958), Smelser (1962), Gurr (1970), some of the readings in Davies (1971), and, of course, Karl Marx. For our purposes, the prototypical case is represented by a class or group of people in a social condition that could be greatly improved, given the organizational and physical resources of the society. The potential for improvement exists (which means that a conscious demand for change is not unrealistic), but the political character of the social order precludes attainment of this improvement through standard political means. Moreover, "natural" growth and change processes in the society do not point toward remedy in the reasonably near future.

APPENDIX   A NOTE ON RESEARCH METHODS

Analysis of both the social context and the inner life of the anticonscription protest movement required information drawn from a variety of sources. In contructing profiles of conscription during the Vietnam era and of the role of the radical student movement in generating the Resistance, the following types of material were especially useful.

1. Federal government studies and reports, including the annual statement of the Selective Service System; congressional hearings on extension of the draft and the volunteer army; research conducted in the offices of the Department of Defense and the Veterans Administration; reports of several national commissions concerned with compulsory military service; and federally sponsored studies conducted by external organizations, such as the National Opinion Research Center and the University of Michigan's Institute for Social Research.

2. Journals and newsletters of the Resistance, as well as publications of radical student organizations, draft counseling and antidraft groups, pacifist organizations, and various leftwing groups, plus independent periodicals concerned with antiwar, leftwing, and pacifist developments in the United States. Among the several dozen helpful publications were *Win Magazine, The Guardian, The Peacemaker, Liberation, Resist, New Left Notes, Final Draft, Downdraft, Draft Counselor's Newsletter,* and *AMEX-Canada.*

3. Academic studies of military manpower and the student movement, ranging in focus from the administrative practices of the Selective Service System to the economic

costs of being drafted and the individual and institutional correlates of student activism.

4. Surveys of opinion on the draft and the Vietnam War and secondary analyses of trends in these national and special polls.

5. Historical studies covering the Resistance, reaction to conscription in previous American wars, and movements similar to the Resistance in other societies (Britain, France, and Australia).

Although these sources yielded much useful information, an understanding of the Resistance organization and the experience of its members necessitated a more direct look at the movement itself. Local Resistance groups existed in a number of cities and on many campuses, but differences among chapters were not extreme. Since detailed examination of a single chapter was desirable (given resource limitations), and since one of the major groupings was conveniently located in Boston, the field research focused on draft resisters and the movement in this metropolitan region. A variety of methods were used, but all were designed to supplement a single primary instrument —structured interviews with nearly 100 draft resisters who were affiliated with the Resistance.

The secondary field methods included a number of activities, as follows. Approximately 20 lengthy informal interviews were held with people affiliated with the Resistance in the Boston area. We observed or participated in a number of movement events, such as internal policy meetings of the two major local Resistance organizations, public demonstrations, and organizing efforts (e. g., talking with draftees assembled at their local board for transportation to an induction center). The Resistance was loosely aligned with radical student and antiwar groups at Harvard University and in the Boston region, and fairly extensive involvement with their activities provided direct information on the relationship between the Resistance and other New Left organizations. In addition, as part of an interview pretest, several days were spent visiting with resisters involved in the small movement chapters at Brown University and Michigan State University. Five resisters were interviewed, and discussions were conducted with several others acquainted with the local movements at Brown and Michigan State.

We selected structured interviewing as the major field method because it allowed for deep and systematic exploration of the ideological and interpersonal changes accompanying membership in the movement, a topic of central interest. Reliance on participant observation would not have produced sufficiently systematic information on membership conversion. A mailed questionnaire survey was inappropriate because it excluded the possibility of in-depth probing and because some of the resisters (those who were under federal indictment or anticipating this event) would have hesitated to supply written answers to certain sensitive questions. Interviews were conducted with approximately 100 draft resisters, and 97 usable interviews were completed. The interview schedule included both highly structured and unstructured sections, and an interview required two hours on the average. The unusual method of selecting respondents requires brief description.

Within the Boston movement it was commonly estimated that 500 to 1000 men had resisted the draft by the time of this study. Interviews were conducted with only young men who had taken some formal act of resistance against the draft. (Of those interviewed, 75 percent had returned or burned their draft cards at one of the Resistance rallies; the remainder had chosen other modes, such as direct mailing to the Justice Department or draft board. Eighty percent had taken the step between October 1967 and May 1968.) It proved difficult to compile a roster of those who had resisted, and in part to circumvent this problem and in part to generate data on social networks, a snowballing sampling procedure was used (for other instances of application, see Katz and Lazarsfeld, 1955; Trow, 1957; and Mullins, 1966, 1968). Essentially, this technique consists of selecting a small set of individuals for interviewing, interviewing a second set of people chosen by the starting group, interviewing in turn the choices of the second set, and continuing in this manner until the desired sample size is reached.

Three conditions must be specified in snowball sampling: the rules for selecting the starting interviews, the number of individuals a respondent is asked to choose for the next wave of interviewing, and the criteria the respondent should apply in making the selection. Regarding the starting points, preliminary informal discussion indicated that the Resistance community had a substantial cliquing structure. In order to maximize coverage, it was necessary to select starting interviews in as many distinct social groups as could be identified. Nine were located, and a single starting interview was initiated in each (the starter was picked from a list of names assembled from preliminary discussions, observation, and Resistance literature). Five of the contexts were university-based groups, two were centered in the major Resistance action organizations (Boston Draft Resistance Group and New England Resistance), one was a religious community, and a group of working people constituted the ninth. In addition, a nearly complete list of resisters became available for one university, and in order to explore the informal structure within this setting, interviews were initiated with all resisters associated with the institution. From this lead we obtained 19 of the 97 interviews.

Each individual was asked to name three others for the

next wave. This number reflected the need to have a final sample of close to 100, a preference that the snowballing extend to five stages, and the assumption that the inbreeding rate could be as high as 50 percent (implying that on the average half of all people named in a given stage would have been interviewed in prior stages or also named by others in the same stage). However, because of unexpectedly high inbreeding, the failure of some respondents to name three other individuals, and other factors, the chains merged early. All chains had at least one link into another chain by the second wave. The ratio of the number of people interviewed in a given stage to the number interviewed in the previous stage dropped from 2.3 in the second stage to 0.9 in the fourth wave and 0.4 by the sixth stage (for further detail see Useem, 1970, Ch. 2 and 3). Trow (1957, 243) encountered a similar development in his snowball sampling.

The criteria employed in selecting people for a subsequent stage of interviews were friendship with the respondent and an act of draft resistance. During the middle of the interview, the resisters were asked to list anonymously their closest friends residing in the Boston area. They were then requested to assess a number of social characteristics of these friends and to state whether each had resisted the draft. At the end of the interview it was explained that a snowballing process was being used and that it would be helpful if contact could be made with the listed friends who were also resisters. If the respondent listed fewer than three resister "friends," the names of up to three resister "acquaintances" were requested, to bring the total up to three. Approximately three in five names produced were in the friendship category. A total of 274 names was generated during the snowballing, although only 224 referred to those in the final 97 person sample. Nearly half (10 unique individuals) of the 50-name attrition was due to refusal to participate in a requested interview; the remainder was composed of people who could not be located or who, as it turned out, had not actually resisted the draft.

Although snowballing in the manner described circumvented the problem of locating a cross section of the population prior to interviewing, it also led to a somewhat biased sample. Hard data are lacking, yet there seemed to be a tendency, when naming "acquaintances," to select people who might be more amenable to an interview, as well as more active in Resistance programs and of greater prominence in the movement. ("Friends" had been named before it was mentioned that an interview would be sought.) Thus there is probably some bias toward the more activist center of the Resistance. In addition, owing to the heavy concentration of starting interviews among university resistance groups and to the complete coverage of resisters at one school, there is probably some bias toward student resisters. Of the resisters interviewed, 60 percent were attending college at the time of the interview. The New England Resistance tabulated the school or work situation of its members in mid-1968 and found that 55 percent were enrolled in college, which suggests that students were slightly overrepresented in our sample (*Journal of the New England Resistance*, October 1968).

TWO

We, the students of the United States, refuse to be drafted. We do not recognize the right of the government to draft our fellow students. We refuse to be turned into killers and corpses for a war that is not ours.

May Second Movement leaflet, 1964.

[Those who sat in at an Ann Arbor, Michigan, draft board] have violated the terms of their parole, and they have no business to have a deferment after that. . . . Reclassification is quicker at stopping sit-ins than some indictment that takes effect six months later. And we haven't heard of any sit-ins since the one in Ann Arbor.

Director of the U.S. Selective Service System, 1965.

DISCONTENT ON CAMPUS:
Higher Education and the Student Movement

The formation of a protest movement is generally contingent on the preexistence of a group of people united around a set of political principles dealing with a solution to a social problem. Some protests erupt spontaneously and reflect little conscious effort by a politicized leadership. But many movements, the Resistance included, are instituted only after a lengthy maturation process in which a substantial number of people come to view a new protest program as valid and realistic. An analysis of the emergence of this protest ideology is therefore central to an understanding of a movement's origins.

One major source of the political principles underlying a new protest movement often is the collective wisdom of earlier protest organizations. As was the case for the Resistance, a new movement's initial leadership frequently comes from former members of such groups. Several basic concepts of the Resistance program had been formulated in leftist student organizations just before mid–1967, and many of the early Resistance organizers had been activists

in these groups. Since the new concepts were in large part
a product of the interaction between the radical student
movement and its political context, we must examine both
the precursor organizations and their political environment. Analysis of the latter factor is also important for understanding how it was that people who were not already
politically engaged could be drawn to the new movement.
Particularly, we want to know whether conditions were
sufficiently adverse to encourage people to seek new remedies, and whether the program of the new movement
was an effective response to the discontent.

In the present chapter we initially focus on conflicts in
higher education and the influence these exerted on the
evolving political perspective of the radical student movement. The conflicts facilitated emergence of a viewpoint
that set the stage for a resistance-type strategy—namely,
the belief that students were a potentially radical force in
American society and that they could be mobilized by programs oriented around solving their problems.

One major problem for students after 1964 was the
Vietnam War, and campus organizations devoted considerable effort to a consequence especially distressing for
many students—the war-time draft. In the latter part of
this chapter we consider some of the means by which the
radical student movement attacked the draft during the
1965–1967 period. There were many ways of organizing
against the war and conscription, and the experience gained
in this period by campus organizations (and some off-
campus groups as well) helped clear the way for experi-
mentation with draft resistance in 1967. However, although
several of the basic justifications for resistance against the
draft were formulated within these pre-resistance organizations, a number of more specific strategic questions remained for the new leadership to settle on its own. But
again, the political environment in which the Resistance

was to operate heavily influenced the ideas it espoused. Some of the organizational and contextual elements that shaped the solution of these strategic issues are taken up in Chapter 4.

CONFLICT IN HIGHER EDUCATION

The student assault on conscription was predicated on the notion that students were an oppressed class rather than a privileged elite. A corollary of this thesis was that students could be mobilized through traditional means of class conflict protest. That is, students were viewed as having a set of common interests that could not be realized within the society's existing framework. Only through coordinated collective efforts with other groups in comparable circumstances could students wield enough power to create the social change necessary to improve their common situation. The role of the protest movement was to organize this attack on the status quo, which would inevitably bring students into an open clash with the society's dominant institutions. This, it was felt, would lead to progressive change in education and in the social order.

To understand how such a perspective came to be shared by a number of people, we must consider the radical student movement and its political context during the 1960s. Let us start with a brief overview of conflicts in the organization of higher education in the United States, and then turn to the student movement's relationship to this setting. Although students and college administrations shared many interests, there were also several major points of diverging concern, and students and administrative authorities were at fundamental odds over how college education was best organized.

An analysis of the school system by Parsons (1959) concludes that formal education plays two critical functions in American life. First, it instills in students the "commitments and capacities which are essential prerequisites of their future role performance." Second, the education system places new members of the labor force in appropriate adult work positions. Underlying this analysis is a set of theoretical assumptions about the compatibility of the structure of schooling, the private economy, and the social needs of both students and the society. For instance, the channeling of students into a highly stratified occupational market is presumed to be in the best interests of students and society alike. Existing differences in income and wealth are considered necessary for the effective allocation of people to work roles in the economy. Varying rewards are attached to different positions to ensure that the most "competent" people assume the most "important" jobs and that they conform to role expectations (for illustrative arguments see Davis and Moore, 1945; Parsons, 1953; Barber, 1957, and Keller, 1963).

This view that American society is based on a consensus of values and shared set of social interests has been challenged by a number of analysts. They have criticized the assumption that the present organization of economic production is capable of meeting the social and economic demands of employees and those of the American people as a whole (e.g., Kolko, 1962; Baran and Sweezy, 1966; Zeitlin, 1970a; Anderson, 1971; Sherman, 1972; Mankoff, 1972; Edwards, Reich, and Weisskopf, 1972). Employing agencies—corporations, government bureaucracies, factories—are not viewed as well-integrated social organizations but as institutions that embody a fundamental conflict between management and most employees. The antagonism revolves around a contradiction in the organization of work. The employees' situation would be improved by higher wages, delegation of control over jobs as well as major organizational decisions, and more pleasant physical and mental working conditions. Such proposed changes often seem to be inherently at odds with efficient management as presently defined. Arguments supporting this analysis of the American economy cannot be discussed here, but it is our position that major conflicts of this type are present in the United States.

There are important implications for the school system. If people are being socialized and channeled into work roles compatible with their values and aspirations, higher education should function smoothly. If instead, however, people are being prepared for undesirable work conditions, problems can be expected. Students may balk at their occupational prospects, blaming the college for routing them in such directions. In addition, effective preparation of future workers requires that many qualities of the work world be experienced in school. Thus some of the alienating aspects of work are likely to have parallels in college.

It can be objected that higher education is actually preparing people for elite positions, and in earlier eras, this was its primary role. Colleges continue to perform this function (most elite positions are filled by college-trained people), but the simultaneous expansion of the white collar sector and the increase in the numbers of those exposed to higher education has given the college system a new role —training people for subordinate positions in the labor force. About 40 percent of the current generation is completing some college on its way into the labor market. A fraction will enter elite positions, but the majority are destined for white collar jobs that offer some of the same undesirable work conditions that blue collar workers face. Included here are such white collar occupational groups as clerical workers, public employees, technicians, nurses, social workers, and engineers. In most instances, income is relatively low and job security is minimal; the employee has virtually no voice in the organization's policies; career incentives are small. This perspective on the quality of white collar work life has been most fully developed for advanced capitalist societies by such writers as Mallet (1965), Gorz (1965, 1968), and Touraine (1971a, 1971b). The thesis, often labeled "new working class" theory, has been applied to the United States in the writing of Oppenheimer (1970), Gintis (1970), Denitch (1971), Flacks (1971a, 1971b), and Birnbaum (1971); for representative critiques, see Aronowitz (1971), Bell (1972), and Szymanski (1972).

If American colleges prepare the new generation for entry into the labor force, what connections between employers and the campus ensure that socialization and allocation are effectively accomplished? A number of unarticulated and unorganized factors converge to produce a close meshing of educational policies and the occupational world. For instance, teachers generally accept dominant American values (those that do not are often prevented from teaching), and they pass them on to students through both the content and the organization of the classroom. Students and their families correctly perceive that a good education is key to one's occupational chances, and they place consumer pressures on schools to provide what is required for job success. School administrators are naturally attuned to the interests of their financial sources, and business perspectives in turn tend to be dominant in state and local governments, federal agencies, and foundations, which are the sources of much of the funding of higher education.

There are also more explicit mechanisms by which the linkage is maintained. One means of integrating the policies of banks and corporations is the establishment of interlocking directorates. Similarly, placement of business representatives on college boards of trustees helps maintain a tie between educational policies and manpower needs of private industry. Studies of college boards of trustees consistently have found that majorities of these bodies are closely identified with business interests. An analysis of the occupational affiliations of nearly 2500 trustees of large universities and colleges in 1915 revealed that businessmen and lawyers held a commanding majority (Nearing, 1917).

Another investigator, who checked the occupations of trustees of 20 representative institutions at 10-year intervals from 1860 to 1930, learned that businessmen, bankers, and lawyers controlled more than two-thirds of the seats at state institutions throughout the period. At private colleges this group steadily gained strength, and by 1930 they held three out of four positions (McGrath, 1936). A 1967 survey detected little change three decades later. Nearly 4000 trustees at public and non-Catholic private colleges and universities responded, and of these, half held positions in business, law, or government (Hartnett, 1969). This 1967 study also revealed that the outlook of the trustees was not divorced from business philosophy. Indeed, nearly half the trustees surveyed agreed that running a college was like operating a business. Nor were the trustees hesitant to involve themselves in decisions about teaching. Well over a majority felt that they and/or the administration should have sole authority in making decisions involving faculty tenure.

The linkage of the campus with the economy is responsible for several latent organizational conflicts between students and the administration. Social needs and values of students cannot be adequately satisfied within the existing college organization, and yet the administration is unable to ensure a steady flow of educated labor without such policies. Under certain circumstances, the resulting organizational tensions can become the source of open political struggle between students and administrations.

One point of conflict results from higher education's occupational channeling function. Since the job structure is highly stratified, so too is higher education. Studies of American social mobility repeatedly indicate that educational level is one of the strongest predictors of occupational achievement. In 1966 a man with one to three years of college training could anticipate lifetime earnings only three-quarters of that gained by a man who had completed four or more years (Miller, 1971, 177).

Not only do schools rank students for exit into the job market, but they also stratify those interested in attending college according to their parents' standing in the occupational system. This occurs both in terms of who is allowed to attend college at all and who is selected to attend the "better" colleges. On the latter point, for instance, one study examined the family backgrounds of students attending various types of schools. The proportion of the student body whose fathers were employed as blue collar workers ranged from 20 percent at private universities to 55 percent at public two-year colleges. Conversely, the proportion with professional or managerial fathers varied from 49 percent at private universities to 16 percent at two-year schools (1).

In general, higher education appears to be preserving the social class and ethnic relations of the broader society in terms of both intake and output of students (for supporting evidence, see Folger, Astin, and Bayer, 1970, Ch. 10; Collins, 1971; Bowles, 1972a; Milner, 1972; Karabel, 1972). Social class and ethnic inequalities are a major source of conflict in American society, and the presence of parallel inequities within the area of higher education results in similar tensions there. The pressures for open admissions can be viewed as one political manifestation.

Another element of antagonism relates to the education

that students acquire during their schooling. There is a difference between the administration's view of what students will need for their future and what students perceive is best learned, given their social origins and future expectations. These differences can become politicized. For instance, many college courses generate untested images of American life. A time of national crisis (e.g., the late 1960s) can force a comparison between what is taught and what appears to be the real situation, and in some cases the contrast is sharp. Thus, for example, the impression that black Americans were rapidly being incorporated into the country's mainstream seemed to be contradicted by the inner-city uprisings in Detroit, Newark, and elsewhere. In this connection, it can be noted that some of the demands for "relevance" in course offerings, establishment of ethnic studies programs, and participation in faculty hiring are examples of conflict over teaching content.

Finally, the issue of control is potentially troublesome. To the extent that students feel strongly opposed to certain educational practices of the administration, it can be expected that students will push for greater political voice in order to implement their own policies. At the same time, the administration can be expected to tenaciously resist erosion of its influence, since any loss of control can mean major policy changes. In addition, however, the relatively powerless state of students within the college context is accompanied by its own instabilities. Participation can become valued for its own sake. Students who accept democratic ideals find that they are almost totally excluded from major decisions in the institution that is most central to their own lives. The many campaigns demanding student power on campuses during the 1960s were partly due to political reactions to this powerless condition (2).

THE REVOLUTIONARY POTENTIAL
OF STUDENTS

The experience of radical campus organizations before mid-1967 was crucial to the formation of a resistance ideology. Out of practical attempts by these groups to instigate social change, a belief spread that students constituted a potentially revolutionary sector of American society. A changing political environment made organizing students more practical than involvement in off-campus work, and the existing cleavage between students and college administrations provided the rationale that persuaded the leftist movement to undertake student organizing.

Between revitalization of student activism around 1960 and foundation of the Resistance in 1967, two important changes occurred in the operating environment of the leftist student movement. A primary focus of early student political work—civil rights for the black minority—had become closed to most white activists. And on campus there was an increasingly volatile atmosphere of discontent. A critical juncture of both changes occurred around 1964–1966, bringing several consequences for ideological currents in the leftist student movement. First, there was increasing emphasis on the problems faced by students themselves. The student was no longer seen as a person who could be mobilized only around the plight of others. He or she came to be viewed as someone who could be motivated to act on the basis of his or her own discontent. Students were perceived to share with other oppressed sectors a set of interests that would lead them to fight for a transformation of the American social order. Second, an amorphous grouping of political principles was replaced by a more coherent and elaborate analysis. Activists began to find that forces that perpetuated the status quo were rooted in fundamental structures of the social order, such as the private economy. Finally, strategies shifted toward a more confrontational style, each successive stage being marked by an escalation in militancy and risks. All three developments encouraged formulation of an attack on governmental power through the anticonscription strike.

Action Locale: Return to the Campus

At the turn of the decade, the cold war was a prime focus for political protest sentiment on the American campus. Cold war phenomena, such as nuclear testing and attempted abridgement of civil liberties by the House Committee on Un-American Activities, were the target of much dissent. The Student Peace Union, founded in 1959, was the largest leftist student organization of the period. (SPU gained peak strength in 1962, when it had about 5000 members in 100 campus chapters: Altbach and Peterson, 1971, 12). Little interest was directed at organizing students around issues of particular concern to them as students, although attention to these issues was not entirely lacking. For example, the quality of life on campus was explicitly mentioned in the "Port Huron Statement," a manifesto endorsed by an early convention of another organization, Students for a Democratic Society (SDS). The university was condemned for preparing "the student for 'citizenship' through perpetual rehearsals and usually, through emasculation of what creative spirit there is in the individual. . . . The academic world is founded on a teacher–student relation analgous to the parent–child relation" (reprinted in Jacobs and Landau, 1966). Yet neither analysis nor campaigns developed around the student condition.

Rapid acceleration in civil rights activity after 1959,

sparked by the first Southern sit-ins, removed student activism even further from campus, both geographically and
ideologically. During the early 1960s, college students concerned with improving the quality of American life faced
uninviting prospects on campus: not certain whether universities oppressed or conferred privileges on its students,
and aware of the pervasive apathy among students, activists
found the burgeoning civil rights movement a more attractive political arena. The civil rights field contained important qualities absent in campus issues. The status of poor
blacks was not ambiguous—they experienced daily discrimination, degradation, and economic exploitation. In
addition, the depth of national concern made real political
gains a strong possibility.

In this context, the class interests of students played a
minimal role in the conscious rationale for white involvement in the civil rights movement. Students, it was
commonly held, joined the struggle to alleviate the condition of others rather than to help liberate their own community. Some of course entered the civil rights movement
armed with a complete system critique which characterized the black minority as only the most exploited sector
of many exploited sectors in American society. But scholars of the civil rights movement generally agree that most
white students became involved because of their liberal,
idealistic commitments. Summarizing an intensive study of
the Congress on Racial Equality (CORE) during the
1961–1963 period, one investigator concluded:

> [W]hites generally came to the movement with fairly
> stable, well-defined liberal views. They usually came
> from, and continued to have their roots in, the intel-
> lectual liberal-left community. Their participation in
> the movement, which usually overshadowed other
> commitments, was one of a range of liberal political
> activities. . . . They were, on the other hand, under

no direct, personal, emotional pressure with regard to the race question . . . (Bell 1968, 126–127).

By 1965 the situation was reversing. Although experimental efforts to organize off-campus continued (e.g., SDS's Economic Research and Action Project among the poor), the radical student movement gradually moved back on campus. Several factors encouraged the retreat.

One element was the ascendance of antiwhite sentiment within a number of civil rights organizations. This itself was a consequence of problems typical of protest movements that have "outsiders" assisting in the struggle of a disenfranchised group (see Marx and Useem, 1971). In 1965 and 1966 latent internal tensions between black and white activists had become overt, and several organizations (e.g., CORE and the Student Non-Violent Coordinating Committee [SNCC]) adopted programs that either relegated whites to a subordinate role or excluded them altogether.

A second factor was the Free Speech Movement (FSM) that developed at the Berkeley campus of the University of California in the fall of 1964. For the first time it became clear that university life could generate a massive revolt. The University of California administration had hindered leftist politics on campus for some time before the FSM, and in the fall of 1964 a university move to prohibit on-campus recruiting for off-campus political activities catalyzed a rebellion against administration authority. The ensuing protest elicited an extensive critique of the structure and functioning of the university. Students attacked what they saw as the impersonality of the school bureaucracy, the distance between students and faculty, control over university affairs by a remote Board of Regents, and overemphasis on career training. Campus chapters of CORE and Friends of SNCC played central roles in the FSM leadership, and many of the students active in the revolt were veterans of civil rights campaigns (3).

A third factor encouraging a return to the campus was expansion of U.S. participation in the Vietnam War in 1965. A significant minority of the student population was deeply distressed by the build-up. One survey of administrators at all the accredited four-year institutions in the country revealed that one in every five schools experienced protest over American policy in Vietnam as early as 1965 (Peterson, 1970, 222). Discontent increased with each new escalation, dissolving one of the earlier barriers to campus organizing—student apathy.

Ideology: Students as an Alienated Class

By the mid-1960s leftist student organizations were caught in a strategic dilemma. Recognizing their organizational weakness, they could chose from among several tactical alternatives. One was to rely on the cooperation of established avenues for political action, such as the government and the Democratic party. Yet civil rights and early anti-war agitation had indicated that these institutions were often unresponsive to change. Another alternative lay in the mobilization of disadvantaged people who had not yet been organized. The natural constituency for a campus-based movement, students, did not seem to be an attractive recruiting target in the early 1960s. However, the situation had reversed by 1966, with the reduction of white participation in the civil rights movement and the appearance of a new political vitality on campus.

Within radical student organizations, political thinking evolved to account for this shift in organizing focus. Student–administration conflicts helped make credible an analysis in which students formed an oppressed stratum capable of engineering major societal changes. Trial programs based on this analysis seemed to work. The emergence of the theory is apparent in SDS, which had become the primary national organization of leftist students by the middle of the decade (4).

A prominent theme in the national SDS convention during the summer of 1966 was the mobilization of students by agitation relating to their powerlessness in the university. Since the system of higher education was characterized as a means for preparing students for the society's labor force, it was believed that democratization of the university would undermine the functions imposed on it from outside. In the long run, this in turn would erode the elite's ability to replenish its supply of docile, educated labor. Although few specific programs were immediately developed around this analysis, its general ascendance was reflected at the 1966 SDS convention in the election of a vice-president who advocated this position (O'Brien, 1969) (5).

By early 1967 proponents of student power were characterizing their approach in "new working class" terms. A major position paper prepared for the summer 1967 SDS convention contended:

> The need to train [educated workers] makes higher education structurally crucial to the functioning of the system. . . . The tremendous expansion of higher education is related to the need to train (both technically and socially) people for the new crucial jobs in the economy. The student is a human commodity in the factory of the university. But unlike a car, students are not inert objects. The student rebellion stems from a variety of factors, primarily developing out of the manipulative training of students to fit them into American society. Students perceiving both the *productive* potential of a society, and the *social* uselessness of the jobs for which they're being trained, are alienated from a system that offers no socially meaningful work.

> The organizing of students on the campus around the
> questions of student control, the draft, and the uni-
> versities' serving of the military can develop a radical
> consciousness concerning the role and nature of their
> future work positions. The starting point for radical
> consciousness is the sense of student powerlessness re-
> vealed by these functions of the university (Gottlieb,
> Tenney, and Gilbert, 1967).

By mid-1967 the radical wing of the student movement
had moved toward the politics of class conflict. College
students joined other sectors already identified as alienated
by undemocratic institutions and the workings of the capitalist economy. But what problems were of greatest concern to students? Besides their powerlessness in the college
setting, it was apparent after 1964 that one of the most
vexing issues was America's involvement in Southeast Asia.

The war impinged on students' lives in several ways. It
was indirectly felt in the formal and informal arrangements
that administrations and faculty members at some institutions maintained with war-related federal agencies. For instance, many campuses permitted military recruiting,
maintained a reserve officer training program (ROTC—
a primary source of officers for Vietnam), hosted military
and related research in special institutes, and housed faculty members who also were consultants to the Department of Defense. Although such activities were considered
outrageous to some students, they did not directly affect
the mass of the student body at most schools.

However, conscription influenced the lives of millions,
and it was in this regard that the war's intensification was
most clearly disturbing. The threat of induction and the
incentives of the deferment system could not be ignored
by draft-age male students. Almost from the beginning of
U.S. involvement in Southeast Asia, radical student groups

debated and implemented programs to thwart compulsory military service.

GROUNDWORK: EARLY AGITATION AGAINST CONSCRIPTION

By early 1967 SDS and other elements in the radical student movement were contemplating a resistance strategy. The questions of the appropriateness of such a measure had already been settled. The politics of class mobilization and conflict were needed to transform America, and students could be organized into a radical protest movement around their problems with the draft. But left unresolved were more specific tactical issues. Since resources were limited, all modes of attack on conscription and the war could not be pursued simultaneously. Student organizers had to decide which option would have the greatest payoff for the movement.

Three types of question affected selection of a particular strategy. First, what gains could be expected? Given the strength of the student leftist movement and the campus atmosphere in the 1965–1967 period, this question could be answered with respect to the benefits anticipated for three more limited goals—radicalization of student political values, recruitment of new people to the struggle, and erosion of the government's ability to continue the Vietnam conflict. Second, what negative consequences could be expected, especially in terms of governmental repression of the movement or prosecution of individuals within it? Finally, on a purely pragmatic plane, could the specific tactic be implemented? Were resources adequate and were people really committed to the idea?

Good information on such questions was unavailable in

1967. Radical activists had already been assaulting conscription for several years, however, and a few unconnected episodes of confrontation with the draft had received widespread publicity. This early antidraft experience was used in movement circles to give partial answers to some of the questions just formulated (6).

Early Episodes of Individual Resistance

During the 1964–1966 period a series of isolated but public draft card destructions took place. Political justifications varied, but conscription and the war were usually cited. The burnings were generally the spontaneous act of a few individuals; there was little prior planning, and organizational endorsement was generally lacking. In May 1964, 12 young men lit their cards at a New York rally sponsored by the Student Peace Union and other groups. A year later, 40 participants in a Berkeley demonstration against American intervention in the Dominican Republic destroyed their draft credentials before a local draft board. Public notoriety, however, came with several widely reported draft card burnings that occurred at antiwar rallies during the summer of 1965. In response to the burnings, Congress passed a bill in August 1965 making destruction or mutilation of a draft card a felony, punishable by a sentence of up to five years. David Miller, a pacifist and civil rights activist, promptly challenged the new law. He sent his papers up in flames at an October rally being held as part of the "International Days of Protest." Miller eventually served a 30-month sentence. A few weeks later a fivesome repeated the incendiary act, and the ensuing prosecution led to several imprisonments. Another widely publicized action, in early 1966, was the simultaneous public draft card destruction in Boston by four members of a pacifist action group. All eventually served prison terms (7).

The movement learned a good deal from these early actions. For example, it was seen that front-page coverage could be obtained by open acts of resistance, indicating that individual behavior could serve as a medium for conveying a political message. Moreover, feelings about the war were revealed to be sufficiently intense to compel at least some young men to resist, although in 1965 this path was primarily chosen by radical pacifists. Finally, it was found that reaction tended to be harsh. Vitriolic epithets were often directed at the demonstrators; four Boston draft card burners were pummeled by a group of passing high school students; press comment and editorial opinion were unfavorable; and Congress urged prompt prosecution of all offenders. Some eventually went to prison, although not all were even indicted. By 1970 the Justice Department reported that only 46 prosecutions had been initiated (with 33 convictions) for mutilation or destruction of draft cards, although hundreds of other individuals had taken such action during the height of the Resistance movement in 1967–1968 (U.S. House Committee on Armed Services, 1970, 12861).

Antidraft Organizing

Within various radical student organizations, programs against the draft were being fashioned, argued, and, in a few instances, implemented. One of the earliest attempts actually antedates the 1965 Vietnam escalation. In 1961 several activists in the Student Peace Union urged collective noncooperation by a large-scale return of draft cards as a means for ensuring international peace. To guarantee that resisters would not stand alone, a novel protection was devised—no cards would be returned until at least 500 had been pledged. The proposal generated little enthusiasm, however, and it never left the mental drawing board.

One young man involved in some of the SPU resistance deliberations, David Mitchell, III, helped found a group called End the Draft. Two years later, in 1964, its newsletter was calling (unsuccessfully) for a resistance movement against the draft. American military policy in Vietnam was a major justification for the proposed resistance. Mitchell himself refused induction in early 1965 on the grounds that serving would make him complicit under international law with crimes the United States was committing in Southeast Asia.

Several student organizations formulated radical antidraft positions and programs as the war intensified. One of the earliest of these was adopted by the May Second Movement, a short-lived group that was ideologically akin to the Progressive Labor party (PLP), a militant Marxist-Leninist organization. Shortly after forming, the May Second Movement circulated a petition stating that the signers would refuse to serve in Vietnam with the American military. It obtained more than 1000 signatures of draft-age men but little public attention.

Civil rights groups also were affected by the escalation of the war. At the end of 1965 SNCC issued a statement condemning the war and expressing solidarity with draft resisters: "We are in sympathy with and support the men in this country who are unwilling to respond to the military draft which would compel them to contribute their lives to U.S. aggression in the name of the 'freedom' we find so false in this country" (8). By the summer of 1966 SNCC sentiment had taken a militant turn, and the slogan "Hell no, we won't go!" was heard in demonstrations against induction centers. But of all major organizations, only SDS planned a systematic assault on the draft system as a primary focus of activity. The selection of an appropriate mode of attack was the subject of much SDS debate between 1965 and 1968.

Beginning in the spring of 1966, in addition to the obvious contact with Selective Service through direct dealings with local boards, students had to contend with a revived qualifying examination to determine eligibility for deferment. At about the same time, the Selective Service System began to use college academic standing as a criterion for draft selection—a practice that brought the higher education system into the induction process. Between 1965 and 1967 SDS experimented with programs designed to interfere with each of these contacts between students and the draft.

In the fall of 1965 the National Council of SDS adopted a program to encourage large-scale applications for conscientious objector (CO) status. Legal means were used— leafletting, debate, and circulation of instruction manuals. The program involved a symbolic protest against the war and sought to undercut the armed forces' supply of fresh manpower. The appeal was directed at the student's personal connection with the draft, and it was made in a way that entailed minimum risk. It also extended the possibility of personal gain, since the student deferment eventually had to be relinquished, but a person holding a CO classification could never be conscripted.

This SDS plan was condemned by many in Congress; Senator John Stennis declared that the government ought to "jerk this movement up by the roots and grind it to bits before it has the opportunity to spread further." Yet the CO classification was always difficult to obtain, and it appears that few students successfully acquired it. It is unknown how many applied because of the SDS campaign, but the relative number of COs remained static through at least mid-1966. After that there was some growth in the number of COs but not a great deal (see p. 131). No prosecutions resulted from this first SDS foray against the draft.

In the spring of 1966 the Selective Service announced that it was reviving the nationally administered aptitude examination it had given students from 1951 through 1963 (the Selective Service College Qualification Test). The Selective Service made clear that the buildup of the war was responsible for the resurrection of the exam. For the first time students were threatened with the loss of their deferred status (2S), and the depth of concern was reflected in the turnout for the test—768,000 students took the exam that spring.

Because the war, 2S status, and conscription were manifestly related by this exam, SDS was presented with a unique opportunity for mobilizing students against the draft. But the nature of the connection was problematic. Students may chafe at the thought of such an examination, but it appeared that refusal to take it would entail reclassification into a draftable category. On the other hand, the student deferment was in many ways a class-based privilege and as such was the source of considerable ambivalence among SDS activists. Stressing the privileged aspect, SDS considered encouraging students to avoid the examination altogether. The anticipated personal repercussion was loss of the 2S deferment, but this was seen as an acceptable risk.

A two-pronged rationale was proposed to justify incurring the risk of becoming eligible for the draft. The radical student movement would be more threatening—that is, powerful—if its active members committed daring acts such as voluntarily relinquishing their protection against conscription. In addition, some SDS members believed that other students might be drawn to the movement by the commitment thus demonstrated. Those in SDS opposing the boycott argued that few students who were not already in radical politics would follow the lead, and therefore SDS would only alienate the great majority of students, who would not refuse to take the exam. In the end, the action was limited to passing out antiwar and antidraft literature at exam time.

In a few isolated instances, local SDS chapters were able to mobilize fairly large groups of students to take militant action against college policies of ranking students for the draft. The best-known incident was the occupation of the administration building at the University of Chicago by several hundred students in May 1966. The protest was initially led by SDS, and the action was repeated shortly thereafter on half a dozen other campuses. However, the issue did not become part of SDS national policy (9).

In late 1966 and early 1967 SDS again organized around direct connections between students and the draft, focusing this time on a new form of agitation—draft resistance. In a period when numerous signs pointed toward the imminent drafting of students because of the Vietnam War, SDS national policy emphasized induction, the final tie between students and the Selective Service. After prolonged debate in December 1966, the SDS National Council passed an antidraft resolution, committing the organization to resistance. But it was intended to be a limited act of defiance, to be taken only when the chips were down. "Unions of draft resisters" would be organized among young men pledged to refuse induction. Members would announce their intentions through "We Won't Go" statements, and they would engage in militant protests at induction centers, demonstrate against military recruiters and draft boards, and direct educational campaigns featuring antidraft and antiwar issues. Local and national resources of the organization were to be committed to implementing the new antidraft program, which was heralded by the national secretary as a decisive shift from "protest to resistance." The resolution declared:

> SDS reaffirms its opposition to conscription in any form. We maintain that all conscription is coercive and anti-democratic, and that it is used by the United States Government to oppress people in the United States and around the world. . . . SDS opposes, and will organize against, any attempt to legitimize the Selective Service System by reforms. . . . SDS therefore encourages all young men to resist the draft. Since individual protest cannot develop the movement needed to end the draft and the war, SDS adopts the following program: A. SDS members will organize unions of draft resisters . . . (10).

Many local SDS chapters introduced parts of the program, but the major thrust was the formation of unions around the circulation of "We Won't Go" statements. The We Won't Go pledge (the slogan was first used on the May Second Movement petition circulated in 1964) committed the signer to refuse induction if called. One statement read: "Our war in Vietnam is unjust and immoral: I believe that the United States should immediately withdraw from Vietnam and that no one should be drafted to fight in this war. As long as the United States is involved in this war I will not serve in the armed forces" (11). The act of resistance was not to be preemptive—confrontation would occur only as the last alternative to induction. It was an attractive strategy for mobilization of students, since it focused on distress over the war and draft without compelling an act of self-sacrifice. It was theorized that the strength of the student movement could be increased while a threat was being directed against the government (12).

Prospects for Preemptive Resistance

Along with the increase in the number of those committed to resist, there were discussions within antiwar and radical student organizations over the logical extreme of the resistance strategy. The government had the initiative if a man postponed resistance until induction, and not many students were expected to reach that point soon. Illegal severance of connections with the Selective Service would precipitate an immediate conflict that was more than symbolic, and, if numbers proved sufficient, it might seriously reduce the pool of potential conscripts. However, to refuse further cooperation with the draft was clearly a violation of federal law and would surely lead to prosecution and imprisonment. Thus the potential gains from a militant conscription strike had to be weighed against the difficulties of recruiting numerous individuals to undertake the risky endeavor. This raised the issue of how many young men could be expected to join such an effort.

For a preemptive antidraft strategy to have any impact, substantial numbers of participants were required. Evidence of the strategy's appeal, then, was critical to potential organizers. Although the Resistance was formally organized in the fall of 1967, many of those who formed its initial backbone had been interested in the possibility of such a strategy for several years. The situation had ripened slowly, and it took time for the political logic of preemptive resistance to become sufficiently convincing.

In July 1966 a small group convened in New Haven to consider resistance and decided to endorse a statement calling for a preemptive resistance action. "On November 16 we will return our draft cards to our local boards with a notice of our refusal to cooperate until American invasions are ended. . . . We men of draft age disavow all military obligations to our government until it ceases wars against people seeking to determine their own destinies" (quoted in Friedman, 1971, 126, and Ferber and Lynd, 1971, 52). Beyond the eight who signed, would others respond?

The planners traveled the country for several weeks, and at a second meeting in New Haven they remained optimistic on the prospects for a November draft card return. However, at a national meeting of antidraft activists held the following month, the general opinion was expressed that a November action was premature. The protest would have more impact, it was argued, if people other than the initial organizers joined in; moreover, building the necessary commitment through such means as antidraft unions required more time. The New Haven strategy was sound in principle, but as a practical matter, it was felt that few were ready to face jail. This judgment necessarily was based on impressions, and there was an understandable desire to err on the conservative side (13).

Some activists drew on experiences of other movements that used draft resistance as a political weapon. At a We Won't Go conference held at the University of Chicago in December 1966, a person who was to become a central figure in the American Resistance, historian Staughton Lynd, read a paper prepared by a French anthropologist on the political use of draft defiance and desertion during the Algerian war. The fighting in the colony was unpopular in France, and manpower was secured through conscription. The method of defiance used by the French was close to that contemplated for the American scene, and references to the impact and problems of the French movement seeped into debates in this country (14).

Finally, in mid-spring 1967, the confrontation strategy underwent a crucial test. Several Cornell University students (one had been active in SDS for several years) issued a national call for the burning of draft cards on April 15. The call was not the program of a national organization, but rather materialized out of intensive internal discussions by a small campus antidraft union. The Spring Mobilization Committee to End the War in Vietnam had planned massive antiwar demonstrations for April 15 in New York City and San Francisco. The Cornell statement urged resistance on that date and included a degree of protection for participants:

> The armies of the United States have, through conscription, already oppressed or destroyed the lives and consciences of millions of Americans and Vietnamese. . . . Powerful resistance is now demanded: radical, illegal, unpleasant, sustained. . . . WE URGE ALL PEOPLE WHO HAVE CONTEMPLATED THE ACT OF DESTROYING THEIR DRAFT CARDS TO CARRY OUT THIS ACT ON APRIL 15, WITH THE UNDERSTANDING THAT THIS PLEDGE BECOMES BINDING WHEN 500 PEOPLE HAVE MADE IT (15).

By April 14 the accumulated pledges numbered around 120, far below the specified minimum. Nevertheless, a final meeting produced 57 volunteers willing to destroy their cards if 50 acted in concert. The burning took place next day in Central Park, in New York, attracting more than 150 participants (the march itself drew 200,000 protesters, according to one of several widely varying estimates). The turnout encouraged resistance organizers.

Other events in the spring of 1967 offered further evidence that sizable numbers would be willing to undertake similar confrontations. One hundred campus leaders (student body presidents, newspaper editors) sent an open letter to the administration suggesting that "unless this conflict can be ceased, the United States will find some of her most loyal and courageous young people choosing to go to jail rather than to bear the country's arms" (16). *New York Times* columnists Tom Wicker (1967) and James Reston (1967) warned of widespread draft refusal, especially among college students. The SDS newspaper, *New*

Left Notes, filled with discussions of resistance theory and activities; in March 1967 a lengthy special issue was devoted to antidraft organizing. The lead article argued that draft resistance had many advantages as a strategy; however, it also warned against "martyrdom" and unnecessarily losing people into prison (Davidson, 1967b).

Let us recapitulate briefly by recalling that by mid-1967 two developments had converged to facilitate adoption of a draft resistance strategy. A significant fraction of America's draft-eligible youth were attending college, and, as we shall see in the next chapter, induction and service in Vietnam posed an increasingly grave threat. At the same time, leftist campus organizations were shifting attention toward the student condition. Reduced off-campus opportunities and greater ferment on campus made organizing among students more attractive, and existing conflicts between students and administrations provided the framework for justifying programs oriented around student grievances. Since these cleavages stemmed from the relation between higher education and the private economy, the mobilization of students pointed toward radical change and not just reform of the university. Thus a radical protest movement became rooted in and concerned with a sector of America's draft-eligible youth just as this sector's draft problems were assuming dire proportions.

Although antidraft work with students came to be seen as a valid program, other questions remained. How, for example, was such work best undertaken? By the time of the Spring Mobilization, groups comprising the student left had acquired substantial experience in agitating with respect to both the war and conscription. The trial-and-error implementation of a variety of programs, accompanied by extensive assessment of the merits of each, gave these organizations a fairly clear picture of their operating environment.

Protest actions revealed that many students were anxious about the draft, but there were serious impediments to effectively organizing against it. For instance, discussions about means of opposing the Selective Service student aptitude examination clarified the contradictory situation facing those with draft deferments: it was in the collective interest of all students to boycott the examination, yet it was still in each individual's immediate self-interest to take the test, since doing so appeared to be necessary to retain a deferment. This meant that effective organizing of students against conscription would need to overcome potent disincentives stemming from the individual registrant's relationship with the draft system. Similarly, the limits of symbolic action had been revealed by the marginal impact of the campaign to compile declarations of intended noncooperation. Although outright draft resistance was riskier than promising resistance if called for induction, the former action was less likely to be ignored by the government. If all draft registrants collectively refused their services to the state—as opposed to merely threatening noncooperation—the government would be faced with a crippling strike by its prospective troops during wartime.

Thus the practical experience of the radical student movement in dealing with its constituencies and opponents was crucial in illuminating the potential of draft resistance and in generating the belief that progressive change could come through this strategy. Many of the early resistance organizers came from the ranks of these leftist student organizations. This circumstance, viewed in the context of the actual development of the movement, suggests that the ideological origins of a protest movement are heavily influenced by the state of political thinking in previous kindred movements. This thinking itself is a product of the political circumstances confronting the prior movements, as well as their experience in attempting to create change.

NOTES

1. Leland L. Medsker and James L. Trent, The Influence of Different Types of Public Higher Institutions on College Attendance from Varying Socioeconomic and Ability Levels (Berkeley: Center for Research and Development in Higher Education, 1965); data reproduced in Karabel (1972).

2. Discussion of these and related conflicts in higher education is taken up in Horowitz and Friedland (1970), Miles (1971), and Bowles (1972b).

3. There is some evidence that involvement in civil rights campaigns eroded student confidence in the college system. In one survey, about 160 volunteers who were active in a 1965 summer project were asked about the relevance of college for them. The question was asked before and after the summer experience. Twelve percent felt that college had become more relevant, but 40 percent believed it had become less so. This was the largest change recorded among a number of attitude dismensions examined (Demerath, Marwell, and Aiken, 1971, 163).

4. Other organizations were forming chapters on campuses around the nation, such as the May Second Movement and DuBois Clubs, but none approached the strength of SDS. The original SDS membership (early 1960s) numbered fewer than 100 students from a dozen campuses; but by 1964 membership had climbed to 2000 at 75 institutions, and by 1966 its rolls contained nearly 20,-000 names on 200 campuses (Shoben, Werdell, and Long, 1970, 208). In early 1967 the SDS national office reported 6000 dues-paying members and some 30,000 who considered themselves to be affiliated with SDS (Davidson, 1967a).

5. The new SDS vice-president argued:

> Our [knowledge] factories produce the know-how that enables the corporate state to expand, to grow, and to exploit more efficiently and extensively both in our own country and in the third world. . . . [P]erhaps we can see the vital connections our [knowledge] factories have with the present conditions of corporate liberalism when we ask ourselves what would happen if: the military found itself without ROTC students; the CIA found itself without recruits;

paternalistic welfare departments found themselves
without social workers; or the Democratic Party
found itself without young liberal apologists and campaign workers? In short, what would happen to a manipulative society if its means of creating *manipulable*
people were done away with? We might then have a
fighting chance to change the system! (Davidson,
1966).

6. The accounts by O'Brien (1969), Ferber and Lynd (1971), Lauter and Howe (1971), and Friedman (1971) of early antidraft activities were important resources for this section.

7. Justifications for these actions by some of the participants
can be found in Finn (1968a), Cornell (1968), Lynd (1968), and
Schlissel (1968).

8. Reprinted in *Liberation*, February 1966, p. 5.

9. Class ranking of students by college administrations for the Selective Service came under attack from many quarters. In the spring
of 1966 approximately 140 professors in the Chicago area issued
a statement condemning the practice on pedagogical grounds:
"When deferment is tied to performance in class an atmosphere is
generated which seriously interferes with the educational process.
. . . For the sake of the national welfare there should be as radical a separation of the activities of the Selective Service Administration from the educational enterprise as possible" (reprinted
in Wallerstein and Starr, 1971, 207–208).

Several university faculties resolved that class rankings be withheld as did the president of one college (Wayne State University);
one board of trustees (Columbia University) moved to discontinue
student rankings altogether. Apparently, however, the withdrawal
of cooperation was not widespread. In 1970 a congressional committee attempted to learn the degree to which colleges were voluntarily supplying information on the status of their students (regarding enrollment, termination of studies, lack of full-time status,
and unsatisfactory performance). Colleges were not legally obliged
to supply this information, but the survey (undertaken by Selective Service personnel) revealed that there was full cooperation of
nearly all colleges in all states (U.S. House Committee on Armed
Services, 1970, 12597–12598).

10. "Anti-draft resolution," *New Left Notes*, January 13, 1967.

11.   This pledge was circulated by the Harvard Draft Union during the spring of 1968. More than 440 undergraduate men signed the statement (9 percent of the male student body) and more than 200 Radcliffe women (17 percent of the female student body) pledged themselves to involvement in draft resistance activities. A month earlier, more than 400 faculty members had published a statement of support for Harvard students who "refuse cooperation with Selective Service because they consider the war unjust and immoral" (*Harvard Crimson*, April 15, May 15, 1968).

12.   The We Won't Go campaign had already gained momentum before the SDS endorsement, and several campus groups somewhat spontaneously circulated and published petitions in mid-fall 1966. An antidraft group at the University of Chicago called a We Won't Go conference in early December 1966. Although no concrete programs emerged from this session, the conference had "the effect of 'legitimizing' the draft resistor into a draft resistance movement," according to one participant (Howe, 1966). The new SDS antidraft program added fuel, and it is estimated by several persons involved in the movement that there were more than 40 We Won't Go groups by summer 1967, with several thousand men pledged to resist induction (cited in Ferber and Lynd, 1971, 64).

13.   Other circles were also convening to consider the potential of antidraft agitation against the war. In October 1966 a conference on "The University and the Draft," held at the City College of New York, was jointly sponsored by local chapters of a national antiwar faculty organization and SDS. At about the same time, several pacifist groups (War Resisters League, Committee for Nonviolent Action, Peacemakers) gathered in the Eastern Conference on Noncooperation with Conscription.

14.   For instance, initial reports on the We Won't Go conference to SDS membership (through *New Left Notes*) summarized the French experience and contrasted it with the situation facing the American antiwar movement (Howe, 1966; Tobis, 1967). The paper on French resistance was soon reprinted in *Liberation* (Verlet, 1967), *New Left Notes* (March 27, 1967), and an SDS antidraft organizing pamphlet (Students for a Democratic Society, 1967).

15.   "A call to burn draft cards," *Liberation*, February 1967, p. 7.

16.   A few months later several hundred student leaders signed a similar open letter. Reflecting the change in spirit over the next

two years, more than 250 student editors and campus presidents declared in the spring of 1969 that they themselves would choose imprisonment over induction. By the spring of 1971 the resistance rhetoric was gone, but a letter condemning the administration's policies in Southeast Asia then accumulated more than 400 signatures of campus leaders. (*New York Times*, April 23, 1969; April 2, 1971).

THREE

Throughout his career as a student, the pressure—the threat of loss of deferment—continues. It continues with equal intensity after graduation. . . . The psychology of granting wide choice under pressure to take action is the American or indirect way of achieving what is done by direction in foreign countries where choice is not permitted.

U.S. Selective Service System memorandum, 1965.

The halcyon days for the better educated and economically secure young men are now past. . . . [An] expert on the draft . . . believes that, if the Vietnam hostilities continue, 50 to 80 per cent of the draftees by next September will be college students.

New York Times article, 1968.

VIETNAM AND CONSCRIPTION

Understanding why a radical student movement should form around an anticonscription strike requires careful examination of the relation between the state and its draft-liable citizens. We must first consider the real impact of the draft on young men during the Vietnam War years. Which groups of youths were most affected by conscription? How did college students fare? As the war progressed, were there sharp fluctuations in the number of men inducted?

We must also examine the intensity and form of the resulting discontent among those who were subject to the draft. Although protest movements themselves can increase political consciousness, a new movement has a major advantage if alienation is already well developed. Activists will prepare to undertake a project as ambitious as a draft resistance movement only if they have visible assurance of the existence of a sizable pool of potential recruits. Trends in the scale and effects of conscription, as well as the level of discontent with this institution, are of interest both for what they tell us about the period and for what they were signaling to would-be organizers.

We begin with a brief historical overview of compulsory military service in the United States, with particular focus on conscription during the Vietnam era. The selective impact of the draft and its personal costs are then examined, especially with regard to college students. Finally, the level of discontent is assessed by considering both attitudinal and behavioral reactions.

COMPULSORY MILITARY SERVICE

Conscription in America is not unique to the modern wars of the twentieth century (1). By 1663 the Plymouth Colony had introduced a law requiring that "all and every person within the colony be subject to such military order for trayning and exercise of arms as shall be thought meet agreed on and prescribed by the Governor and Assistants" (quoted in Duggan, 1946, xvi). Conscription was the subject of more than 650 laws and provisions of the American colonies at the outbreak of the Revolution, although in practice military service was chiefly symbolic. Washington's army had depended in part on state militia units raised through conscription, but it was not until the War of 1812 that compulsory service on a national scale came under serious debate. Congress nearly passed a national draft law in 1814.

National conscription finally entered the American way of life during the Civil War, as the number of volunteers waned, apace with dwindling enthusiasm for the war. The Confederacy enacted draft legislation in 1862 (14 percent of the 1.2 million serving in the Confederate Army were conscripts), and the Union introduced it in two stages, the first in 1862. Congress passed an act in July 1862 giving Lincoln the power to demand quotas of militiamen by states, to be raised either through voluntary enlistment or through the drafting of men between 18 and 45. One clause permitted individuals to hire substitutes, creating a high-priced market for those who were willing to serve as alternates. The Militia Act was difficult to administer, and its provisions appeared to depress the flow of volunteers. Within a year, Congress passed the nation's first draft act (March 1863). In addition to retaining the option of hiring substitutes, the bill included a provision allowing for the payment of a $300 fee in lieu of service. Such escape clauses generated considerable bitterness. As a popular adage of the period put it, the Civil War was prosecuted with "the rich man's money and the poor man's blood." Opposition to the act was violent and massive. The New York draft riots of July 1863 were the most extreme reaction (approximately 1200 dead), but these events were only the protest's most visible edge.

With this backdrop, the new draft machinery failed. Nearly 300,000 names came up in the first national draft call (July 1863). Roughly 3 percent were inducted and 9 percent provided substitutes. Another 18 percent paid the requisite fee, and 70 percent found medical and other exemptions and disqualifications. Later calls fared little better, and altogether, of the more than 2 million men who served in the Union army during the Civil War, only 50,000 (2.3 percent) had been drafted (Lindsay, 1968b, 131–137).

Compulsory service was reintroduced in 1917, shortly after the country entered World War I. The Selective Draft Act, which became law in May 1917, contained many provisions that were to become familiar to the draftee of the Vietnam period. Males between the ages of 21 and 31 registered with decentralized boards of local citizens, and conscripts were drawn from this universal pool according to military needs. (The upper age limit was raised to 45 in 1918.) Full exemptions were provided for ministers, divinity students, and public officials, and non-combatant status within the military was allowed for conscientious objectors presenting claims based on membership in the major pacifist churches. Commutation fees and substitutes were abolished, thereby eliminating a major source of inequity and public opposition. In addition, critical occupations were identified. The President received authorization to exempt employees in industries considered vital to the nation, including agriculture. By the time of the armistice, the number of men registered with 4000 plus local boards exceeded 24 million. Of the 4.7 million who saw service in the armed forces, more than half (2.8 million) were involuntary recruits.

The cessation of hostilities spelled the end of conscription for two decades. However, ominous developments in Europe led to the creation in 1940 of America's first peacetime compulsory military service. Divided domestic opinion on America's potential role in the European conflict and on compulsory service helped restrict the scope of the enabling legislation, the Selective Service and Training Act. Registration of all men between 21 and 35 was mandated, but the law limited to 900,000 the number of draftees that could be in uniform at any one time. It also limited service to one year, and confined all duty to the United States.

Congress reluctantly extended the act in mid–1941, but extensive modifications put conscription on wartime footing soon after Pearl Harbor. Service was lengthened to the life of the war plus six months, and the minimum draft age later was lowered to 18. Deferments were available to those in occupations deemed essential to the national interest. Draft calls peaked at nearly half a million men per month in late 1942, and of the 16 million plus who had served by the end of 1946, approximately 10 million had been drafted.

The 1940 Selective Service Act survived two reviews in 1945 and 1946, but expired and was not renewed in early 1947. Little more than a year later, conscription reappeared in the form of the Selective Service Act of 1948, urged by the Truman administration in an atmosphere of declining volunteer rates and looming cold war (2). Basic elements of this legislation have been periodically renewed since then and have constituted a continuing basis for conscription through the Korean War, a decade of peace, and the Indochina conflict. The 1948 act included some guidelines on implementation, but major administrative questions were to be resolved by executive order of the President. Since the act provided for service on a selective rather than a universal basis, these administrative judgments were highly significant, especially as they affected the matter of who was drafted.

The President was authorized to conscript the men required for maintaining an established level of military strength, and those between 18 and 26 were to register for potential service. This pool always exceeded the number of inductees deemed necessary, however, and various criteria were established to reduce the pool and to create an order of induction priority. The Department of Defense specified mental and physical induction standards, and exemptions were provided for those occupying various official posts (e.g., members of state legislatures), as well as several other categories, including members of reserve units, ministers, and divinity students. A limited conscientious objector clause provided noncombatant service or total exemption to those who did not wish to join the armed forces for religious reasons. Secular and selective objection, and opposition based on "political, sociological, or philosophical views or a merely personal moral code" did not constitute grounds for exemption. High school and college students received a restricted protection against induction.

Secondary school students were deferred until they graduated or reached age 20, and college students could complete an academic year if called for service, provided their academic performance was adequate. Beyond this statuory protection, the President could expand student deferments as such a measure served the "national interest." In addition, the act provided that conscription should be "consistent with the maintenance of an effective national economy." Accordingly, the President was granted discretionary authority to declare deferable certain occupations in industry, agriculture, and research. Finally, an individual's family situation was to come under consideration in cases of hardship.

Draft calls were issued in December 1948 and in January 1949. After that, until the outbreak of the Korean War in June 1950, the voluntary enlistment rate was high enough to cancel the need for further nonvoluntary induction. When the Korean conflict began, however, draft induction rates soared to nearly 90,000 per month. During the Korean War approximately 27 percent of the servicemen were draftees.

In the summer of 1951 Congress amended and retitled the 1948 legislation. The Universal Military Training and Service Act of 1951 contained few significant substantive modifications, and for 20 years this act served as America's basic conscription authority. Periodic reviews and extensions in 1955, 1959, 1963, 1967 (when the title was shortened to Military Selective Service Act, since the universal aspect had never been realized), 1969, and 1971 preserved the basis concepts underlying the original formulation of selective service. Important reforms were introduced in the three later reviews, particularly in the realm of student deferments and in the method of assigning eligibility priorities. In 1969 a lottery system was initiated in which induction order was randomly assigned according to day of birth. For those without the protection of a deferment draft-eligibility was limited to a single year. New occupational deferments were eliminated in 1970 and new student deferments were abolished a year later. But while greater equity was being introduced into Selective Service policies, draft calls entered a period of sharp decline as U.S. troops were withdrawn from Vietnam, servicemen were provided higher levels of compensation, and the armed forces were substantially cut in size. In 1971 fewer than 100,000 men were conscripted, and in 1972 the total dropped to 50,000. Immediately after the United States signed the Indochina peace accords in early 1973 the Defense Department suspended all further draft calls and the armed forces were shifted to an all-volunteer recruitment basis.

CONSCRIPTION IN THE VIETNAM ERA

Overall Impact

During the 1960s the number of draftees never comprised a major proportion of those who were subject to conscription. Although draft susceptibility extended to the age of 35 for anyone who had ever received a deferment, few over the age of 26 were inducted (3). In 1960 the American male population between the ages of 18 and 26 was a little above 9.3 million, climbing to more than 11 million in 1965 and exceeding 14 million in 1970 (U.S. House Committee on Armed Services, 1966, 10003). The number of inductees never topped 340,000 in any fiscal year. The average annual induction from fiscal 1960 to 1965 was a little over 100,000, and for 1966 to 1970 just under 300,000.

In addition to those who were directly drafted, many men entered the service because they expected to be drafted. It is difficult to determine the exact proportion so motivated, but the Department of Defense conducted two surveys among those in uniform which provide a rough measure. First-term enlistees, officers, and reservists were asked whether they would have entered in the absence of a military draft (4). In 1964 the fractions of "reluctant volunteers" were 38, 41, and 71 percent, respectively; these amounts increased to 54, 60, and 80 percent in the 1968 sample survey (U.S. House Committee on Armed Services, 1966, 10038; 1970, 12638). Using the figures for the number of men entering the service during the two years preceding each survey, we find that for every person drafted during fiscal 1962–1963, another two reluctantly volunteered; the ratio was slightly greater than 1 : 1 for fiscal 1966–1967 (5). Combining induction and reluctant volunteer figures, we obtain the numbers of men entering annually because of conscription during the early period and during the later period: approximately 345,000 and 670,000 respectively. Assuming a relatively static situation—the former figure holding for the period 1962–1965 and the latter number valid for 1965–1969—we see that of the 11 million plus men within the eligible age range, roughly 4 million reluctantly entered military service. Conscription singled out one of every three young men in the United States.

Another way to approach this question is to examine the incidence of military experience among those reaching the age of 26. A Pentagon analysis based on U.S. Census figures concluded that 58 percent of 26-year-old males in 1962 had some military experience. The percentages declined to 52 and 46 percent in 1964 and 1966, respectively (U.S. House Committee on Armed Services, 1966, 10005). During the 1960–1965 fiscal-year period, the armed forces gained one-fifth of their new personnel directly through the draft, and the figure for the fiscal 1966–1970 period increased to one-third (6). Given the above-mentioned ratios of reluctant volunteers to draftees, these figures suggest that roughly 60 percent of those who served did so directly or indirectly because of conscription. For the age groups reaching 26 in the mid-1960s, this estimate implies that slightly more than one in four (e.g., 60 percent of the 46 percent who had served in the 1966 cohort) were so affected—roughly the proportion calculated earlier. Thus during the 1960s, at least, one-quarter to one-third of America's young men entered the military because of the draft.

However, the late 1960s were marked by a sharp jump in the number of conscripts. Escalation of the Vietnam War introduced a discontinuity in induction rates around 1965–1966. At the end of 1964 the United States had slightly more than 23,000 troops stationed in Vietnam, but within four years the total stood at well over half a million, peaking at 543,400 (see Figure 3.1). In 1960 there were 2.5

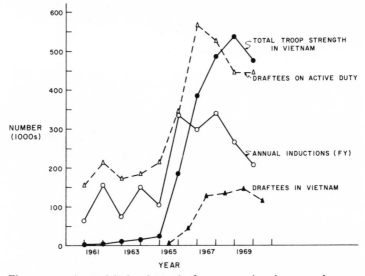

Figure 3.1   Annual inductions, draftees on active duty, total troop strength in Vietnam, and draftees in Vietnam, 1960–1970. SOURCE. U.S. Department of Defense, 1971; Glass, 1970 (draftees in Vietnam).

million American military personnel on active duty. In 1964, before the alleged Gulf of Tonkin incident and before any visible sign of impending escalation (the "Pentagon Papers" suggest that the administration of Lyndon B. Johnson was privately completing such plans), overall strength had edged up to 2.7 million. By mid-1968 more than 3.5 million people were in uniform. In February 1965, the Selective Service called up some 3600 men; within 20 months this monthly number had reached 49,000. Thus the sudden intensification of the war brought immediate consequences for America's draft-eligible population. Within two years the probability of induction had tripled—a change that could hardly escape notice by most the country's youth.

The sharpness of this increase in the number of draftees must be put in perspective, however. From February 1949 through July 1950, inductions had dropped to zero despite the existence of authority to conscript. The entry of U.S. troops into Korea was followed by calls of nearly 50,000 in September 1950 and 87,000 by January 1951. Within a year of the revival of conscription, almost 650,000 had been summoned. Even steeper induction rates accompanied the outbreak of hostilities during World Wars I and II. In late 1941, for instance, monthly quotas were averaging approximately 50,000. In the month immediately following the attack on Pearl Harbor and the declaration of war, 87,000 were inducted. The following month, 160,000 were called up, and by August 1941 more men were being drafted monthly (380,000) than during an entire year at the peak of the Vietnam War. Between mid-1941 and mid-1942, 4.5 million men entered service through induction. Thus the dramatic impact of the Vietnam War on conscription rates was not without precedent. If anything, the draft's growth was more modest than it had been at the start of the Korean War.

Distributive Impact

In a statistically random selection system (the draft has never been random, even under the lottery, since large segments were excluded by deferment or exemption), conscription would affect a cross section of the age-eligible youth of the country, allowing for minor fluctuations from call to call. What has actually been the incidence over the Vietnam decade in the United States?

It is expected on theoretical grounds that social class criteria should infuse many realms of American life, including federal government policies (see, e.g., Miliband's discussion, 1969). Empirically this hypothesis has been repeatedly demonstrated in domains ranging from treatment of mental illness to the system of school tracking. In the case of conscription, therefore, it should be anticipated that state selection procedures will be significantly related to the class background of draft registrants.

During the Civil War, Union legislation explicitly introduced such class-based policies as the commutation fee and substitute hiring. However, resistance to conscription and especially to these policies was so intense that few were ever drafted. Consequently, the social class composition of the Union army was attributable primarily to volunteer rather than induction differentials. At the other extreme, when the demand for manpower pushed conscription to very high levels during World War II, selective service approached universal service, and this tended to minimize class factors, at least in terms of who wore a uniform (the rank of the wearer was another matter). Intermediate situations prevailed during Korea and Vietnam. Although conscription was a major source of troops during both wars, the limited scale of these engagements made a full-scale mobilization of military-age youth unnecessary. The opportunity for social class criteria to enter the selection of personnel for waging these wars was at a maximum.

An Eisenhower nominee for a top Defense Department post declared in 1953 Senate hearings "that there is too much validity in the statement often made that the son of the well-to-do family goes to college and the sons of some of the rest go to Korea" (7). Using data from the city of Detroit, two researchers concluded that the charge was indeed valid—at least with respect to casualty rates. Mayer and Hoult (1955) gathered the names of Detroit men officially listed as dead, missing, or captured in Korea through April 1954. Using census data, they determined median income, value of housing, and racial composition of the neighborhoods of the 441 Detroit residents lost in Korea. Casualty rates reveal a marked linear relation to census track income. For those coming from communities in which the median incomes were under $2500, the rate was 14.6 casualties for every 10,000 dwelling units. For the $3500 to $4000 range, the average dropped to 8.6, and for $5500 and above the rate reached its lowest level, 4.6. In other words, a young man from a poor background bore a 300 percent higher risk of dying or disappearing in Korea than a man from affluent regions of Detroit (8). Moreover, the probability for a black person was approximately half again as high as that of a white with similar economic background. The rate per 10,000 for blacks from areas in which homes were valued between $8000 and $15,000 was 7.7, whereas for whites under the same conditions the level stood at 5.4.

Indirect evidence indicates that the draft played a major role in producing this pattern during the Korean War. In late 1964, as part of a major study of military manpower sponsored by the Department of Defense, the Bureau of the Census administered a lengthy questionnaire to a national sample of civilian men between the ages of 16 and 34 (Klassen, 1966). Those aged 31 to 34 in 1964 were 17 to 20 at the time of the outbreak of the Korean War, and their military experience reflected induction policies during that period. Social class background is related only weakly to whether this age group had military experience. For instance, of those who served, 76 percent had fathers who were blue collar workers or were in the military; for clerical and sales workers, the proportion stood at 75 percent, and for professional, technical, and managerial fathers the fraction dropped to 67 percent (Klassen, 1966, 232). Only sons of farm workers were significantly less prone to have had military service (56 percent). A similar pattern existed when the background variable was the father's education or race. However, of those who entered active service, there was a significant association between class background and being drafted. Thus 36 percent of the blue collar sons were drafted, in contrast to 21 percent of the sons of professionals and managers. Two in five whose fathers had an eighth-grade education or less were conscripts, but of those with college-trained fathers, only one in seven entered by way of the draft. It was the same with race— half the blacks who served were drafted, whereas only a third of the whites were conscripts. The class differences in the casualty rates probably occurred in part because draftees were more likely to be assigned infantry roles and were less likely to become officers.

The evidence relating to Vietnam points toward a curvilinear pattern, the heaviest conscription rates falling on the children of blue collar and lower-eschelon white collar workers. For example, one newspaper reported on the more than 400 Long Island men killed in Vietnam through mid-1969 and assembled the following portrait of the war casualties:

> As a group, Long Island's war dead have been overwhelmingly white, working class young men. Their parents were typically blue collar or clerical workers,

mailmen, factory workers, building tradesmen, and so
on. Most of the dead could have been expected to do
similar work, perhaps inching up the income scales a
notch or two. . . . Five of every six of the enlisted men
for whom the information is available were high school
graduates. . . . Perhaps one in eight of the enlisted men
had taken some college courses. . . . Long Island is
about 35 percent Catholic. The percentage of the war
dead that was Catholic is much higher—well over 50
percent. Whatever the national picture may be, there is
no evidence that Long Island's war dead have been disproportionately poor or black (Owens, 1969, 5R).

To evaluate the national pattern, we start with the 1964
Defense Department survey. Focusing on the group aged
24 to 26 in 1964 (those vulnerable to the draft in the late
1950s and early 1960s), 55 percent entered active military
service; of these, 11 percent were drafted (Klassen, 1966,
232, 252). The survey shows an inverse association between the probability that a young man will be drafted
and the occupational level of his father. Only 3 percent of
the sons of professionals, technicians, managers, and proprietors were inducted, but 4.4 percent of the sons of clerical and sales workers, along with 7.1 percent of the sons of
blue collar and military personnel, were drafted. For those
coming from homes without fathers or with unemployed
fathers, the rate was 8.0 percent.

If education level is used as a measure of class background, however, a strong curvilinear tendency emerges
(9). Service and draft rates as they relate to educational attainment before military service are shown in Table 3.1 for
those aged 24 to 26. The probability of serving is substantially reduced for those who enter college, and it is drastically reduced for those who pursue graduate work. On the
other hand, having little education also lowers the chance
of serving. The distribution of the draft by extent of
schooling is more ambiguous. Few college graduates ever

receive official greetings, but the figures suggest that the probabilities are roughly the same from eighth grade through a few years of college. However, a clearer curvilinear pattern is apparent if we look at slightly older men —those aged 27 to 30 in 1964 (few in this group would be likely to enter the service *after* the time of the survey). The proportion drafted rose steadily from 7 percent of those with an eighth grade education to 15 percent of those with two to three years of college; it then abruptly dropped to 6 percent of the college graduates.

Table 3.1 Percent Serving in the Armed Forces and Percent Drafted by Level of Education, for those Aged 24–26 in 1964

Education Level *	Served in Armed Forces (%)	Drafted (%)
Less than eighth grade	21	—
Eighth grade	37	7
Ninth–eleventh grade	58	7
High school graduate	67	7
College, under two years	62	4
College, two years or more	43	8
College graduate (B.A., B.S.)	43	2
Graduate study	14	0

SOURCE. Klassen (1966, 230, 250).
* For those who served, level of education is educational attainment before entry into the armed forces.

Yet this picture is incomplete. Besides those inducted, we must consider the men whose decision to volunteer for service was influenced by the existence of the draft; and we find that "reluctant volunteer" rates also vary with social background. In both the 1964 and 1968 Defense Department surveys, there was a strong correlation between educational level and "reluctant volunteer" status. For fewer than 12 years of schooling, the 1964 Army rate in this category was 28 percent. This rose sharply for those who had completed high school (47 percent) and even more sharply for those who had some college (64 percent). In 1968 the respective proportions were 34, 58, and 78 percent (Sullivan, 1970, I-2-7).

We compare the overall number of draftees and reluctant volunteers at varying levels of education with the corresponding total male population in the United States. The distribution of reluctant military participants is taken from estimates made by Oi (1967), who based his figures on the previously cited 1964 servicemen survey. Although the ratios are sensitive to the specific male cohort used for comparison, the general pattern persists, whatever reasonable control group is employed. The median age of enlistees in the early 1960s was near 19; inductee ages were between 22 and 23. Therefore, the comparison group used here consists of American males aged 20 to 24 in 1964. The ratio of draftees and reluctant volunteers to total number of eligible males by amount of education is given in Table 3.2, and the curvilinear pattern is apparent. College gradu-

Table 3.2   Reluctant Service Participants Compared with Total Male Age Cohort, by Level of Education

Education Level	Distribution (%)			Ratio	
	A: Draftees and Reluctant Volunteers	Males, 20–24 years B: White	C: Black	A : B	A : C
8 years or fewer	3.7	9.3	17.0	0.40	0.22
9–11 years	20.8	15.3	30.4	1.36	0.68
12 years	55.0	40.7	36.4	1.35	1.51
13–15 years	17.4	27.3	13.0	0.64	1.34
16 years or more	3.1	9.6	3.9	0.32	0.79

SOURCE. Column *A* from Oi (1967, 46, 56), columns *B* and *C* from Ferriss (1971, 311).

ates and those who had not entered high school were much less likely to have been coerced into service than those who had attained intermediate levels of training. This suggests that upper blue collar and lower white collar segments of American society were bearing the brunt of conscription, at least during the first half of the 1960s. Summing up several such studies, including their own detailed analysis of conscription in Wisconsin, Davis and Dolbeare arrived at a similar conclusion (1968, 129).

The class impact, of course, was not a simple product of conscious decisions by draft officials. As in the case of any major institutional complex, numerous small decisions combined to yield the procedural rules of the system. If the decisions sometimes favored and sometimes discriminated against certain segments of the draft-eligible population, the net outcome should be a conscription pattern that approximated a lottery. However, Selective Service decisions were not randomly related, and various biases led to systematic protection of some groups and exposure of others. Three major factors taken together account in large part for the draft distribution in the 1960s.

First, the armed services insisted that those entering the military meet minimal mental standards (primarily assessed by score on the Armed Forces Qualification Test), and this resulted in the relative exclusion of the poor from conscription. During the latter half of the 1960s, annual preinduction rejection rates for mental and physical reasons varied from 35 to 45 percent. Roughly a quarter of the rejections stemmed from mental disqualification and virtually all the remainder were due to physical rejection (prior to the reduction of mental standards in 1965 and 1966, closer to half of the preinduction rejections were for failure to meet the mental requirements).

Indirect evidence suggests that medical deferments did not go disproportionately to the poor; if anything, the reverse appears to have been true. In 1968, for instance, whites were medically disqualified at twice the rate of blacks. However, blacks were five times as likely to fail the mental tests, and the net outcome was a greater overall (mental and medical) rejection rate for blacks compared to whites (54 versus 40 percent; U.S. Department of the Army, 1969, 40). Assuming this pattern was in large part related to the lower economic status of blacks, it is likely that social class was inversely correlated with disqualification for mental reasons among whites, as well. This distribution does appear in pre-Vietnam data. Among those aged 16 to 23 in 1964 who had been evaluated for military service, 25 percent of the middle- and upper-class whites were declared unfit for either physical or mental reasons. Forty percent of the poor whites and blacks were so classified (Klassen, 1966, 204).

Second, a complex system of deferments and exemptions, some statutory and some based on executive decision, excluded major blocs of age-eligible persons. In June 1966, for example, one in three registrants was shielded by a deferment not relating to mental or physical qualification. Two types of deferments were particularly significant because of their close relationship with the social class of the registrants—0.3 million held an occupational deferment and nearly 2 million were deferred as students.

These exemptions protected the offspring of middle- and upper-class families. For example, the occupational deferment was earmarked for those whose employment was found to be "necessary to the maintenance of the national health, safety, or interest." The national interest was defined in a way that favored occupations requiring extensive training. Until 1968 the Department of Commerce issued a list of "essential" sectors in the economy; it included such areas as education, missile production, and the chemical industry. The Labor Department, too, interpreted the national interest by specifying certain occupational roles that might serve as guidelines when deferments were issued. The list of titles shows a preference for positions requiring college experience, such as astronomer, geologist, mathematician, nurse, scientific linguist, and high school teacher (10). The college student deferment was clearly class linked, given the strong association between college attendance and social class. In addition, the student often could prolong his protection by parlaying the college deferment into an occupational deferment. Among those aged 26 in mid-1964, 11 percent of the college graduates, but less than 1 percent of those not completing college, held occupational deferments (U.S. House Committee on Armed Services, 1966, 10011).

The third major element linking social class and draft eligibility lay in the considerable discretionary authority of the more than 4000 local boards and their unrepresentative social composition. Local board members were recruited through a variety of ways, which were by no means uniform from state to state. The Selective Service appointed members nominated by state governors, and governors normally assigned state selective service directors the job of finding nominees. Various procedures were used, but in almost every case, the boards that were created were dominated by the local elite. The California procedure was typical. State Superior Court judges nominated members from their jurisdictions. These judges are elected in nonpartisan elections, and since they are usually prominent attorneys, they tended to nominate local notables. The result was that board members in rural counties were likely to be farmers who owned large amounts of land; in urban areas, businessmen and professionals predominated (Jacobs and Gallagher, 1968, 125).

Similar elite composition prevailed in local boards across the country. This is shown in one complete survey of the country's more than 16,000 board members in 1966 (the return rate was better than 96 percent). In metropolitan regions, almost seven out of ten members were professionals, technical workers, officials, managers, or proprietors; the national census classified only one in four American male employees in these occupations. Conversely, 7 percent of the urban board members were classified as blue collar or service workers, although nationally nearly 55 percent of the work force in 1965 held such positions (National Advisory Commission on Selective Service, 1967, 75; U.S. Bureau of the Census, 1970, 225). The black representation was 1.3 percent, although the national proportion was more than eight times that figure.

Without careful analysis, it remains an unproved hypothesis that board members' class positions shaped their decisions about who was to be drafted. However, some evidence suggests that this was the case. For instance, a survey in the fall of 1966 asked Wisconsin draft board members and a cross section of the general public how important it was to defer college students. Fifty-five percent of the board representatives backed such deferments. Forty-six percent of the professionals among the public agreed, and 43 percent of the proprietors and managers concurred; but among blue collar workers, the level of support dropped to 35 percent (Davis and Dolbeare, 1968, 92).

In any case, student and occupational deferments, along with the discretionary authority of local boards, combined to create a pattern of exemption that was the reverse of that generated by mental deferments. Among a sample of age-eligible youth in 1964, the fraction possessing deferments for reasons other than mental and physical disqualification ranged from 66 percent (fathers had an eighth-grade education or less) to 75 percent (high-school educated fathers) and 89 percent (fathers had received professional or graduate training) (Klassen, 1966, 236).

Thus with mental standards truncating class eligibility from below, and student and other deferments offering extra protection at the top, the sons of economically more secure blue collar workers and lower-echelon white collar employees were most vulnerable to conscription.

STUDENT DEFERMENT

Official justification for the policy of temporarily excusing students from induction came as a corollary to occupational deferment. It was reasoned that students successfully pursuing certain lines of training were acquiring skills critical to the maintenance of a strong private economy and defense infrastructure. The policy had its origins in World War I and carried into World War II, when students were deferred "not as students, but rather because of their prospective contributions to the war effort" (Blum, 1967, 63). The special protection for students received its clearest articulation in cold war conscription policies, since available manpower far exceeded what was required. The chairman of the committee which fashioned the deferment scheme that was adopted in the early 1950s (and remained a central feature of selective service until 1967) offered the basic rationale: "Men of high ability constitute a national resource that is in short supply. From among them come our leaders and experts in every field of endeavor"; therefore, students must be allowed to continue their training (Trytten, 1952, 45).

The 2S deferment was not to be a blanket exemption, and individual ability was identified as the chief criterion for selecting students whose education was in the "national interest." Ability was measured in two ways—by scholastic rank within the school and on performance on a nationally administered aptitude examination. From 1951 through 1963 more than 600,000 students submitted to the test, and poor academic performance or low test scores led to the conscription of some students. By 1963, however, manpower needs were sufficiently light to allow exemption of all students (providing satisfactory progress was being made toward a degree). In the spring of 1963 about 2000 students (less than one examinee for every two local boards in the country) took the qualifying exam, which was finally suspended the next year. A February 1966 study found that among a 5-percent sample of army inductees (drafted over the previous 12 months), 12 percent had some college training and only 2 percent held a bachelor's degree (U.S. House Committee on Armed Services, 1966, 10012).

The sense of relative immunity from conscription, widespread among students during the 1963–1965 period, was shattered by the Vietnam buildup. At the end of June 1965, the Selective Service had an available manpower pool of 2.2 million, but the sudden increase in calls and consequent scrambling for deferments over the next 12 months reduced the pool to 1.4 million. This 40 percent attrition was a direct result of the Vietnam buildup (U.S. Selective Service System, 1967, 20). Since student deferments were not statutory, one way of ensuring the ready availability of new personnel for the growing engagement in Southeast Asia was to dip into this protected class (11). Local boards were instructed to "tighten up" on students, and several states introduced fairly drastic alterations in student policies (Wamsley, 1968, 147–148). A 1966 Department of Defense study of the draft observed that "in March, 1966, a tightening of student deferment policies was indicated to ensure an adequate supply of manpower for possible future draft calls for the Vietnam buildup. Accordingly, the Director of Selective Service . . . reinstituted the student deferment criteria based on class standing or test scores" (U.S. House Committee on Armed Services, 1966, 10013). That, indeed, he did. In the 13 years of the testing program between 1951 and 1963, 600,000+ students took the examination. Yet on three testing dates in late spring 1966, more than 750,000 men took the revived qualifying exam.

Despite widespread tension on campus, it is unclear how many students were actually drafted. A study of the reclassification procedures of a national sample of 199 draft boards was made for the period between October 1965 and September 1966, a period coinciding with the sharp escalation of draft calls for Vietnam and moves to increase the pressure on students. Of those who became eligible for induction through loss of their 2S deferments during this period, local boards had documents indicating that one in four was still a student (National Advisory Commission on the Selective Service, 1967, 95). Because local draft records were often incomplete, this is a conservative estimate of the fraction reclassified (since some of those reclassified without full information on file were probably in school). In June 1966 approximately 1.8 million students were protected with a 2S classification (about three-quarters of the full-time male undergraduates at four-year institutions).

Let us assume that approximately a fifth of those with deferment (i.e., 360,000) ceased being students in any given year; we also suppose that at least half this group (i.e., 180,000) moved into a draft-eligible status. Then the one-quarter of those reclassified 2S to 1A while still students represented roughly 45,000 young men, or around 2 percent of America's full-time male undergraduates. During the first year of the Vietnam engagement, every fiftieth student was conscripted out of his studies—a trend probably visible to most undergraduates, given the strong self-interested concern with the topic.

On several more occasions during the fall of 1966 and

spring of 1967, the Selective Service administered its qualifying exam to a total of 167,000 additional students. But
the 1967 renewal of the draft act revamped the student deferment system and made the tests unnecessary. With the
cold war turning hot and weekly American battle deaths
exceeding 100, the fairness of the draft had become a bit-
terly debated national issue. "Certainly any system is open
to question when it sends one youth into steaming jungles
infested with Viet Cong but lets another stay home because he's studying English sonnets at college," observed
one newspaper editorial in mid-1966 (12).

The attack on the inequities inherent in college deferments was particularly strident. Despite a presidential commission, a congressional commission, several national conferences, hundreds of newspaper editorials, dozens of
protest demonstrations, and lengthy congressional hearings,
the 1967 legislation contained few basic changes. However,
two features were novel. The President was granted authority to defer all undergraduates requesting deferment
and making normal progress in their education; thus individual ability and scholastic performance were eliminated
as criteria for selection. President Johnson issued an executive order declaring such a deferment, and after two years
of anxious uncertainty, undergraduates were abruptly
equipped with nearly ironclad protection. At the same
time, the act and consequent executive orders led to the
abolition of most graduate deferments, except in medicine
and related fields. Those entering their second year of
graduate school in the fall of 1967 were provided grand-
father clause protection and could retain a student deferment, but protection was stripped from incoming and future graduate students. However, there was a one-year
moratorium on these actions until the fall of 1968. Thus,
while the threat of immediate conscription was removed
for undergraduates, the sense of impending exposure in-

creased, particularly among juniors and seniors. Perhaps hardest hit by the news were upperclassmen at elite colleges and universities, for here majorities had traditionally continued on for postgraduate training, and expectations of near-permanent exemption had been high (13).

What was the real effect of the policy shifts on students? In 1963–1964 approximately 2 percent of first-term servicemen held college degrees (Sjaastad and Hansen, 1970, IV-1–13). Newspaper reports placed the fraction of new draftees with college degrees at 5 percent in fiscal 1967, and the amount rose to 16 percent during the fall of 1968— when graduate deferments were severely curtailed for the first time (Rosenbaum, 1969). Another report concluded that in fiscal 1969 about 9 percent of the new army inductees held college degrees (Glass, 1970).

An indirect measure comes from a comparison of reluctant volunteer rates before and after initiation of the Vietnam War. The army nonofficer rate for those having at least some college education was 64 percent in 1964; in 1968 it stood at 78 percent. Combining these figures with the number of army volunteers in 1964–1965 and 1967–1968 (Sullivan, 1970, I-2-7,8), it is found that the annual number of men with college experience who were indirectly pressed into army service tripled during the first years of escalation. If marine, navy, and air force rates for enlisted personnel are added, the total increase was by a factor of 2.5.

The relative liability of students can also be gauged by examining the proportion of students holding deferments during the latter part of the 1960s. Table 3.3 shows a fairly sharp decline in the proportion of students with a deferred status who were pursuing bachelor's and first professional degrees—from 75 percent in 1965 to 61 percent in 1967.

Other evidence indicates that conscription had a greater impact on college students than on noncollege youth as the

Table 3.3   Proportion of Male College Students Holding Student Deferments, 1964–1970

	Students with 2S Deferment as Percentage of Total Male Enrollment *	
Year	Four-Year Institutions	All Institutions †
1964	66%	49%
1965	75	54
1966	66	47
1967	61	48
1968	63	44
1969	64	45
1970	62	43

SOURCE. U.S. House Committee on Armed Services (1970, 12601).

* These figures are based on male students enrolled in four-year undergraduate and first professional degree (e.g., MD, LL.B.) programs. The 2S totals are from Selective Service records for December of each year, except 1970 (May).

† Included among the all-institution enrollment totals are part-time and junior college students who are not in a program leading to a bachelor degree. Both groups were ineligible for a student deferment.

war escalated. Consider the educational attainment of servicemen at the time of separation from the armed services. Two trends are clearly apparent in the 1965–1971 period. First, the proportion of men leaving uniform with at least some college rose steadily, beginning in 1967. Assuming a two- to three-year gap between entry and separation, the *proportion* of men entering military service in 1968 with college backgrounds increased by approximately 50 percent over that of the 1964–1965 period (Figure 3.2).

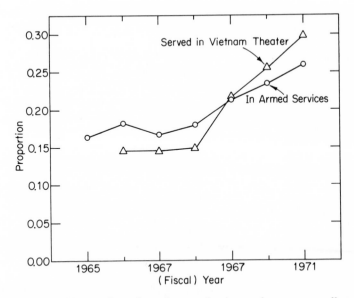

Figure 3.2   Proportion of servicemen having at least some college education when they left the armed forces, 1965–1971. SOURCE. U.S. Veterans Administration, 1972.

Because of the sharp expansion in military strength during the late 1960s, the *number* of former college students rose drastically (Figure 3.3). For instance, 90,000 were separated in fiscal 1967, but well over twice this number (237,000) left uniform in fiscal 1970. Moreover, the number of men who served in Vietnam and left the service in fiscal 1968 jumped from 48,000 to 151,000 by fiscal 1971.

Second, those having some college were *less* likely to serve in Vietnam in the war's early years than servicemen with fewer than 16 years of education, but this trend reversed among those separating by fiscal 1969. In 1966 the ratio of the proportion of those in Vietnam with college training to their overall representation in the military was

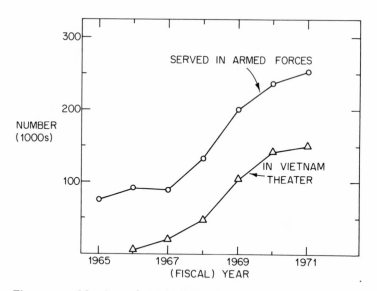

Figure 3.3   Number of servicemen having at least some college education when they left the armed forces, 1965–1971. SOURCE. U.S. Veterans Administration, 1972.

0.80. By 1969 this had risen to 1.01, and in 1971 it reached 1.15 (from U.S. Veterans Administration, 1972) (14).

From the data, it is apparent that the relatively privileged draft status of American students was seriously undermined by the increasing U.S. role in Southeast Asia. In 1965 the Selective Service was virtually guaranteeing deferments to all full-time students who were making satisfactory progress. This provided not only temporary security for undergraduates, but nearly complete exemption for those planning professional or academic careers. From 1965 on, however, the Selective Service and other federal agencies began to signal an end to immunity. Shifting conscription policies increased anxiety among students through renewal of the qualifying examination, tighter board policies on granting 2S deferments, and mounting student call-ups. By curtailing the escape into graduate and professional training, the 1967 draft legislation and executive orders reduced uncertainty for students as undergraduates but increased their postgraduate liability. In this way the war heightened the probability that all draft-age men might be inducted and shifted the draft's impact proportionally toward the student population. Yet the effects of the draft on students never reached extreme levels, since many continued to discover means for evading conscription.

BURDEN OF THE DRAFT

As an institution drafting 0.3 million men annually in the late 1960s and deferring millions of others, the Selective Service System was not without major influence on American life. Naturally, the impact on those facing induction was especially profound. The character of this impact is central to understanding why some came to rebel against the government's authority.

Even before a young man was called up, his life was affected by the pressures of the deferment system. In fact, the Selective Service took some pride in the role of deferments in shaping career choices of young men. An internal Selective Service memorandum (which became popular reading in the antiwar movement) furnished some revealing sociology on the unacknowledged functions of the draft in American life:

> While the best known purpose of Selective Service is to procure manpower for the armed forces, a variety of related processes take place outside delivery of manpower to the active armed forces. Many of these may be put under the heading of "channeling manpower." Many young men would not have pursued a

higher education if there had not been a program of student deferment. Many young scientists, engineers, tool and die makers, and other possessors of scarce skills would not remain in their jobs in the defense effort if it were not for a program of occupational deferments. Even though the salary of a teacher has historically been meager, many young men remain in that job, seeking the reward of a deferment. . . . The club of induction has been used to drive out of areas considered to be less important to the areas of greater importance in which deferments were given, the individuals who did not or could not participate in activities which were considered essential to the defense of the Nation. . . . Throughout his career as a student, the pressure—the threat of loss of deferment— continues. It continues with equal intensity after graduation. . . . He is impelled to pursue his skill rather than embark upon some less important enterprise and is encouraged to apply his skill in an essential activity in the national interest. (The entire memorandum is reprinted in Wallerstein and Starr, 1971, 195–202).

The document further argues that a relatively late induction age enhances the "channeling" effect. If their draft status is uncertain, registrants will seek the protection of a deferred status, the memorandum maintains. Then an older induction age, by sustaining the threat of military service for a longer period, enables the Selective Service to exert influence over more career decisions. The document's self-congratulatory tone exaggerates the real impact of the draft but accurately describes its essential effect.

One study estimated that just before the Vietnam expansion, the wasteful by-product of deferment seeking was an annual cost to those involved of around $2 to 3 billion (Sjaastad and Hansen, 1970; President's Commission on an All-Volunteer Armed Force, 1970, 27). Other studies illustrate how these costs were created. For example, draft-liable young men were at a disadvantage in the labor market.

Half the college placement offices in a 1964 survey reported that some employers had restrictions on hiring draft-eligible graduates during the 1964 academic year. A survey of civilians in the same year revealed that one in five men between the ages of 19 and 25 had been refused a job at least once because of unfavorable draft status. The discrimination was more acute for older and college-educated men. Among enlisted armed forces personnel, preservice job difficulties were experienced by 11 percent of those having a high school education or less, aged 17 to 18. Thirty-four percent of those recording a similar education level but aged 22 to 25 had this problem, and among college graduates the proportion reached 45 percent. Sixty-nine percent of the college graduates aged 22 to 25 replied affirmatively when asked the vaguer question of whether they had had personal difficulties owing to draft uncertainty (U.S. House Committee on Armed Services, 1966, 10008–10010).

Further evidence demonstrates the serious impact that "channeling" may have on registrants, even in such personal domains as marriage. Since the Korean War period the Selective Service had treated married men without children the same as single men. However, in 1963 President John F. Kennedy issued an executive order that placed married men without children after single men in the order of induction. Since the number of single men was more than adequate to meet draft calls at that time, this policy had the effect of deferring married men without children. The Defense Department checked the marriage rates for the nine months following the decree. A comparison of the marriage rates with those of two years before revealed no significant effect except in a narrow age range—those aged 20 and 21, for whom the rates increased by 7.5 and 10.9 percent, respectively. The median age of inductees in 1964 was 22 (U.S. House Committee on Armed Services, 1966, 10014–10015).

Besides career and marital "channeling," the existence of the draft had a second major consequence—the suppression of dissent. The Selective Service not only responded harshly to protest against the draft but also opposition to the Vietnam War. One of the earliest and most widely publicized episodes during the Vietnam period stemmed from an antiwar sit-in at a local board in Ann Arbor, Michigan, in the autumn of 1965. Several dozen demonstrators were arrested, and the State Director of Selective Service subsequently suggested to the participants' local boards that the individuals be made eligible for immediate induction. At least 11 demonstrators lost their deferments, although most eventually succeeded in having the action reversed by the courts (Merrill, 1966; Ross, 1966). The annual report of the Selective Service made clear its punitive reclassification policy: "[T]hose who . . . engage in sit-ins in any Selective Service office which impede the operations of the System . . . may be treated legitimately as delinquents and ordered for accelerated induction" (U.S. Selective Service System, 1967, 43).

Faced by intensified attacks on the war and associated institutions such as conscription and the military, and with outright defiance of compulsory service on the horizon, the draft administration reacted with further repressive measures. In late October 1967, just 10 days after the first national Resistance draft card return, the Selective Service director advised local boards that young men involved in illegal protests against the draft or military recruiting could be dropped from a deferred status, since violation of draft regulations was not in the "national interest." Moreover, he argued that violators should be given induction priority (through classification as "draft delinquents"). There was much adverse public reaction to this application of the draft. At a subsequent news conference, the director asserted that he had consulted with the White House prior to sending the directive. But public pressures had so intensified by late fall that the Justice Department and the Selective Service issued a joint declaration suggesting that the punitive policy was being dropped. However, the director reverted to his earlier position in later public statements. The year-end report of the Selective Service asserted that "when ordinarily peaceful and orderly demonstrations and dissentions [sic] degenerate into activities which hamper, impede, or obstruct the System's or related military manpower procurement processes, this does constitute a failure of the registrant to meet the conduct required to retain a deferment and in addition may become the basis for a determination of delinquency" (U.S. Selective Service System, 1968b, 22).

In one publicized case, an Oberlin College student who had been involved in a demonstration against military recruitment on campus was subsequently reclassified as a delinquent. In defending its action, the local board referred to the 1967 national directive (the reclassification notice was eventually rescinded; Marmion, 1968, 163). In another instance, a radical activist at the University of Oklahoma lost his deferment when the local board decided that his "activity as a member of Students for a Democratic Society [was not] to the best interests of the U.S. Government" (15).

In other publicized cases the evidence that the draft was used as a weapon against dissent was more circumstantial, but it was strong enough to arouse suspicion. Thus several organizers with the Southern Conference Educational Fund (SCEF), a progressive interracial organization working against poverty and discrimination in the South, reported harassment by the Selective Service (Reeves and Hess, 1970, 80–85; Southern Conference Educational Fund, n.d.). In one instance an SCEF leader was charged with "sedition" after he had initiated a campaign against strip mining in Kentucky. Shortly thereafter the federal courts ruled the sedition law unconstitutional, but the organizer then received an induction order. He refused induction and was sentenced to five years in jail, but the conviction was subsequently overturned by the U.S. Supreme Court.

Such cases, in conjunction with official pronouncements and an administrative system characterized by semisecret, highly variable, and seemingly arbitrary operations, fostered an image of official repression. A 1966 survey of 570 University of Wisconsin students registered with the Selective Service illustrates the sentiment prevalent on many campuses: nearly two in five believed that picketing as a peaceful protest against the Vietnam War would lead to the withdrawal of their student deferments (Davis and Dolbeare, 1968, 98) (16).

Once inducted, a young man suffered additional disadvantages. First, he typically sacrificed substantial civilian income. Second, he was exposed in time of war to injury and death, usually at a level higher than that experienced by volunteer servicemen and officers. Finally, if he were morally and politically opposed to prosecution of the Vietnam War, conscription entailed compulsory participation in an activity he regarded as fundamentally objectionable.

The economic cost of being drafted can be assessed in several ways. One of the simplest is to compare foregone civilian earnings with military compensation. The financial loss borne by conscripts reached its highest level in American history at the time of the Vietnam War escalation. The ratio of enlisted earnings (pay and allowances) to average wages in manufacturing declined from a high of 1.02 during the Civil War to 0.89 in World War I, 0.64 in World War II, 0.69 during the Korean War, 0.60 in 1960, and 0.58 in 1965 (Rafuse, 1970, III-1-41). Using data from around the 1960 period, Hansen and Weisbrod (1967) estimated that draftees and reluctant volunteers were paying an average tax of 38 percent on their potential civilian income. In the same period, civilians were being taxed at an overall rate of approximately 10 percent. Draftees during the early 1960s were "taxed" at an even higher rate than that imposed on reluctant volunteers—45 versus 28 percent (because of different earning capacities and opportunities within the service; Oi, 1967, 59).

Given the large range in civilian incomes and the comparatively narrow range in the armed services, the older and more highly educated draftees and reluctant volunteers were taxed more heavily, since their civilian earning capacity was generally greater. For draft-affected servicemen in 1959, the tax for college graduates was nearly 1.5 times that for high school graduates. Potential civilian income was taxed at a highly progressive rate that went from zero on $2000 to 9 percent on $2650 to 20 percent on $3000, and so on up to 80 percent on a salary of $12,000 (Hansen and Weisbrod, 1967, 418–419). However, there was a curvilinear aggregate cost to the strata of the society from which draftees were taken. That is, although college graduates had to forego more of their civilian income if inducted, a proportionally smaller number actually served.

Using pre-Vietnam data, Berney (1969) weighted the tax rate with the probability of being a reluctant service participant within various education levels and found an aggregate tax distribution that fell most heavily on the high school graduate stratum. The result of the calculation is somewhat dependent on the nonservice comparison group employed (Berney used a much broader group for calculating participation rates than we did in Table 3.2); however, the general pattern is unmistakable: setting the aggregate conscription tax at 1.0 for those with 8 or fewer years of education, the relative rates for those with 9–11 years, 12 years, 13–15 years, and 16+ years of education are 3.3, 4.7, 3.6, and 1.1, respectively.

When a peacetime draft was converted to wartime conscription, induction also entailed the risk of combat injury and death. However, it was not simply a matter of being conscripted at a time when the military was sustaining casualties on the front lines. Draftees were more likely to assume combat roles than volunteers. Survey data collected just before the Vietnam escalation show that among enlisted army personnel, combat positions were held by 28 percent of draftees, 25 percent of the first-term volunteers, and 21 percent of the career regulars (Moskos, 1970, 203). Many of those who enlisted and reenlisted were given some choice in the occupational specialties they entered, and these men tended to avoid infantry, artillery, and armor assignments.

Consequently, in mid-1970 25 percent of the army volunteers were serving in Vietnam, whereas 30 percent of the conscripts were stationed there. At the end of fiscal 1970 fewer than one-third (32 percent) of active-duty army personnel had entered the service as draftees, but more than two-thirds (70 percent) of the army combat roles—infantry, armor, and artillery—were filled by conscripts (Glass, 1970, 1752). During the late 1960s, according to one estimate, the average draftee had a 50 to 80 percent chance of being shipped to the war zone (Glass, 1970, 1758). The consequences can be seen in Vietnam casualty figures. In 1965 draftees accounted for one in six of those killed in action (the bulk of those sent to the front lines when the war began were regular army troops). In 1966 it was one in four, and by 1969 it was running at two in five (Table 3.4). In the army, conscripts accounted for 28 percent of the deaths during 1965 but 62 percent by 1969. On a cumulative basis, nearly half of army battle deaths in Vietnam through 1970 were drafted men.

The meaning of these figures for the prospective conscript is more apparent when the individual casualty prob-

Table 3.4   Annual Draftee and Total Battle Deaths in the Vietnam War

Year	Total Number, All Services	Draftees (%)	
		All Services	Army
1965	1,369	16	28
1966	5,008	21	34
1967	9,378	34	57
1968	14,592	34	58
1969	9,414	40	62
1970	4,221	43	57

SOURCE. Columns 1 and 2, U.S. Bureau of the Census, 1971, 253; Column 3, U.S. House Committee on Armed Services, 1971, 172.

ability is calculated. In 1968, the heaviest year of fighting, the Army volunteer had an 8.4 percent chance of becoming a casualty during his 12 month tour of duty in the war zone (1.6 percent chance of death and 6.8 percent of injury). For the conscript, the rate was 15.7 percent (3.9 death, 11.8 injury). Thus during the heaviest ground combat period in Vietnam, for every army volunteer wounded or killed in action, nearly two (1.8) army draftees were casualties; for the five years of most active fighting, the overall ratio stood at 1 : 1.5 (Glass, 1970). Combining the chance of being shipped to Vietnam with the probability of suffering serious injury or death, the person drafted during the height of the war stood a 5 to 10 percent chance of becoming a casualty.

Given this relation between conscription and Vietnam casualty rates and the incidence of conscription by social class, we would expect that injuries and deaths in Vietnam would weigh heaviest on the sons of families in the middle of the class system. Within the service, the distribution should be shifted somewhat toward the poor end because of the differential class allocation of manpower. For example, 1964 data indicated that a draftee having some college training was half as likely to be assigned a combat specialty as a fellow draftee with only high school training; the same college-trained individual had 40 percent the chance of the conscript with less than a high school education (the same pattern applied to volunteers; Moskos, 1970, 203).

As in the Korean case, fragmentary evidence is consistent with the foregoing expectation. The Long Island study of Vietnam casualties already mentioned found a disproportionately high death rate among sons from the upper levels of the working class, and a similar pattern is revealed in a study of Vietnam dead who had lived in Salt Lake City. All but two of the 67 killed through 1968 had come from areas in which the median family income lay between $4000 and $8000 (using 1960 census data) whereas only 80 percent of the total population lived in these neighborhoods. The impact was particularly heavy— over half—in the $5000 to $6000 range; none of the war dead came from areas with less than $4000 income, and only two lived in the over-$8000 areas (Clayton and Smith, 1970).

An analysis of Wisconsin servicemen killed in Vietnam through 1967 indicates that the "poor" were overrepresented by a factor of about 2 relative to their proportion in the state population (Zeitlin, 1970b). One study analyzed casualty rates state by state. Leigh and Berney (1971) compared these rates with several indices of the social composition of each state—such as per capita income, unemployment, and fraction that failed the Armed Forces Qualification Test. The results show that poorer states sustained higher casualty levels (even when the proportion of a state's population in uniform was controlled), but the trends suggested by the aggregate data may not apply to individual casualty patterns.

It is unclear how many college students ever saw the front lines. The proportion of conscripts with at least some college rose after 1966, and the rate at which students were sent to Vietnam was increasing more rapidly than for servicemen as a whole. By 1968 ex-students were overrepresented in Indochina in relation to their numbers in uniform, although still underrepresented in relation to the civilian population (Figures 3.2, 3.3). Pre-Vietnam data would suggest than their roles in the war theater tended to be in support rather than combat areas. Thus college students were probably underexposed to the battlefield, but it was clear that the war's escalation substantially increased their vulnerability year by year (17).

The third major source of potential discontent among those who were eligible for the draft was the controversy over U.S. involvement in the Southeast Asian war. In mid-1965 one in four Americans believed that the dispatch of U.S. troops to Vietnam was a mistake. Shortly after the Tet offensive, more than half had adopted this view, and by 1970 the proportion was approaching three in five (Mueller, 1971). Although disenchantment with the war grew in virtually all social class, racial, age, and political groups (Wright, 1972), some were consistently more opposed than others. Blacks, women, the less educated, and those of lower economic status were significantly more dovish throughout the war (Verba et al., 1967; Hamilton, 1968; Hahn, 1970; Rosenberg, Verba, and Converse, 1970, Ch. 3). What about those for whom nonvoluntary service in the war was at least a possibility?

American youth was not exceptionally antiwar. In fact, during the war's early years young people were slightly more favorable toward U.S. involvement than their grandparents' generation—and even a bit more than some in their parents' generation. For instance, in 1964 more than a third of those aged 18 to 24 urged that the United States

take a stronger stand, even if this meant invading North
Vietnam. Those aged 25 to 29 were slightly more hawkish,
but support for escalation declined in older age groups. A
quarter of those between 45 and 49 and only a fifth of
those over 65 were in the hawks' camp (Hamilton, 1968).
This pattern was maintained through much of the war, although by 1969 the relationship approached curvilinearity;
that is, both the nation's young and elderly populations
were more antiwar than the middle-aged (Erskine, 1970;
Wright, 1972).

However, youth was far from united on such political
issues, and educational factors were a major source of dif-
ferentiation. Although national polls repeatedly found that
those with more education were inclined to support the
government's war policies, those actually in college during
the war years were somewhat more antiwar than their
noncollege peers. Consider one national poll conducted in
the fall of 1968 among a cross section of college and noncollege youth. Within the college group, the survey distinguished between those who saw their education in career
terms and those who saw it as an opportunity to change
American life (the split was roughly 60/40). When asked
about the war, 46 percent of the noncollege group indicated "strong support for the U.S. position." Among the
students, the same view was held by 26 percent of the ca-
reer-oriented and 14 percent of the change-oriented individuals (*Fortune Magazine*, 1969).

The *Fortune* survey also illustrates the diversity within
the campus population. Opinion differed along both individual and institutional lines (though decreasingly so toward the close of the decade). Many of the typical attributes of student activists (e.g., upper-middle-class
background, high scholastic achievement) correlated with
opposition to the war. The antiwar climates at colleges and
universities were related to similar factors (e.g., size, policy

of selective admissions, presence of research-oriented faculty). In one national survey, Converse and Schuman (1970) examined war opinion as a function of the type of college attended. Generally, the more elite the campus, the more dovish the sentiment of its alumni. Education's "upper crust" was to the left of the noncollege population, but the "lower crust" leaned rightward.

Comparable differences can be noted in the incidence of campus antiwar and antidraft protest. Peterson (1970) surveyed deans of students at four-year accredited colleges and universities about episodes of organized student protest during the 1967–1968 academic year. The proportion of campuses on which antidraft protests occurred ranged from 6 percent at teachers' colleges and 15 percent at Catholic institutions to 36 percent at public and 55 percent at private universities. Demonstrations against Vietnam policies occurred at less than a third of teachers' and Catholic schools (21 and 28 percent) but at more than half of the public and private universities (53 and 68 percent).

Intense antiwar sentiment was prevalent in some collegiate circles and on at least some campuses. Moreover, a 1971 study found that the political and moral issues on which opposition to the war was based were much broader at one institution (the University of Michigan) than among the population at large (Schuman, 1972). The students who believed that sending troops to Vietnam had been a mistake were asked to indicate the reason for their opinion, and their responses were compared with those of a sample of Detroit area residents. Among the respondents naming as one reason the war's cost in lives, three-quarters of the Detroit residents mentioned *only* American lives, whereas the same fraction of Michigan students referred to *both* U.S. and Vietnamese deaths.

For at least a segment of the student population, then, conscription included the prospect of forced participation in a war antithetical to deeply held values. It became a dishonorable calling. Taking the risk of personal injury or death could no longer be justified as patriotic sacrifice.

Even the 90 percent of draftees who survived their tour uninjured had to face additional problems on their return. Despite the advantages conferred by serving—such as preferential hiring policies for veterans, special educational and health benefits, and the carryover of skills acquired in the military—there were also some obvious costs. These included delays in acquiring college training, loss of several years' experience in the civilian work force, and, at least initially, a higher chance of unemployment—in 1970 the unemployment rate among veterans aged 20 to 24 was 16 percent above the male nonveteran rate (U.S. Department of Labor, 1971, 26). It was also learned that except for a few specialized areas such as electronics, the carryover of military skills was minimal. In one survey of army veterans who left the service between 1962 and 1965, among those who had served one term as enlisted men, fewer than one in six reported finding a civilian job requiring skills related to his service occupation (Kassing, 1970). Inductees were much more likely to be assigned tasks having no civilian application. In reviewing a number of studies of veterans' earnings, Kassing concluded that military service does not increase a young man's position in the civilian occupational market, and there was some evidence that it was detrimental. A 1964 study of veterans and nonveterans, in which education was controlled, showed that among whites the nonveterans were receiving salaries about 10 percent higher than those earned by veterans. On the basis of several other studies, however, Janowitz (1971) concluded that military service does have a small positive effect on the lives of persons from low socioeconomic backgrounds. Military service results in a slight upward occupational mobility for the poor, although there is no apparent effect for those from higher class backgrounds. Yet on the whole, the evidence does not point toward any significant economic gains as a consequence of service in the armed forces. In addition, polling evidence suggests that the Vietnam veteran did not receive the same social status accorded veterans serving during other war periods.

A national Harris survey in 1971 found half the American people agreeing that "veterans of this war were made suckers, having to risk their lives in the wrong war in the wrong place at the wrong time." Such sentiment was strongest among those with whom the veteran was most likely to have contact—his peers. Although opinion overwhelmingly favored granting Vietnam veterans the same homecoming given returning soldiers in the past, few believed this was happening. Asked to compare the relative receptions, half felt that Vietnam veterans were less enthusiastically welcomed than veterans of earlier wars had been. Corroborating evidence comes from a survey of Vietnam era veterans conducted simultaneously by Harris. They were asked whether people "at home made you feel proud you had served your country in the armed forces." More than one-quarter expressed mild or strong disagreement, and college graduates most often rejected the statement (Harris and Associates, 1971a, reprinted in U.S. Senate Committee on Veterans Affairs, 1972).

DELEGITIMATION

The importance of public acceptance for the effective functioning of conscription cannot be overestimated. As an institution mobilizing the activities of millions of young men, it faced classic problems of social control, yet the solutions available to the Selective Service System were limited. The draft did not offer material incentives since, as we have already seen, conscription and military service in the late 1960s entailed substantial personal loss. Two other possible methods of control remained. One was dependent on widespread acceptance of the purposes of military activity and its methods of recruitment, and the other was contingent on the availability of coercive devices.

If selective service is considered to be a legitimate institution by the public and by draft registrants, an induction order would not seem to be an unreasonable request by the state. More generally, if military service is an honored calling, being conscripted constitutes little more than a push in the direction of one's patriotic duty. Should the level of commitment of draft-eligible youth diminish, parents, friends, teachers, and employers help restore it. When the legitimacy of compulsory service is unquestioned, an incipient antidraft movement faces a difficult fight. However, conscious antagonism in some social quarters promises the movement at least a foothold from which it can hope to gain sufficient strength to inflict concrete damage on the draft machinery. Thus it is appropriate to consider several issues regarding legitimacy. To what degree and how rapidly did acceptance of the draft deteriorate during the Vietnam era? In what quarters was hostility strongest? Such trends were crucial for a resistance movement, since the fate of an anticonscription strike was contingent on the occurrence of a rapid snowballing of membership rolls. In producing the needed expansion, the movement had to be able to exploit the breakdown (already underway) of the draft's hegemony.

When conscription is neither profitable nor widely accepted, coercion offers a final means of control. Penalties —lengthy incarceration, damaged work opportunities— are designed to outweigh the costs of submitting to induction. However, even this mode of restraint is inadequate under some circumstances. For instance, when the disadvantages of conscription rise rapidly, as during an unpopular foreign war, some will see jail or exile as less painful than serving. Furthermore, if dissent is sufficiently strong, prison and self-exile may become sanctioned. Then resistance to the draft not only involves fewer personal penalties but becomes more highly esteemed than entering the armed forces. In such a situation, the potential for a draft resistance movement is considerably heightened.

Loss of Public Confidence

Several Harris polls suggest that as the war lengthened, confidence in conscription waned. Table 3.5 shows that

Table 3.5 American Public Opinion on the Selective Service System, 1965–1969

Date		Percentage Favoring Present Draft System	
		Question A *	Question B †
March	1965	64%	
December	1965	90	
August	1966		79%
February	1967		58
May	1968		53
February	1969		57

SOURCE. Harris surveys; for 1965, *Washington Post*, December 20, 1965; for 1966 and 1967, *Washington Post*, February 20, 1967; for 1968, *Philadelphia Inquirer*, May 13, 1968; for 1969, *Boston Globe*, March 3, 1969.

* "Do you feel that all young men who are able-bodied should be eligible to be drafted for military service (or offered noncombat service for religious reasons), or do you oppose the draft?"

† "As you know, young men 18 years old and over, if physically qualified, are subject to the military draft. In general, do you favor or oppose the draft as it now works?"

the initial major commitment of American troops to Southeast Asia in late 1965 was accompanied by a surge of enthusiasm for the draft, a trend consistent with the initial public rallying behind the involvement in Vietnam (18). There is a better than 25 percent increase in support between March and December, which is to be expected during the opening months of any war (Campbell and Cain, 1965). This can be illustrated by noting that in October 1939, just after the German invasion of Poland, two in five Americans favored a universal draft; within eight months, after the fall of France, more than two in three were so inclined (Key, 1961, 277). However, the nearly universal support for conscription at the end of 1965 soon entered a decline brought on by such factors as disillusionment with the war, heavy casualty figures, and heightened visibility of draft inequities, especially those related to college student deferments. By mid-1968 overall backing had fallen to a little more than half those polled. Although a slight rise in support was registered in early 1969, other evidence suggests that the basic downward trend continued through 1970. For several years the American Council on Education asked an annual national sample of college freshman what they thought about a volunteer military organization. In 1968 support for the idea came from 37 percent and this figure reached 53 percent in the fall of 1969 and 65 percent in 1970 (Bayer, Astin, and Boruch, 1971). To the degree —perhaps quite limited—that college freshman opinion reflects national trends, the pattern indicates a steady decline in public acceptance of induction.

The vitality of public debate over amnesty also suggests waning support. Limited amnesty decrees eventually followed both World Wars, but growth of proamnesty sentiment in the midst of the Vietnam conflict is probably without precedent. A 1971 White House-sponsored youth conclave recommended an all-volunteer military and a presidential declaration of amnesty for "draft violators and exiles" (White House Conference on Youth, 1971, 22), a major issue in the 1972 presidential campaign was treatment of draft and military resisters, and numerous political and religious organizations were actively promoting amnesty by 1971.

Opinion polls reveal that public tolerance for those who avoided service was already fairly widespread several years before the War's conclusion. For example, a Gallup survey in the 1970 spring found little sentiment for punishment of those refusing induction. Only 7 percent of students and 17 percent of adults advocated jail (official policy at the time), and 29 and 8 percent, respectively, preferred no penalty whatsoever. Majorities of both groups favored noncombatant civilian service alternatives (19).

In late 1971 another Gallup survey revealed that 28 percent of the American people favored amnesty for jailed and exiled draft resisters (23 percent would extend this to deserters) (20). With the question refined to distinguish between amnesty coupled with a national service and unconditional amnesty, only 7 percent selected the latter. However, a full 64 percent backed some form of provisional amnesty (such as a period in national service). Just under one in four remained staunchly opposed to any such plan. Further erosion of opposition to unconditional amnesty was apparent in a Gallup poll conducted half a year later. Some 36 percent favored open return without penalty— a sharp increase from the 7 percent holding this position six months previously. And youth between 18 and 24 had become evenly split on the issue. However, an early 1973 Gallup survey revealed a slight reversal in this trend; the proportion backing unconditional amnesty slipped from 36 percent in mid-1972 to 29 percent in February 1973 (21). In general, proamnesty attitudes paralleled opinion on the war. For example, in the 1972 study those earning more

than $15,000 annually were opposed to amnesty by a
2-to-1 margin, wheras those with incomes under $3000 di-
vided evenly. Strongest backing for unconditional release
came from nonwhites, manual workers, and those with
grade school education—the same sectors most against
the war during the Vietnam period.

Legitimation of the Resister on Campus

As public disaffection with the draft spread, distaste in
some student sectors verged on outright hostility. The
Selective Service's coercive control declined so greatly that
increasing numbers of student registrants saw the alternative to induction as less costly than being drafted. At the
same time, draft avoidance came to be morally and politically respectable on some campuses.

By 1967 a significant minority of students at certain elite
institutions were asserting their commitment to avoid or
refuse induction. In late 1967 a poll was conducted among
Harvard seniors, and although the response rate was low
(43 percent), the results indicated widespread and militant
opposition. More than nine in ten condemned U.S. policy
in Vietnam. What if a call came to serve? One in ten said
he would go to jail, another one in ten chose exile, and
nearly three in five said they would make a determined effort to avoid service. One-third said that if drafted they
would refuse orders to fight in Vietnam (22). Similar levels
of opposition were recorded on several other elite colleges
that year. Fifteen percent of the Amherst seniors queried
stated that they would refuse service. Thirty-five percent
of Cornell seniors (Furst, 1968) and 60 percent of University of Chicago seniors and first-year graduate students
who responded said that they would refuse to serve in

Vietnam. Well over a third of the Chicago students preferred exile or imprisonment (23).

There is some evidence that the resistance ethos was filtering into high schools by 1969. A nationwide survey of high school seniors revealed that by spring of that year 4 percent claimed they would balk at induction if called. However, when asked about their friends, two in five indicated that at least a few of their associates would refuse to serve (Johnston and Bachman, 1970, 14, 102).

Evidence on the state of mind of a national cross section of college students comes from a spring 1968 survey of seniors by Harris. He concluded that "between 20 and 30 percent of the college groups called up for service in the next few months will be seriously contemplating whether or not to refuse to serve." He observed that if even a third acted on their threats, "the size of this crisis will exceed any this nation has ever faced in terms of resistance to the draft" (24). The eventual crisis did not exceed that of the Civil War, but the number of college students who said they were prepared to resist did remain large. Another Harris survey of undergraduates in late spring 1970 (this one not limited to seniors) found that one in five intended to seek exile or prison if called for conscription (Harris and Associates, 1970).

Thus it appears that a potential beachhead for a resistance movement did exist from at least 1967. A substantial pool of young men had decided to accept the harsh consequences of noncooperation if called. At the same time, registrants arriving at this position were finding increasingly supportive atmospheres on campus. A November 1967 "referendum" at 23 northeastern colleges included one somewhat ambiguous question on what people would do to express dissent from—or support of—America's current foreign policy. Nearly a quarter suggested moderate civil disobedience, including sit-ins, draft card burning, and draft resistance (Marshall and Pennie, 1968). By the fall of 1968 approximately half the students queried in a national survey felt that draft resistance was justified under some circumstances (*Fortune Magazine*, 1969, 35). The shifting atmosphere was most clearly evident in three Harris polls of college seniors. Shortly before graduation the respondents were asked "How do you feel about these individuals who are refusing to go into the armed forces when drafted, because of their opposition to the war in Vietnam? Do you respect them more or less because of the stand they are taking?" In 1968, in the first survey, 29 percent of the seniors said they felt more respect for resisters. In 1969 half the seniors leaned this way, and by 1970 three in five supported resisters (25).

Antipathy toward conscription was stronger on campus than off, and it was more advanced in institutions and circles that were dominated by leftist political views. These patterns can be seen in several national surveys conducted between 1968 and 1970. These studies were made after the Resistance had peaked, but other investigations of campus opinion over the period suggest that the relative distribution of the beliefs can be applied to 1967–1968, although the absolute levels cannot be.

The split between college and noncollege youth (aged 17 to 23 or 24) was sharp, resistance sentiment being much stronger on campus (Table 3.6). There was also considerable variation in opinion among college students themselves. Institutional traits associated with campus unrest were predictive of support for draft resisters, and, to a lesser extent personal willingness to resist (Table 3.7). An ambience conducive to resistance was most developed on large, highly selective, nondenominational private colleges.

Individual political and social values also related to attitudes regarding draft resistance. In the 1969 survey, for in-

Table 3.6   Attitudes of American Youth on Draft Resistance, 1968–1969

Question	Date	Non-college Youth (%)	College Youth (%)		
			All	"Practical" Students	"Change-Oriented" Students *
Do you feel that draft resistance is justified under any circumstances? .... Yes	October 1968	17		36	67
Resisting the draft is basically wrong—a citizen is obligated to serve his country regardless of his personal views about the justness of a war.	March–April 1969	72	44		
Using the draft as a political weapon is always or sometimes justified.	March–April 1969	29	49		

SOURCE. 1968 data from *Fortune Magazine* (1969, 35); 1969 data from Columbia Broadcasting System (1969, 22, 31).

* The distinction between "practical" and "change-oriented" college students is based on which of the following two statements respondents identified as most representative of their views on college and career: "For me, college is mainly a practical matter. With a college education I can earn more money, have a more interesting career, and enjoy a better position in society." "I'm not really concerned with the practical benefits of college. I suppose I take them for granted. College for me means something more intangible, perhaps the opportunity to change things rather than make out well within the existing system."

Table 3.7   Undergraduate Attitudes Toward Draft Resisters and Own Resistance If Called for Induction, 1970

	Respect for Draft Resisters * (%)	Exile or Jail Likely if Called for Induction (Males) † (%)
Nationwide undergraduate college students	57	20
Type of college		
Size		
10,000 and over	70	27
3000–9999	50	16
Under 3000	44	12
Control		
Private nondenominational	63	19
Public	57	21
Denominational	46	16
Selectivity ‡		
Above average	67	25
Average	65	22
Below average	46	15
Individual politics		
Political perspective		
Far left	93	63
Liberal	73	23
Middle of the road	35	4
Conservative/far right	22	0
Protest participation		
Participated in protest	79	35
Protest occurred but did not participate	36	5

SOURCE. Harris and Associates (1971b, 305–306).
* "How do you feel about those individuals who are refusing to go into the armed forces when drafted, because of their opposition to the war in Vietnam? Do you tend to respect them more or less because of the stand they are taking?" The table figures represent the percentages indicating "more" respect.

stance, the pollsters divided respondents into five political groupings on the basis of their responses to a number of social issue questions. Support for resistance as a political strategy ranged from 56 percent of the "revolutionaries" to 9 percent among "moderate reformers" and 3 percent of "conservatives." (An even stronger pattern is apparent in the 1970 poll; see Table 3.7.) College students who were more concerned with personal career than with social change tended to oppose resistance on both moral and political grounds. On some elite campuses, however, the backing for resistance actions had grown very strong by the end of the decade. For example, a sample of University of Chicago undergraduate and graduate students were asked at the end of the 1970 spring term whether they were sympathetic with the "destruction of draft board files" and whether they advocated "nonviolent demonstrations and resistance to precipitate faster changes" in American society. Two in three supported each measure (Aron, 1970, 16–17).

---

† "If you were called up for the draft, which of the following courses of action would you be likely to take? (1) Accept the draft call and serve; (2) attempt to avoid induction, but serve if these attempts failed; (3) leave the country rather than serve; (4) go to jail; (5) not sure." The percentages presented represent the proportion selecting the third option (14 percent nationwide) and fourth option (6 percent nationwide).

‡ Above-average schools (28 percent)—SAT or ACT scores of entering freshmen generally above 574; average (25 percent)— scores generally between 500 and 574; below average (47 percent)—scores generally below 500. The survey was conducted in June.

Although general political ideology was a major source of variation in antidraft sentiment, two additional factors accounted for a disparity in attitudes between college students and noncollege registrants. One was the apparent existence of a social class influence on opinion about the draft. A limited 1966 survey of Wisconsin adults aged 35 to 49 found level of education to be associated with belief in the fairness of the Selective Service System. A quarter of those with less than a high school education felt the system itself unfair, but half the respondents with at least come college believed it to be unjust (Davis and Dolbeare, 1968, 168).

A second factor affecting attitudes toward conscription was the cost to the individual of being drafted. A 1964 study shows that the degree of personal loss on induction was related to feelings that the draft was unfair (Oppenheim, 1966). The higher one's education, the more he expected further education, and the more one had planned to enter a professional career, the greater the discontent over the draft. For instance, 82 percent of prospective blue collar workers and 79 percent of prospective nonprofessional white collar workers felt that the draft was fair. But 65 percent of those expecting to become professionals or business executives were content with the draft.

Part of this variation related to social class background, but a portion stemmed from the direct costs of being conscripted. Oppenheim examined the level of opposition when the actual chances of being drafted were taken into account. She used three indices reflecting the probability of induction—whether the respondents expected to do military service, their age, and their level of family responsibility (marriage was still grounds for deferment). Among those whose career and salary losses would be greatest if drafted, protection from the draft was correlated with belief in its fairness; for those who had less to lose, the correlation was substantially weaker. For example, of the young men likely to enter college, the group in a more secure circumstance believed the system to be more just. For those unlikely to complete high school (i.e., those who stood to lose relatively less), their exposure to the draft had little bearing on their feelings of fairness. Thus conscription generated its own opposition among those threatened by it, and the reaction was particularly marked among youth who would be forced to forego the most in certain material terms.

Action: Outright Avoidance

Draft registrants faced three sets of avoidance options. One was direct resistance, which included induction refusal, destruction or return of draft papers, failure to respond to local board communications, nonregistration, and related actions. These forms of opposition entailed probable prosecution. A second option was legal evasion through classification in a deferable status. The final choice was to enter exile.

Direct Resistance. As young men turned 18 they were required by law to register with a local board. Understandably, it was difficult to determine how many failed to do so, but one estimate placed the total higher than 50,000 (26). However, the Resistance considered induction refusal to be more relevant to its objectives, and this was more readily measured. In 1970, giving testimony before a House subcommittee on the draft, a Justice Department official took note of some trends of concern to his agency: "Prior to 1967, the handling of selective service cases was not of any great significance. Since that time, however, the number of such cases has mushroomed. The great increase in these cases seemed to coincide with the great increase in draft calls in the fall of 1965. . . . The antipathy to the Vietnam War in some quarters must be considered a major factor" (U.S. House Committee on Armed Services, 1970, 12841).

Figure 3.4 confirms the foregoing observation. Until the war's escalation, the Justice Department was initiating about 300 prosecutions annually for draft law violations.

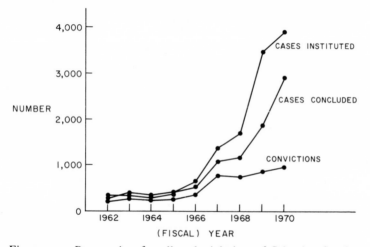

Figure 3.4   Prosecution for alleged violation of Selective Service laws, 1962–1970. SOURCE. U.S. House Committee on Armed Services, 1967, 2493–2494 (for 1962–1964); U.S. House Committee on Armed Services, 1970, 12853 (for 1965–1970).

The caseload skyrocketed after 1965, reaching nearly 4000 in fiscal 1970. Even then, the Justice Department pursued only a fraction of the cases brought to its attention. In the late 1960s, the Selective Service was lodging complaints against well over 20,000 registrants annually, yet in none of these years did the number of cases filed in court exceed 4000 (U.S. House Committee on Armed Services, 1970, 12860).

It should be noted that the growth in Selective Service violations was not simply a product of enlarged induction calls. In fiscal 1966 the number of complaints filed per 100 inductees stood at 4.0. By 1970 the rate was 12.9—a tripling of relative volume (Figure 3.5). A similar pattern exists when the prosecution load for a year is compared with

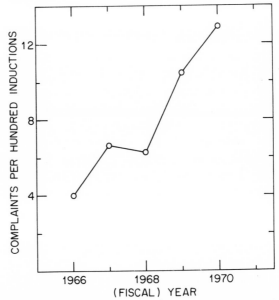

Figure 3.5 Selective Service complaints of draft law violations, per 100 inductions, 1966–1970. SOURCE. U.S. Department of Defense, 1971; U.S. House Committee on Armed Services, 1970, 12860; U.S. House Committee on Armed Services, 1967, 243.

the previous year's conscription total (up from a rate of 0.6/100 inductees in fiscal 1965 to 1.5 in 1969) (27).

In the late 1960s draft violations increased much more rapidly than the average crime rate. In fiscal 1964 Selective Service prosecutions constituted about 1 percent of all criminal cases filed by the Justice Department. By 1968 they had risen above 6 percent (at a time when prosecutions under the Civil Rights Act of 1964 dropped by a third from the previous year to a four-year low). Ten percent of all federal cases were connected with the draft by 1970 (28). This put draft evasion in the realm of major crime—it ranked fourth after auto theft and violations of immigration and narcotics laws. In San Francisco, by early 1971 more than half the criminal cases awaiting trial were for draft violations (U.S. House Committee on Armed Services, 1971, 775).

The government's reaction to draft resistance is indicative of the seriousness with which it took the threat to its authority. Punishment of "deviance" serves both to deter like actions in the future and to affirm the moral basis of the existing order. Thus the growing severity in penalties for resisting was one manifestation of the scale of opposition—the harshness of the punitive measures increased as the degree of the probable challenge was perceived as greater. This tendency was apparent in both congressional and judicial action. In 1965, shortly after some of the first antiwar demonstrations that had included highly publicized draft card burnings, Congress amended the draft law to include stiff criminal penalties for mutilation or destruction of draft credentials.

In 1967, disturbed over the inability of the Justice Department and the courts to curb the breakdown of control, Congress instructed the Justice Department to prosecute all draft resisters as rapidly as possible and ordered top priority for their cases in federal courts. The 1967 report of a House Armed Services Committee special commission on the draft included language characteristic of the period's sentiment: "The Panel was deeply concerned by what appeared to be a soft attitude on the part of public officials toward individuals who contrive to escape the privileges and responsibilities of military service. . . . The Panel reserved for this matter its strongest recommendation that 'teeth' be put into procedures for identifying all such offenders and that a vigorous program of punitive action against them be undertaken" (Civilian Advisory Panel on Military Manpower Procurement, 1967, 9–10). The Justice Department prosecuted increasing numbers of cases, and even initiated an action against those accused of inciting young men to drop out of the draft, as in the unsuccessful prosecution of Benjamin Spock, Michael Ferber, and three others for their role in the Resistance movement.

The courts also responded. During World War II the average sentence for draft violations peaked at 32 months (in 1945). In the late 1940s it dropped to a little more than 14 months; the Korean War drove it back up to 31, but during the interwar period it settled down to an average of 22 or 23 months. By fiscal 1964 it reached a 15-year low of 21 months. However, in fiscal 1966 the average violator was being sent off for 26 months; 32 in 1967, 37 in 1968, and 36 in 1969 (U.S. Senate Committee of the Judiciary, 1969, 348; U.S. Bureau of the Census, 1972, 266).

A 1969 survey of the opinions of one-third of the more than 300 federal district judges indicates that a major cause for the increase noted was a desire to stem the rise of resistance. Two-thirds of those polled agreed that "high sentences will deter potential violators more than light sentences," and most judges believed that the primary purpose of sentencing in selective service cases was to discourage future violations. As one judge put it, if the offender "is able to avoid military duty by his own decisions, the ability of the nation to have a proper military force is jeopardized." Moreover, politically motivated resistance was subject to harsher reprisal. Sixty percent of the judges who distinguished between induction refusal as an act of selective conscientious objection and refusal intended as antiwar protest believed that the latter deserved a more severe penalty. One-fifth of the judges asserted that the burning of

draft cards as a protest was more serious than refusing induction or falsifying information to the local board (*Columbia Journal of Law and Social Problems*, 1969,
182–190) (29).

Legal Evasion. Outright resistance was met with severe
penalties, and many American youths selected channels
provided by law for avoiding conscription. Trends in the
use of legal outlets during the Vietnam era suggest that the
draft was under increasing pressure from the acts of registrants seeking administrative remedies for avoiding induction.

The rights and definitions of conscientious objection
came under vigorous debate in the courts, the Congress,
the Selective Service System, and the public domain during
the Vietnam period (see Finn, 1968b; Walzer, 1970; Schlissel, 1968; Rohr, 1971). The war thrust upon draft-eligible
young men the question of whether they were conscien-
tiously opposed to killing. Many who would not have requested a CO status in peacetime discovered that they
were indeed pacifists. However, for many others who
were unable to obtain a deferment and were opposed to
serving in the armed services or fighting in Indochina, the
CO status became a potential escape route. This alternative
was particularly attractive to well-educated and affluent
youth who had the resources and background necessary
to file effectively for the status. Among other conditions,
applicants were requested to file a properly worded expression of their religious and pacifist beliefs (30).

Thus trends in CO claims probably reflected not only
shifts in pacifist sentiment but also changes in selective
objection (conscientious objection to participating in the
Vietnam war), secular objection (based on political, philosophical, moral, or sociological beliefs), and feigned objection. Smith (1971) found a moderate increase in the num-

ber of registrants holding a CO compared to the total number of young men registered. In mid-1964 only 6 of 10,000 registrants were COs. This number rose to 7 and 10 of 10,000 in 1968 and 1970, respectively. The total CO strength grew from 17,900 in 1964 to 40,600 in 1970 (U.S. Selective Service System, 1970, 56).

However, obtaining a CO status was difficult, and other statistics show that these ratios underestimated the number of CO aspirants. For instance, according to a Selective Service announcement in 1971, 4 to 5 percent of the new 18 year-old registrants were applying for CO status (31). A survey of Stanford University students in the fall of 1970 revealed even more widespread objection. All male students were asked to provide information on their draft situation. At the graduate level, 27 percent stated that they considered themselves to be conscientious objectors, although only 5 percent had sought this status with the Selective Service. At the undergraduate level the respective proportions were 41 and 7 percent (U.S. House Committee on Armed Services, 1971, 791).

Delay through appeal was another means of avoiding call-up. A registrant who objected to being made eligible for induction could take his case to a state appeals board. Again, action in this area represented both delaying tactics and valid claims to reclassification. Smith (1971), who divided the number of 1A registrants into the number of appeals over one-year intervals, found a growth from 4 per 10,000 in fiscal 1965 to 45 in 1967 and 102 in 1969.

Exile. When the second option failed—and induction or prison appeared likely—some young men left the country. Canada was the primary destination, although draft exiles settled in a number of countries. A State Department official claimed in 1970 that the best estimate of the number of draft exiles in Canada was about 2000 (32).

At about the same time, a Canadian television network estimated that the combined resister and deserter figure was nearer 60,000 (Williams, 1971, 83–84), and some estimates were considerably higher. Official Canadian immigration records show that the number of American draft-age males annually receiving "landed immigrant" status (similar to becoming a permanent resident alien in the United States) increased substantially in the late 1960s. One estimate, based on those aged 18 to 29, showed a growth from 1800 in 1965 to 2700 by 1967 and 4100 by 1969; the greatest increase was among those between ages 20 and 24 (Killmer, Lecky, and Wiley, 1971, 110).

These figures include those who deserted from the armed services. Absentee (AWOL) and desertion (absent for more than 30 days) rates soared during the Vietnam era, roughly tripling between 1965 and 1970 (for all branches except the navy). The army absentee rate grew from 5.7 percent in fiscal 1966 to 9.0 in 1968 and 13.3 by 1970. Similarly, desertion rates rose from 1.5 to 2.9 and 5.2 during the same periods. More than 70,000 men deserted from the army in fiscal 1971—a rate of 7.4 percent, which is slightly higher than World War II desertion peak rate and more than triple the highest Korean War level (33).

Those acquainted with the exile scene in Canada and elsewhere have generally surmised that deserters came disproportionately from poor and working-class backgrounds, in contrast to the more middle-class composition of the group which had avoided induction. For instance, the director of the American Civil Liberties Union's amnesty project reported in Senate testimony that "good education, middle class and white race in a general way . . . characterize those who refused to submit to compulsory military service and went to prison or into exile or underground. It is . . . the poor, less educated, and the members of minority groups who contribute a much larger proportion of the deserters, of those who submitted to induction and became aware only *in* the military of the cruelties and irrationalities of the war" (Schwarzschild, 1972, 3–4) (34).

One Defense Department study, although not conclusive, found patterns consistent with the picture just presented. The analysis covered selected characteristics of army enlisted personnel who entered the service during fiscal 1968 and 1969 and who had received "unsuitability" discharges (administrative discharges resulting from such activities as drug use, alcoholism, or frequent arrest) or were classified as deserters as of January 1971. Two-thirds of the 64,000+ men in this sample were deserters. Blacks were twice as likely to have deserted or to have been discharged (11.1 percent, versus 6.5 percent for whites), and those scoring in the lowest category of the Armed Forces Qualification Test were nearly five times as likely as the highest scoring group to have deserted or been discharged. Of the men having 12 or more years of education, the rate was 3.2 percent, whereas among those who had not graduated from high school, 15.7 percent had deserted or had been discharged as unsuitable (Flyer, 1972).

It may well be that opposition to military service and conscription was substantial for youth from all economic sectors but became manifest in different forms at different times. The wealthier individuals were more prone to resist prior to induction, and the poorer ones were more apt to rebel after entry into service. This in part reflected divergent experience in uniform. Poor and working-class men were more often assigned combat roles, and the army reports that a majority of those who went AWOL did so after receiving orders for Vietnam (35).

CONCLUSION

The conscription situation was in flux. Prior to the Indo-china buildup, roughly one in four registrants was drafted and served in the military. War-related manpower demands doubled the number of those conscripted, however, and the 1965–1968 period was marked by particularly sharp increments in draft levels, as U.S. troop strength in the war zone soared above 500,000.

Conscription, as noted, hit hardest in the center of the class structure. The very poor tended to be disqualified from service, whereas the rich were more easily able to obtain de facto exemption through a complex deferment system. Consequently the middle was the most vulnerable. Once in uniform, the higher a person's social class standing, the more likely he was to be placed in noncombatant roles, and the higher his probable rank.

Available evidence indicates that troop shortages brought on by the war increased the impact of the draft on college students. Between 1965 and 1970 the number of former students in uniform tripled, and their proportional representation doubled. In addition, certain costs of the draft fell heaviest on the collegiate population. Channeling, the state's punitive use of conscription, and the draft's extremely progressive taxation were all most acutely felt by this sector. Moreover, some student circles, especially on elite campuses, were highly critical of American policy in Southeast Asia; for them, the draft constituted impressment and forced service for objectives considered to be unjust if not repugnant.

A casualty rate for college students is hard to determine. Compared to the registrant pool as a whole, they were less likely to be drafted, since deferments provided differential protection of the affluent throughout the Vietnam era. And although students in uniform were more likely than nonstudents to wind up in the war zone as the war progressed, those who arrived overseas were less likely to see front line service. For these reasons, students probably suffered relatively fewer casualties than nonstudents. Several limited studies of Vietnam battle deaths as a function of class background consistently revealed that the middle to lower reaches of the class structure bore the greatest losses. Nevertheless, college students, like all registrants, were experiencing increasing exposure to compulsory service in Vietnam, as well as possible death. In addition, various government actions, such as reinstitution of the Selective Service College Qualification Test and abolition of the graduate deferment, encouraged the impression in 1966–1968 that induction of graduating seniors soon would occur on a massive scale. (In fact, however, it fell far short of anticipated levels.)

At the same time, conscious opposition to the draft was evolving. Public acceptance of compulsory service was being replaced by widespread doubt about the system's fairness and by a growing unwillingness to support punishment for those violating its rules. On campus, again particularly at the major universities, hostility approached a counterlegitimacy, and resistance was becoming normatively sanctioned behavior. Significant fractions of age-eligible students (one in four according to a national survey done in 1968) were seriously considering induction refusal.

These developments did not go unnoticed. Polling data and Selective Service policies received widespread press coverage, and columnists provided continuous comment on the war and its domestic effects. In the spring of 1968 Walter Lippmann alerted his readers to an incipient draft crisis. He observed that the Johnson administration was confronted with a pervasive resistance, both open and hidden, among the country's military-age generation, and for the first time in this century "it was fashionable not to go to war and entirely acceptable to avoid it."

Other indices show a corresponding expansion in the number of cases of individual avoidance. The rates of Selective Service complaints about violations tripled during the late 1960s. Government prosecution increased, and longer sentences were meted out. Similar trends appeared in other forms of individual struggle against compulsory service. Desertion, preinduction exile, and search for non-draftable classifications were all on the upswing.

The major manpower buildup in Vietnam ended in 1968, and induction calls and other pressures on draftees leveled or dropped thereafter. However, the decline in Selective Service authority continued through at least 1970. The proportion of college seniors that esteemed draft resisters in 1970 was double that of 1968. Desertion and AWOL rates in 1970 were higher than in any previous year of the war. It appears that initial conflicts connected with the war's escalation had triggered a much more far-reaching reaction to military service.

It may seem paradoxical that the class sector hardest hit by the war and conscription—upper blue collar and lower white collar occupations—did not spawn a registrant revolt. Rather, collective insurgency erupted among a sector of registrants enjoying a relatively favored status. Draft pressures did not directly translate into discontent and rebellion. There are several possible interpretations, and all probably contributed to the condition.

1. *Institutional Context and Mobilization.* Compared with noncollege youth, draft registrants in college were more readily mobilized for political action. One reason for this was the campus environment. Antiwar and radical sentiment was well developed at some colleges before the Resistance began, and leftist student organizations were actively attempting to organize students around their grievances. The trade union movement might have played

a similar role for noncollege youth. However, organized labor tended to support administration Vietnam policy, and thus unions were unlikely to demonstrate much interest in encouraging young members to oppose military service, regardless of the personal costs conscription involved. In addition, labor organizations typically included a broad age spectrum, in contrast to student organizations whose constituency and membership were much more universally concerned with the draft.

2. *Trends.* The college student was never subject to compulsory service to as great an extent as his noncollege peer. Nonetheless, the Vietnam War increased the probability that he would serve, and the chance that he would serve in Vietnam rose even more rapidly for him than for noncollege youth. For students at elite universities, where antiwar sentiment was typically strongest, a long-standing and previously foolproof protection was being ended by the escalation.

3. *Complex Costs.* The costs of conscription interacted with social class in divergent ways. Some costs hurt poor youths more (e.g., chance of front line service if drafted), but others left affluent youth at a greater relative disadvantage (e.g., disruption of career plans).

4. *Political Response.* Working-class youth were more prone to accept cynically a distasteful situation, whereas students from more affluent backgrounds were more likely to try to circumvent it or to attack the problem head-on. Thus reaction to the costs of conscription was contingent on prior historical and social class factors.

Those considering an anticonscription revolt saw the 1967–1968 period as opportune. Although some ominous trends were barely visible in 1966–1967, others were already apparent (e.g., escalating draft calls with no end in sight), and the situation promised to worsen. It appeared that manpower shortages and pressure for a more equitable draft were soon to expose students to massive induction.

By exacerbating a process already well underway, a movement could hope realistically to attain its logical end —rebellion among hundreds of thousands of draft registrants. The movement simply would need to collectivize and add political coherence to increasingly widespread individual action. A reasonable course for the student left by mid-1967 was to capitalize on the favorable developments.

NOTES

1. This overview of American conscription draws heavily on the work of Duggan (1946), Jacobs and Gallagher (1968), Lindsay (1968a, 1968b), Marmion (1968), Rothenberg (1968), Wamsley (1969), Rafuse (1970), Gerhardt (1971), Canby (1972), U.S. Selective Service System (1961), and Annual and Semi-Annual Reports of the Selective Service System.

2. A monthly enlistment rate of 30,000 was required to maintain the army at its authorized level of 670,000. However, during the 1947–1948 lapse in the draft, enlistments declined as low as 12,000 a month and never exceeded 24,000. By March 1948, one year after the draft ended temporarily, the army was below its authorized level by 130,000 men (Jacobs and Gallagher, 1968, 43).

3. For instance, 1 percent or less of the 1968 army inductees were over the age of 26 (U.S. Department of the Army, 1969, 62–63).

4. The question was: "If there had been no draft and you had not had any military obligation at the time you first entered Active Military Service do you think you would have entered the service (yes, definitely; yes, probably; no, probably; no, definitely; no idea)?" Draft-motivated volunteers were identified as those selecting either of the two negative options, and percentages were calculated after excluding those choosing "no idea" (ranging from 4.6 to 12.4 percent). Another way to calculate reluctant volunteer rates involves analysis of the correlation between draft calls and enlistment rates over a number of time periods. This approach yields slightly lower rates than are obtained from survey data (Fisher, 1969, 250). Its validity is questionable, however, since monthly induction calls were based in part on enlistment rates (see the discussion of Gilman, 1970, II-1-4 to II-1-10).

5. Accession figures are for fiscal 1962–1963 and 1966–1967. Reserve figures represent those entering active duty. Reserve and enlistment data are from U.S. Department of Defense (1971, 46). The officer procurement figures for 1962–1963 are from Oi (1967, 42); data for 1966 are from U.S. House Committee on Armed Services (1966, 10001). Fiscal 1966 figures are used as an estimate of the number of new officers in 1967.

6. Oi, who obtained yearly officer accession figures through 1965, shows that inductions account for 21 percent of all new military personnel during the fiscal 1960–1965 period (1967, 42). If new officer rates for the latter half of the decade are set at 50,000 annually, the induction factor for fiscal 1966–1970 is 31 percent.

7. Quoted in "Why Korea is called 'Poor man's war.'" *U.S. News and World Report*, February 20, 1953, pp. 18–20.

8. The full set of figures:

Median Income ($)	Casualty Rate / 10,000 Occupied Dwelling Units
Under $2500	14.6
2500–2999	10.8
3000–3499	9.1
3500–3999	8.6
4000–4499	7.5
4500–4999	6.6
5000–5499	5.8
5500 and over	4.6

SOURCE. Mayer and Hoult (1955, Table 3).

9. Numerous studies have shown that a close link exists between academic achievement and class origins. For instance, among male students graduating from high school in 1960, those in the highest socioeconomic fifth were more than three times as likely to enter college the following year as youths from the poorest fifth (Folger, Astin, and Bayer, 1970, 310). Moreover, students in the most affluent fifth were more than seven times as likely to have graduated from college within five years of completing high school as those in the bottom quintile.

10. However, it should be noted that even when these lists served as guidelines for assigning occupational deferments, the final decision remained with the local board. One study, using a national sample of nearly 200 draft boards, examined the official

records of reclassified men for the year ending September 1966. Of those reclassified for deferable occupations (2A), only 47 percent were in one of the designated critical occupations; 30 percent were employed in an "essential" industry, and fewer than one in three satisfied both criteria. The variation from board to board in the number of new 2As falling within the national interest categories was considerable (the interboard standard deviation was 27 percent: National Advisory Commission on Selective Service, 1967, 102). In 1968, the lists were abandoned altogether, although the occupational deferment was retained, and local boards were instructed to use their own discretion in continuing to provide exemptions on the basis of "essential community need."

11.   Another option, also used, was to dip into the class protected by medical and mental disqualification. In the summer of 1966 the Defense Department announced it would provide training and assistance to "part of America's subterranean poor" through "Project 100,000." Qualifications (primarily mental) were lowered to allow the induction of an additional 50,000 men annually and the acceptance of an equal number of volunteers who would have otherwise been turned away. Although ostensibly a liberal program to rehabilitate the country's poor, Project 100,000 provided a major source of manpower at a time when shortages due to the buildup were becoming acute. Secretary of Defense Robert McNamara declared, "[W]e can salvage tens of thousands of these men . . . [for] productive military careers and later for productive roles in society." However, the "new standards men," as they were labeled, received little special attention in the service other than assignment to combat roles. More than one in three (37 percent) found themselves in such positions although the rate for the rest of the service was less than one in four (23 percent). The program was cut back in 1971, owing to deescalation of the war and lowered draft calls (U.S. Department of Defense, 1969; Gerhardt, 1971, 279; Starr, 1973, Ch. 6).

12   *Washington Star*, May 22, 1966.

13.   Private conversation and news reporting acquired crisis overtones. In the spring of 1968 an article warning of the abolition of graduate deferments appeared in the radical national weekly *The Guardian:* "About two thirds of the men drafted next year will be college students, and about one third of them will be sent to Vietnam. Graduating college seniors, graduate students and MA recipients have been thrown into the pool, leaving only medical and divinity students untouched" (Furst, 1968). Campus newspapers

carried equally dire warnings on the fate soon to befall those leaving the fold or pursuing unprotected graduate studies. Harvard's student newspaper in late 1968 offered some estimates on students' prospects: "Increasingly large numbers of recent college graduates will be drafted in January, according to Washington draft experts. They predicted yesterday that by June degree-holders will fill from 90 to 100 percent of monthly draft quotas" (*Harvard Crimson*, November 20, 1968). The Pentagon revealed that it expected between a quarter and a third of the 1969 draftees to be college graduates (Rosenbaum, 1968). The campus newspaper at the University of Oregon put it bluntly: "Graduate students can no longer hide behind their student deferments. Now they must step forward and be counted as either supporters or resisters of the draft. . . . They must choose to fight the draft or fight" (quoted in Furst, 1968).

14. Indirect evidence suggests that prior to 1969 a person's social class was a more powerful predictor of Vietnam service than the VA figures would indicate. A 1968 (September–October) national election survey asked respondents whether they or any of their immediate relatives had been in the armed services and stationed in Vietnam over the previous five or six years. There was substantial association between three measures of social class (education, income, and status ranking of occupation) and Vietnam experience. Two of the relationships are as follows.

Social Class Variable	Proportion with Self or Relative in			
	Vietnam	Armed Services	Ratio	(N)
Education				
10th grade or less	14.0%	24.7%	.57	(393)
11th grade	12.9	25.8	.50	(248)
12th grade	12.1	30.9	.39	(528)
At least some college	7.3	27.1	.27	(439)
Family income				
$4000 or less	13.5	27.5	.49	(415)
$4000 to $7000	12.9	26.7	.48	(363)
$7000 to $12,000	10.9	31.7	.34	(524)
$12,000 and over	8.8	26.3	.33	(319)

SOURCE. 1968 National Election Survey, Center for Political Studies, University of Michigan (data made available by Andre Modigliani).

15. *New York Times*, January 19, 1968, p. 11.

16. One study suggests that some fears were well founded. Reisner (1971) inspected the appeals of 178 Selective Service registrants who were denied CO status by their local boards. The reviews were heard by appeal boards in 1968 and 1969. The success rate was low—only 14 percent of those who filed obtained the CO status they sought. The researcher examined the complete Selective Service files on each registrant and determined that 25 percent of the files included information implying opposition to the Vietnam War. Nine out of ten of these cases showed evidence of overt opposition in the form of membership in antiwar organizations or involvement in antiwar demonstrations. Not one of the 46 appeals by these antiwar applicants was successful. Several federal courts have held that opposition to the Vietnam War could not be used as grounds for denying a CO application, suggesting that antiwar students were discriminated against, at least in this administrative area.

17. Within the college population, casualty rates in all likelihood varied not only by a student's social class background but also by the type of college he attended. We might hypothesize, for example, that students at the elite universities stood less chance of entering front line service as conscripts. Stewart Alsop (1970) reported that through mid-1970 a total of two former students of Harvard, Yale, and Princeton had died as draftees in Vietnam (60 volunteers had been killed).

18. A Gallup question on whether the United States should have become involved in Southeast Asia showed a significant jump in support of the administration between late 1964 and late 1965, the period of initial American escalation of the war. However, responses to another question frequently used by Gallup since 1965 indicated that public backing peaked in 1965 and entered a continuous decline thereafter (Mueller, 1971).

19. Gallup Opinion Index, Report 59, June 1970, Princeton, N.J.

20. The question was: "Do you favor or oppose amnesty for Americans who have left the country to avoid the draft and for those who have gone to jail rather than be drafted?" However, nearly half those polled favored granting amnesty for Lt. William Calley and "other Americans" convicted of war crimes in Vietnam; only one in four opposed the idea (*Newsweek*, January 17, 1972, p. 20).

21. The question was: "Do you think young men who have left the United States to avoid the draft (A) SHOULD be allowed to return to this country without some form of punishment, or (B) SHOULD NOT be allowed to return to this country without some form of punishment." The Gallup Opinion Index, Report 86, August 1972, Princeton, N.J.; *Boston Globe*, March 5, 1973.

22. *Harvard Crimson*, January 15, 1968; *New York Times*, January 15, 1968. Caution should be exercised in interpreting these figures on pledges to resist or enter exile. They can be used as a crude measure of the growth of disaffection with conscription and the war, as well as an indication of the degree to which an atmosphere supportive of draft resistance had spread in sectors of the student population. However, it is questionable whether the verbal assertions were translated into action if and when the choice were forced. Reviews of the literature on the association between attitudes and behavior find only moderate consistency between the two (Wicker, 1969).

23. The Chicago study is reported in the *Harvard Crimson*, March 30, 1968.

24. *Boston Globe*, May 16, 1968.

25. *Boston Globe*, July 21, 1970.

26. Cited in Ferber and Lynd (1971, 283).

27. Resistance in some regions and communities was virtually epidemic. For instance, more than a quarter of the total complaints filed by the Selective Service in fiscal 1970 came from California (7400); this was double New York's share. Some figures unearthed by one newspaper illustrate the scale (Elias, 1970). California's draft quota between October 1969 and May 1970 was 7800. Some 18,000 men were ordered for induction, but 40 percent did not appear. Spot checks in affluent Los Angeles suburbs showed that at several local boards more people failed to appear for induction than the combined number of draftees and enlistees. The local U.S. attorney's office indicated that one-fifth of their staff time was consumed by such cases. Other urban areas reported comparable statistics—a Chicago-based draft resistance organization estimated that in early 1971 around 45 percent of those called were not appearing for processing (*The Peacemaker*, 24, February 6, 1971). In Oakland, California, 53 percent of 4500 called did not appear at all, another 5 percent refused to step forward, and 7 percent were rejected as unqualified, leaving 35 percent who finally entered the service (*New York Times*, May 5, 1971).

28. The 1964 and 1968 figures are from U.S. Department of Justice (1964, 1968); the 1970 data come from Justice Department testimony before the House Special Subcommittee on the Draft (U.S. House Committee on Armed Services, 1970, 12861).

29. One case illustrates the extremes to which the government and courts occasionally took their efforts to preserve the draft's authority. In the summer of 1968 a 19-year-old college student tore up his draft card at a rally protesting the Vietnam War and police violence at the Democratic National Convention in Chicago. He turned the shreds over to a police officer, but the next day remorsefully wrote his board and requested a duplicate, saying that he felt the "greatest sadness and confusion" in his life. He was reissued a card within a week, but shortly thereafter his student deferment was withdrawn. The local board acted under a national Selective Service memorandum calling for the quick induction of those who damaged their draft credentials. Normally, the government would delay any prosecution until induction, when it would either drop the case if the registrant entered the service or indict him if he refused to step forward. (From 1965 through mid-1970 the Justice Department initiated fewer than 50 prosecutions for the mutilation or destruction of draft cards.) Several weeks later, however, the student was indicted for misuse of his card and given the maximum punishment—five years in prison and a $10,000 fine. In 1971 his appeal reached the U.S. Supreme Court, and the Solicitor General argued the government's case: the "publicity given to his act—not his views—was reasonably thought to create a risk of widespread imitation." By a vote of six to three, the Court declined to review the case (*Boston Globe*, March 23, 1971; April 13, 1971).

30. The salience of the education factor can be seen in one Selective Service System survey of the educational background of those classified as conscientious objectors and awaiting work assignment in September, 1971:

Level	Distribution (%)
Trade school	4
High school graduate	18
Some college	35
College graduate	42

The average number of schooling years completed stood at 14.8. (*Draft Counselor's Newsletter*, n. 5, 1972, p. 9).

31. *Boston Globe*, April 25, 1971.
32. *New York Times*, February 5, 1970.
33. Trend data on army absenteeism and desertion are as follows:

Fiscal Year	AWOL * (%) Vietnam	Overall	Desertion (%) Vietnam	Overall
1965	1.2	6.0	0.4	1.6
1966	2.8	5.7	0.6	1.5
1967	2.1	7.8	0.6	2.1
1968	3.1	9.0	0.5	2.9
1969	2.7	11.2	0.5	4.2
1970	3.5	13.3	0.4	5.2
1971	—	17.7	—	7.4

SOURCE. Columns 1 and 3, information supplied by Directorate of Defense Information, Assistant Secretary for Public Affairs, U.S. Department of Defense, 1971; columns 2 and 4, U.S. Bureau of the Census 1972, 261.
* Figures are based on army enlisted strength. AWOL is absent without leave for 30 days or less; desertion is absent without permission for over 30 days.

34. Exile organizations in Canada offered similar assessments. Half a dozen American exile organizations in Canada released a statement in early 1972 on the growing amnesty debate in the United States. Objecting to the class bias in some proposals that would exclude deserters from a general amnesty, the statement observed that "deserters, generally are from working- or lower-class backgrounds, and are the first to get drafted and are the most likely to have received orders to go to Indochina. . . . Draft dodgers, on the other hand, generally come from middle-class backgrounds [and] have carried a student deferment to enable them to get an education while temporarily fending off the draft. . . ." ("Restoration of Civil Liberties: A Position Paper," Press Release of January 17, 1972, Toronto, Canada; also see Knight and Colhoun, 1972). Corroborative data come from a small interview study of 12 draft resisters and 21 deserters in Canada (Emerick, 1972). Compared to the deserters, the resisters tended to come from families with

higher education, higher income, and upper white collar employment. The resisters themselves were somewhat better educated and had been more active in political activities before leaving the United States.

35. "Desertions among GIs near high," *Washington Post*, August 11, 1971.

FOUR

---

*I'm through being channelled. You can count on
me to return my draft card on April 3.*

New England Resistance pledge form, 1968.

*It was the first time I had said No in a very per-
sonal and concrete way. . . . You were putting
yourself on the line.*

Boston draft resister.

*We have told the Administration and Selective
Service System where [they] can go, and the
FBI and Justice Department can follow them.*

Newsletter of the New England Resistance,
1967.

*Two hundred and eighty-one people had turned
in their [draft] card and we thought it was all
over for the war.*

Boston draft resistance organizer.

RECRUITMENT AND THE CALCULUS OF NUMBERS

On April 15, 1967, the Spring Mobilization Committee to End the War in Vietnam staged massive street demonstrations in New York City and San Francisco. In New York more than 150 individuals chose the occasion to destroy their draft cards. This event was somewhat spontaneous, but a speaker in San Francisco announced to the more than 50,000 assembled demonstrators that there shortly would be an organization for promoting and coordinating such protests. It was proclaimed that on October 16, because of the Vietnam War, a group of men would jointly return their draft cards to the government and would cease all cooperation with the Selective Service System. The movement would be called the "Resistance."

The speaker was David Harris, a Stanford University undergraduate and a member of a small ad hoc group of San Francisco activists who had decided to organize this new course of action. The group traveled the country during the following months, attempting to persuade existing antidraft groups to sponsor the October rally and, where this proved to be impossible, encouraging individuals to form new groups. Several Boston residents became intrigued by the idea over the summer, and in the early fall a working group of half a dozen was formed. A few members were in graduate studies at the time, most had finished college, and all were veteran activists whose prior engagements ranged from early civil rights efforts to SDS campus and community programs and some antidraft organizing.

The rallies were held on October 16, as planned in dozens of cities throughout the nation, and the Resistance was formally constituted as an organized movement with distinct identity. The initial success elated the Boston organizers. More than 200 young men came forward during a ceremony in a historic Boston church and burned or destroyed their draft cards—this was a more than twentyfold increase over the original organizing cadre. "I had expected 40 resisters, and when several hundred got up I almost passed out," recalls one of the central figures in the Boston movement. "We had pulled off this phenomenal 16th thing, we were still singing the hymns, we had money and people, and we were the hottest thing going. We were really on a trip," recollects another. The euphoric atmosphere was apparent in the comments of a third organizer written shortly after the October event:

> Even now, more than a week later, there's not much we can say about October 16. The rally on Boston Common was the biggest antiwar demonstration New England has ever seen. The march to the church was orderly, peaceful, and totally impressive. . . . The service at the Arlington Street Church is something that simply doesn't bear *post facto* analysis. It had been planned for weeks. . . . But still, except to say that it was a moving, spontaneous, and beautiful thing, nobody can explain very well what happened inside the church last Monday. The most irreligious of us, perhaps, are ready now to believe in miracles (1).

The press was equally astonished by the scale of this movement's opening event. The lead story in the *Boston Globe* the next morning headlined: "67 Burn Draft Cards in Boston, 214 Turn in Cards, 5000 at Rally." "Federal Prosecution Hinted for All Without Draft Card" warned an even larger headline in the evening edition.

In the political currents of mid-1967, the prospects for a draft strike looked reasonably good, and a small band of draft registrants initiated such an action—with a new movement organization to go with it. We have already seen that basic elements of this strategy were precast in trends in the radical student movement and the incipient decline of belief in the draft's legitimacy among college students. Mobilizing the campus had been defined as a valid means for strengthening the radical left. This analysis appeared to receive confirmation in the upsurge of open discontent with the college environment and concern with broader American problems. Survey studies confirm what student organizers already sensed from their own experience. Activism rarely characterized more than a fifth of the student body, but majorities often backed the objectives of radically oriented protest when it broke out (2). At the same time, the prospect of being personally forced to fight was turning the distant war into a concrete issue among student draft registrants. By 1967 the induction of students was on the rise, and measures such as the abolition of graduate deferments and the punitive use of the draft against antiwar dissenters were creating an even more threatening atmosphere. Therefore, political programs against the draft could be seen as attempts to meet real problems felt and faced by the student population. But by 1967 it was also apparent that it would be difficult to design an antidraft program that would affect the war and mobilize uninvolved students. Several prior attempts had shown only marginal success.

General aspects of the goals and strategy of the Resistance derived from previous developments, but specific questions remained to be resolved by the movement itself. Since the movement's final program reflected the political context in which it germinated, an understanding of its form requires examination of the movement's initial relation to its environment. The political context of a protest movement can be broken into three distinct elements.

1. *Opposition.* Significant aspects of the institutions under challenge by a protest movement include their actual and potential power, the modes of control they employ in responding to the protest, the specific interests under attack, and the ease or difficulty with which the institutions are targeted for protest actions.

2. *Constituency.* The *base* constituency is the sector that the movement claims to represent; it is the primary source of recruitment. An *intermediary* constituency is a sector affiliated with neither the movement nor its opponent; it may play a mediating role, or it may be encouraged to influence the actions of one or the other of the parties to the conflict. Campus protest organizations often viewed the student body as the base constituency and the college administration as the opponent, the faculty and broader public being seen as intermediary constituencies.

3. *The broader protest movement community.* Movement organizations are often a part of a more general community of dissenting organizations. CORE, for example, was one group among many which composed the diffusely organized civil rights struggle of the early 1960s. The strength of this broader movement community and its general regard for the specific member organization can significantly affect the life and operations of the latter.

In narrow terms, the opposition of the Resistance was primarily the Selective Service System, its base constituency was student draft registrants, one intermediary constituency was a middle-class "conscience community" perceived to have some influence with the federal government, and the supportive dissident community was the radical student movement. In less restrictive terms, however, the opposition also included those institutions sustaining the course of American foreign policy; nonstudent draft registrants were seen as part of the base constituency as well, and leftist, antiwar, and pacifist groupings of many varieties were part of the broader movement with which the Resistance was identified.

The focus of this chapter is on the influence of these contextual factors on the specific goals adopted by the Resistance. Its broader protest context (the radical student movement) played the decisive role in defining the primary objectives of the Resistance as it formed. These objectives centered on the application of political pressure to the Selective Service System, and this led to the question of how effective pressure could be applied with the resources available. The organizers settled on a vanguard action to be followed by a cascading expansion of draft resistance. The design of this main action strategy was dictated by the nature of the opposition target (the draft system) and the nature of the base constituency (draft registrants). A pivotal issue here was the recruitment to the movement of large numbers of draft registrants who would participate in the proposed strike. We take up the working conceptions regarding recruitment mechanisms held by the early organizers and then turn to the actual processes by which people were drawn to the movement.

THE AIM: EXPANDING INSURGENCY THROUGH THE ANTICONSCRIPTION STRIKE

Radical campus circles were cognizant of growing student malaise over the Vietnam War, but there was also awareness that many previous attempts to mobilize students had had little apparent effect on the war. Consequently, any new program under consideration was obliged to show more promise than previous ones in reaching uninvolved students and in challenging continued escalation of the war. Thus in 1967 there was a strong emphasis on finding means for directly hampering the war effort. An antiwar strategy must be capable of undermining America's role in Vietnam by the application of direct pressure, since previous expressive actions had yielded little visible gain.

However, this viewpoint posed a difficult problem for protest organizations whose membership numbered in the tens of thousands at most and whose composition was primarily young college students, a comparatively powerless sector of the society. The relatively minor scale of the existing leftist student organizations, even in alliance with off-campus antiwar groups, meant that resources for direct influence on state policies were limited. One possible remedy was to expand the student left through recruitment and radicalization of new members and supporters. Another was to devise a form of direct leverage against the national administration. Both these approaches had become important themes in New Left thinking by 1967.

The prospective conscription of college students appeared to offer a unique focal point for a protest program to satisfy both criteria. Draft registrants latently possessed that power which is available to any group of people on whose active cooperation an institution depends— withheld cooperation. If this tactic is undertaken collectively, a united group can exercise veto power over an institution's normal functioning. Creation of this unity is of course a central political problem, for noncooperation rarely spreads spontaneously to major proportions. However, a dedicated organization of prospective noncooperators might introduce the necessary unity. Consequently, it could be reasoned that the organization of draft registrants for noncooperation with the Selective Service System would force the government either to deal with the movement's demands to stop the war or to operate without a major means of manpower procurement. This type of action is often used by subordinate groups in institutions such as factories, bureaucracies, and schools. However, unlike many strikes, the demands of the proposed draft registrant strike would not be negotiable (since the strike would be terminated only if the war were ended or conscription abolished). It would be a permanent strike.

Thus draft resistance appeared to offer a means for applying direct pressure on the government. It also met the second criterion for an effective program in the context of 1967—namely, that of expanding the membership of and support for the student left. Organization of the movement necessary to instigate a conscription strike would require reaching thousands of uninvolved draft registrants. Environmental signals in 1967 suggested that creation of such a strike was a realistic possibility. Growing induction calls amidst shrinking acceptance of conscription promised accelerating momentum in exactly the same direction required to stage the strike—widespread willingness among registrants to take the risks of going out on permanent strike.

However, the administrative procedures of the military draft system introduced ambiguity into the manner of defining a strike. The deferment system placed large numbers of registrants, including most male college students, in a reserve status. Their willingness to serve would not come under immediate test, although future events might force the issue. Three types of strike were possible in this situation. Student registrants on deferment could be organized to threaten that they would refuse to enter the service if called (*threatened* resistance). (This had already been tried in the We Won't Go campaigns, and it was apparent that any effect at all on the war and the draft was minimal.) Another possibility was to organize registrants to refuse induction when called (*reactive* resistance). However, since call-up was a distant prospect for many students and since most would have left college by time they faced the decision (making organizing difficult), this was not a particularly attractive choice. The third alternative, *preemptive* resistance, was based on utilizing the government's definition of "cooperation" with the Selective Service System. Federal laws required that young men register with a local board, carry a draft card, and respond to requests for pertinent information. A strike could be organized among those prepared to renounce this form of cooperation without waiting for the actual induction order. This also meant that students could be reached while still on campus. Given the thinking and experience of the radical student left in 1967, then, *preemptive* resistance appeared to be the most promising strike form, in contrast to the threatened and reactive resistance options.

However, those committed to a preemptive resistance program never became a majority within existing organizations. Individual activists had urged draft resistance as early as 1962 in the Student Peace Union; the idea had been picked up by End the Draft in 1964, and it had gained adherents within SDS and other local antidraft associations by 1967. With the exception of some locally constituted groups (e.g., Chicago Area Draft Resisters, which was to become a mainstay of the national Resistance after October 16), such efforts generally failed. Boston Draft Resistance Group (BDRG), an antidraft organization formed in the spring of 1967, refused to adopt the program.

During the spring and summer of 1967 sentiment in SDS was sympathetic to a preemptive strike, and many argued strenuously on its behalf. SDS had already gone on record supporting a program that encouraged resistance when all other options were closed to a person. But many were opposed to a campaign that would send most participants to jail, saying that the costs would be too great in relation to the gains anticipated, and SDS never officially incorporated a preemptive strategy.

In June 1967 an SDS national convention passed a resolution clearly distinguishing between reactive and preemptive resistance. It also separated support for the preemptive action from support for those who take it, and SDS endorsed only the latter. Articles sharply critical of Resistance politics appeared in the two issues of *New Left Notes* that appeared just before October 16 (Hamilton, 1967; Garcia and Gray, 1967). On the eve of the event that was planned to inaugurate the Resistance, SDS came as close to backing preemptive resistance as it was ever to be; but even then, the group stopped short of full affirmation. On October 8, the SDS National Council went on record with a resolution promising assistance to those taking the step:

> The SDS N.C. encourages all chapters to seek out and support all men participating in the Oct. 16 refusal to co-operate with the [Selective Service System] and should aid them in further resistance to—that is, relevant obstruction and disruption of—the American war machine wherever vulnerable. SDS encourages and will help all members of "The Resistance" to defy all state authority, overt and covert, over the control of their lives, including the power to imprison our brothers in American concentration camps. . . .

But the National Council also warned against unnecessarily precipitous action:

> SDS recognizes the validity of all direct challenges to illegitimate authority, but seeing the insufficiency and misdirection of symbolic-confrontation-oriented movements, urges members of "the Resistance" to involve themselves in local community organizing projects

aiming to build a powerful insurgent white base inside
the United States (3).

Whatever the merits of the case for or against preemptive resistance, it was unlikely that an organization such as
SDS could ever adopt a preemptive program at that time.
SDS and other radical student groups were generally open
to all students sharing a commitment to radical change in
America. A preemptive resistance program would surely
split these organizations. The ranks of SDS included
women, as well as men who were ineligible for the draft,
and thus a major proportion of the members could not
have participated directly in the action. A divisive internal
cleavage would have occurred between those who were
jeopardizing personal security and those who were incapable of lending more than support. Moreover, the commitment shared within SDS did not extend to a general willingness to risk lengthy imprisonment. Many SDS activists
were prepared for such a consequence, but since this attitude was not a prerequisite for membership, large numbers
were not.

For the reasons just suggested and related considerations,
some of the early advocates of preemptive resistance became disenchanted with the proposal. But those remaining
committed to the strategy envisaged one way to circumvent the failure of existing organizations to embrace
resistance—namely, the creation of a new organization.
Since the new movement would be centrally concerned
with generating a nationwide registrant strike, it would
also be most effective (though not mandatory) from an organizing standpoint to limit membership to draft registrants who were actually on strike. It logically followed
that membership should be made contingent only on an act
of noncooperation which placed the registrant on strike. In

the interest of maximizing the scale of the strike, political beliefs other than common opposition to the Vietnam War should not be a prerequisite to membership.

Thus the state of the radical student movement in 1967 created the belief that a preemptive attack on the draft would be a valid program, but since this program at the same time contradicted principles on which existing groups were based, it could only be implemented by a new organizational vehicle. The criteria believed to be mandatory for an effective protest program carried over from the broader student protest culture into this new movement it spawned; as a result, three primary objectives were initially identified with the Resistance:

1. Creation of a tangible setback to U.S. involvement in Indochina.
2. Radicalization of new people, as recruits to the broader protest movement pushing for radical social change in America.
3. Establishment of a new organization to accomplish these tasks on a sustained basis.

These themes weave through the reflections of those we interviewed who were already seasoned activists when they joined the Resistance. "I saw myself as part of a vanguard group which could bring the war machine to a halt," reported one resister. The draft would be the critical linkage, as another recalled:

> Essentially, I saw turning in my card as a political act. From a rather shallow analysis this seemed to be the best way to end the war. . . . I had been thinking that if 50,000 announce their noncooperation it would stop the draft and the best way to halt the war is through the draft.

The overarching political aim was to build an insurgent radical movement. Most broadly, this entailed strengthening the student movement and kindred challenges to the status quo. More narrowly implied were creation and maintenance of a new movement organization. The broader perspective is apparent in the thinking of one veteran SDS activist:

> I'm not in the mainstream of the Resistance but I am in the mainstream of the New Left. I have always been involved in this movement and not the Resistance. . . . I saw [resisting] as both a tactic to end the war and a personal step that had to be taken. The fact that many young people are refusing to submit to the draft is of concern to the people in power. In all I didn't see Resistance as *the* tactic but as *a* potentially good tactic for helping to build the Movement (4).

The narrower viewpoint, stressing the creation of a new organization, was primary for one of the founders of the Resistance:

> People seem to have gotten into resistance for two reasons. First, some wanted nothing to do with the draft or the whole system. Second, some people wanted to weld a movement around a couple of issues in order to become a pain for the government. As an organizer my motivation was primarily the latter—to create trouble and help to end the war.

Similar themes are evident in the calls to resist and statements of purpose appearing in numerous flyers, rally speeches, and articles throughout the latter half of 1967, as the movement was being launched. Left-leaning magazines and journals carried extensive debates and position papers on the merits of draft resistance. These publications included *Dissent, Liberation, The Catholic Worker, The Guardian, New York Review of Books,* and dozens of underground newspapers. The lead article in a special resistance issue of a peace movement paper (*New Patriot*) circulating around Ithaca, New York, summed up the basic Resistance program:

> Because our other forms of protest fail to accomplish the ends we seek, we find ourselves in a position where we must resist. . . . We must act for these two reasons: (1) Our actions can stop or disrupt (at least temporarily) the functioning of the American War machine and/or (2) our actions are of sufficient symbolic value that they will help build our movement. . . . The most important reason I see for resisting the draft is that we are trying to build a movement that can eventually cut into the draft's manpower supply and stop the government from fighting unjustifiable wars. . . . Remember that we are in the early stages of building our movement. For it to grow, we need more and more men of draft age to resist. Public and collective actions of resistance, together with intensive community organizing, can do this (Dancis, 1967).

STRATEGY: CASCADING GROWTH

The most pressing problem for the Resistance in its early days was to fashion a strategy appropriate to the movement's aims. The calculus of numbers necessarily became a focal concern. Consider two of the stated objectives— radicalization and recruitment of new people, and the creation of a Resistance organization. The number of individuals attracted to the student left through draft resistance would be a transparent gauge of the success of the first goal, and the number of committed Resistance members would be one obvious measure of the second. The Resistance organizers faced a problem that activists attempting to strengthen any protest organization must solve.

However, two other factors unique to the strike strategy made the numerical tally an overriding concern. First, the mechanism forseen as tangibly hindering the war effort was a reduction of the pool of potential conscripts. The greater the number on strike, the greater the impact on the war. Second, there were large personal costs in undertaking noncooperation, but these could be reduced considerably if the number of resisters became sufficiently large.

Since the success of the movement was contingent on an effective strike and protection of its membership, specification of the parameters for each became key movement issues. How large would a strike have to be in order to exert real impact on the war and to end the fear of prison for resisters? It was also necessary to devise a plan for instigating the strike. The Resistance had to find a means of attacking the draft system that could not be countered effectively by the government. This would not be an easy task, given the great disparity in resources available to the opposing parties.

The implications for movement strategy of the relationship between the Resistance and its opponent, the government, are taken up in this section. The following section treats the strategic consequences of the relationship of the Resistance to its constituency of student draft registrants.

When a Strike Is a Strike

By 1967 the Vietnam War was substantially dependent on a steady flow of manpower, stimulated in part by the workings of the Selective Service. Annual draft rates were running well over a quarter million men, 130,000 conscripts were stationed in Vietnam, and half the army combat deaths were sustained by draftees. National policy was not intrinsically wedded to staffing the armed forces with conscripts, and it is conceivable that the Indochina engagement could have been waged no less effectively with volunteers alone. But there were obvious advantages in using conscripts, and in any case an administrative complex had evolved over several decades for the induction and utilization of draftees. Consequently, to threaten the pool of potential draftees would not constitute an inherent challenge to the continued prosecution of the war, but it could raise the costs to the government of proceeding with the war effort.

As one of the movement's advocates put it, the tactic of resistance had "the short-run objective of increasing the costs of the war so that the policy-makers will have one more reason for ending it" (Putnam, 1968). The most immediate cost was reduction in the flow of manpower for the war. In the longer run, the Resistance could help erode public belief in conscription, thereby making it easier for draft-eligible men to decide to refuse induction or flee to Canada, as well as creating a climate of public opinion that would make it harder for Congress to renew draft legislation. There were also secondary consequences, such as the possibly disruptive effect of widespread law breaking on the normal functioning of the government. Also, it was reasoned that the jailing of thousands of college students who had opposed the Vietnam War by refusing induction, might have a persuasive symbolic impact on an intermediary constituency, a middle-class "conscience community," which in turn might put additional pressure on the government.

Since the creation of a conscription strike was central to the proposed strategy, the Resistance had to have some idea how large such a strike would need to become in order for the Selective Service to feel the pressure. In mid-1967 the Selective Service had more than 19 million registrants in the draft-eligible age range. A major bloc consisted of veterans and those already in uniform (6 million); a second group was disqualified for physical or mental reasons (2.5 million), and another 6 million held temporary occupational, family, or student deferments. Two million registrants were classified in a special disqualification category that could be lifted during a national emergency. In all, nearly 10 million young men were deferred but theoretically available for service. Only 1.4 million were directly eligible for induction (U.S. Selective Service System, 1968a). Between mid-1966 and mid-1968, monthly draft calls ranged from 11,000 to 48,000, and a total of 0.6 million were inducted during the two-year period. If reluctant volunteer rates are taken into account, approximately 1.2 million men were affected by the draft.

The strategic questions revolved around determining the fraction that would be necessary to constitute a dangerous threat to the government, and, secondarily, around such issues as whether the cost would be linear (directly proportional to the number on strike) and whether a resisting but deferred student would count less than a noncooperating youth who was eligible for immediate induction.

In theory such questions on cost could be answered with a degree of precision, but obviously in practice only the crudest outlines could be considered. Speculation was mandatory, however, since mounting a strike that would reach threatening proportions was the crux of a major Resistance objective. Lacking resources to undertake a comprehensive analysis, the Resistance tended to rely on a few informed guesses. These became part of the movement's lore and were widely circulated.

Two estimates offered by prominent columnists of the *New York Times* provided some of the first quantified

hunches. The paper's reputation gave the numbers an aura
of credibility; and since it had national readership, dissemi-
nation was ensured. In early May 1967, Tom Wicker
wrote a column on the refusal of heavyweight boxer Muhammad Ali to be inducted. A paragraph near the end of
the column was to be repeatedly quoted by Resistance
proponents:

> A hundred thousand Muhammad Alis, of course, could
> be jailed. But if the Johnson administration had to
> prosecute 100,000 Americans in order to maintain its
> authority, its real power to pursue the Vietnamese war
> or any other policy would be crippled if not de-
> stroyed. It would then be faced not with dissent but
> with civil disobedience on a scale amounting to revolt
> (Wicker, 1967).

A few days later *New York Times* readers were also informed of the potential scale of resistance to the war. An
intense national debate on draft reform was underway, focusing on the bill in Congress authorizing continuation of
the Selective Service. *Times* columnist James Reston offered an insider's commentary on why the Johnson administration had backed away from its own advisory commission's recommendations that most student deferments be
abolished. Reston reported that "there is genuine fear [in
Washington] that abolition of all or most college deferments might lead to massive defiance among undergraduates. One estimate here is that if college students were
called like any other nineteen-year-olds, as many as 25 percent of them might refuse to serve" (Reston, 1967). This
was encouraging news for Resistance organizers.

At the end of June 1967, some 1.7 million age-eligible
men held student deferments. They would not all become
immediately available for the draft if their student protection were stripped, since a fraction would qualify for other
deferments. However, assuming that 1 million could not

find such protection, and accepting the estimate cited by Reston, some 250,000 youths would become resisters.

The outcome of the legislative debate on draft extension was to give undergraduates a full deferment protection, but it also seemingly ended graduate student deferments, and this meant that at least seniors would soon face the prospect of induction. A 25-percent rate of resistance among college seniors would ensure rapid growth of the movement, and the figure was cited often by the Resistance in justifying its strategy. For instance, a New York Resistance leaflet urging a massive turnout for a draft card return ceremony in April 1968 (one of the national card return dates) used the estimate published in the *Times* to lend support to the hopeful prospects of the resistance (5).

With little explicit rationale Wicker's 100,000 figure acquired the status of a basic threshold number. Staughton Lynd also advanced the 100,000-strong thesis in early articles advocating a resistance course (1967a, 1967b). Using the figures from the two *Times* columnists as a point of departure in a *New Left Notes* article, Lynd argued that "a little arithmetic makes clear the immense and sobering fact that if there were no student deferments, 100,000 men would refuse to go and the war would end" (1967b). The Boston chapter of the Resistance adopted these calculations and injected some estimates of its own. In building support for the April 1968 resistance ceremony, its newsletter noted that "the nation's leading antidraft attorney" had asserted that if 2 percent of the nation's youth resisted, the Selective Service System would be disrupted (6). If we take the 10 million plus registrants hypothetically available for service, 2 percent would come to several hundred thousand men. If the 2 percent were calculated on the basis of those currently eligible, however, the total would be in the tens of thousands. Another resistance group used induction rates as its baseline. The Wisconsin Draft Resistance Union (centered on the University of Wisconsin Madison campus) set its working figure at a noncooperation rate of 4 percent among draftees (Gabriner and Baran, 1969). This came to an annual total ranging between 10,000 and 15,000.

The inherent ambiguity of the situation led not only to variant estimates of the strike scale necessary to disrupt the draft, but also to estimates that were highly optimistic, especially once the movement's modest scale became apparent. Six months after its inauguration, Resistance membership was in the thousands, but there seemed to be little likelihood of breaking five figures. Hundreds of thousands of potential recruits appeared to be totally out of reach, but tens of thousands might not be, and speculation soon depressed the threshold required for draft disruption to four figures. A column appearing in a Boston Resistance newsletter in mid-spring 1968 offered this assessment at a time when the national movement counted fewer than 3000 resisters in its ranks: "Even Boston attorneys opposed to the cause have expressed astonishment at our success so far in tying up the legal process, and indicate that as few as 5000 resisters nationally could effectively disrupt Selective Service altogether" (7). In general, however, movement strategists expected that a minimum of 100,000 was prerequisite to any concrete impairment of the draft.

Security in Numbers and the Graduated Risk

Destruction of draft credentials, failure to cooperate with local board requests, and refusal of induction were serious violations of Selective Service regulations and constituted grounds for federal prosecution which could lead to a five-year sentence. In the early days of the movement it was unknown how swift government prosecution would be, nor what form it would take, but few doubted that punitive action would be forthcoming. A number of those interviewed reported anticipating imminent arrest on turning in their card. Indeed, one new resister readied a suitcase for the stay in jail, and another resister posted daily notices on his apartment door directing the FBI to his work location.

However, the resources of the FBI, the Justice Department, the federal courts, and the prison system were limited and not particularly elastic. It was presumed within the movement that several thousand resisters could be handled without undue administrative strain but that a more massive turnout would lead to chaos—that is, a positive accomplishment that might result in shortening the war. Also, if the government's facilities for prosecuting draft violators were limited, then beyond a certain point every additional resister lowered the probability of government action against each one. Several thousand resisters could anticipate incarceration, but numbers above this maximum would of necessity remain free. The greater the excess, the smaller the chance each resister had of being prosecuted. Consequently, the logic of this protective element further compelled the movement to concentrate its resources on generating the largest possible number of draft resisters.

The threshold for disrupting the federal prosecution system was substantially lower than that for impairing the conscription system. During the Vietnam era the Selective Service filed more than 20,000 complaints annually for alleged draft violations. The Justice Department never initiated more than a fifth of these cases. Inadequate evidence, improper Selective Service administrative procedures, and registrants' last-minute decisions to cooperate accounted for some of the discrepancy, but the testimony before a congressional committee of a representative of the Justice Department revealed that the department simply could not cope with much of the load:

[T]here are probably 30,000 or 35,000 determinations [of Selective Service charges of draft violations] that have to be made by assistant U.S. attorneys whether to go or not to go. If we were to review all of those, it would require quite an arm of the Justice Department merely to review them, and there is no such unit to do that. . . . We are faced with the situation where there is a continuing, open, obvious expressed intent by many groups to absolutely swamp the system and swamp the courts and the Department of Justice. I do not intend in my section [Government Operations Section, Criminal Division] to be a party to allowing our being swamped. For instance if I went out of this room today and there were 100,000 people out there turning in draft cards . . . [and] if we instituted 100,- 000 cases for 100,000 draft card turn-ins, we would allow these people to accomplish exactly what they wanted to accomplish. . . . [I]f you take, and you try to solve a massive problem with selective prosecution, I think this is the proper way to approach it (U.S. House Committee on Armed Services, 1970, 12852–12853).

The deterrent effect of selective prosecution declined in direct proportion to the number of resisters above some relatively fixed level. This level was probably lower than the 10,000–20,000 range. In district court between mid-1967 and mid-1968, the Justice Department filed more than 1700 criminal cases connected with Selective Service violations; during the same period the total number of federal prosecutions of all types stood at 28,000 (U.S. Department of Justice, 1969). Consequently, as the foregoing testimony suggests, it is doubtful that resources would have been at all adequate for handling the full 21,000 complaints received from the Selective Service during that period. Thus the Resistance stood a much better chance of recruiting enough men to be able to offer its members some protection than of reaching the level required for seriously reducing the supply of fresh troops. However, if the Resistance were to surpass this intermediate protection threshold, it would greatly increase the likelihood of achieving the draft disruption threshold. Recruiting new resisters would be considerably easier once a major disincentive to joining the strike—personal repercussions—was minimized.

Any collective safety that resulted from widespread defiance of the draft would not be uniformly shared. The organizers were in a particularly exposed position. They were the first to act and therefore their names were likely to be the first sent through the prosecution process. Moreover, as leadership they were obvious targets for government attempts to suppress the movement, and they could expect especially harsh sentencing for that reason. This expectation was realistic according to one study of the attitudes of federal district judges. The judges generally shared the position that politically motivated draft resistance deserved a severer penalty than noncooperation based on pacifism or other principles (*Columbia Journal of Law and Social Problems*, 1969). Furthermore, organizers were subject to charges of encouraging draft evasion or conspiring to do so, and both were prosecutable acts (in early 1968 the Justice Department did indict five leaders on these grounds: see Mitford, 1969).

Finally, there was a subjective jeopardy factor that would be faced by early resisters but not by later ones. During the first card returns there was great uncertainty over the proportions the movement would reach, and there was a chance that it would not go much beyond the several hundred initiators, leaving these individuals highly exposed to prosecution. On the other hand, once thousands of cards had been collected and the movement had accumulated working experience, new noncooperators would have a much clearer picture of what their chances of jail would be.

The organizers had already decided on taking an act of

resistance, despite their vulnerable position, which could never be adequately protected even with a massive growth of the movement. But the number of those resolute on noncooperation in mid-1967 could not have exceeded 1000. How was the movement to become at least 100,000 strong? One approach was the solicitation among a large number of young men of conditional pledges to resist, followed by an announcement of the movement's existence. This course involved obvious problems, including the difficulty of recruiting people to a hypothetical organization and guaranteeing that paper commitments could be translated into action once the minimal number had been obtained. In Boston at least, the organizers canvassing for registrants to participate in the first card turn-in on October 16, 1967, found that outright pledges were easier to elicit than contingent ones. The alternative was to formally institute the movement organization and to orient initial activities around generating more resistance. Although this plan could be realized more readily, it was also more hazardous. If others did not join after the first round of resistance, the government had ample resources to prosecute all members; moreover, nothing would have been gained, since the strike would have been too small to exert any effect on the draft system. However, opinion settled on this vanguard alternative, and the first card return involved approximately 1000 registrants nationally; one-fifth of these were in the Boston region.

The critical issue then became how the 1000 resisters could amplify their number one hundredfold. In recognition of the recruiting context, an innovative solution emerged—"snowballing." One of the early Boston organizers summarized the snowballing scenario:

> We are now only a week away [from October 16], and the situation is shaping up. Across the country, about 3000 resisters. This is a long way from the

100,000 that Staughton Lynd was talking about in the April issue of *Liberation* that is needed as a means of causing a massive breakdown in the structure of the draft. But 3000 is all that The Resistance needs to be launched. The 3000 who participate in the October 16th action will become organizers for the next wave of Resistance. It is this, more than anything else, which means The Resistance cannot be stopped. If by the time we repeat our action again in the spring, each member of The Resistance has recruited *only one more person*, the number will have doubled to 6000. And so on. With the momentum gathering and subsequent waves happening more frequently, this kind of geometric progression puts Lynd's 100,000 well in sight. This is an immense and provocative thought. This is what the October 16th beginning is all about (quoted in Thorne, 1971, 96).

Those entering later waves would benefit from minimal personal costs and high certainty of impact, a classic bandwagon effect. Assuming a relatively static joining propensity among an eligible population, the dangerous initial stages would draw those prepared for risky action, and later periods would bring in the increasingly less venturesome.

A scheme tried by the New York Resistance attempted to systematize the relation between numbers and risk. Its leaflet (8) for a nationwide card return planned for April 1968 asked: "How ready are you to assume the risks of effective action? How ready are you to build on the movement initiated by the 2000 who have already returned their cards?" Anticipating that varying levels of readiness would be dependent on the dangers involved, the circular offered a set of graduated pledges. The prospective resister could indicate his willingness to take the step outright. But he could also offer himself on a provisional basis, pledging his participation if similar pledges exceeded a minimum number (the choices ranged between 1000 and 15,000). This mechanism helped short-circuit the wait-and-see attitude intrinsic in a snowballing strategy.

Not only would cascading help circumvent the inhibiting effect of personal endangerment, it represented as well a particularly powerful means of attracting new people to the movement, irrespective of the jeopardy involved. Studies of social movements often reveal that interpersonal influence is a primary means of drawing people into a movement organization (9). Snowballing could provide an outreach network that would optimize the movement's recruitment potential. If each resister persuaded only one or two friends to confront the draft on the next public Resistance occasion, the accelerator effect should overwhelm the Selective Service in half a dozen stages.

STRATEGY: BASIS FOR RECRUITMENT

Any organization attempting to expand its ranks will elaborate beliefs on why people should be drawn to the movement it stands for. These are essential for design of even the simplest recruitment program. The beliefs that emerged in the Resistance reflected its origins in the radical student movement, the use of the preemptive resistance strategy, and the complex relationship of the movement's primary base constituency (draft registrants) to the government.

The shift of SDS and other leftist student organizations toward a class analysis of American society and the situation of college students contained major implications for recruitment ideology. It followed from this leftist perspective that mobilization of students into a radical movement could be best achieved by programs aimed at overcoming their common problems, rather than concentrating on the problems of other groups. Some students would be drawn on an intellectual or moral basis, but the majority would respond only when the protest organization appeared to offer a solution to their own grievances. This of course was a primary reason for selecting the draft as an antiwar issue in the first place. As one campus draft union put it, "We choose to focus on the draft because it represents that point of contact between young men and government where symbolic complicity in the war effort always threatens to become real" (10).

Thus the decision of the Resistance to concentrate on conscription bore the assumptions that male students were irritated or distressed by their draft prospects and that a malaise due to compulsory military service pervaded the entire campus community (this view was essentially correct for at least some colleges, according to our previous chapter). Agitation around the draft, therefore, would bring people to the movement on the basis of a desire to respond to their own situation. One person who was active with the Boston Resistance from the time of its inception argued that the draft presented a unique opportunity for organizing college students:

> Noncooperation reached those people who were much the beneficiaries of the system. Its systematic denial of necessities to them had been unreal—they had it so good they just didn't realize how bad it was, and they needed to be reached. The Resistance was more effective than SDS in reaching these people because resisting made people respond to their own lives through the draft. Oppression could be understood concretely in terms of one's own life, and until you understand it in your own terms you don't get away from altruism and you don't feel it.

In the movement, concern frequently focused on external events that appeared to heighten the draft vulnerability of college students. Monthly draft quotas, the lifting of graduate deferments, rumors of undergraduates being drafted, and the dilemmas facing college seniors were the subjects of much attention. A poster announcing the April 1968 rally on the Boston Common listed the time and speakers for the demonstration and closed with the line: "N.B. SENIORS, GRAD STUDENTS."

However, the use of preemptive rather than reactive resistance introduced a contradictory element into the organizing plan. Among individual college draft registrants, the relationship to the Selective Service varied substantially. New graduate students and seniors faced real induction possibilities, the Selective Service had been threatening wholesale conscription of all students, and the draft channeled and discommoded students in various other ways (e.g., when it was used punitively). In 1967 and 1968, however, a majority of students still held 2S deferments, which provided at least temporary security. For those confronting imminent induction, noncooperation could be seen as both a long-term and an immediate solution to their plight. But for those not likely to be conscripted in the near future, noncooperation was a very costly step, in the short run. It carried the risks of relinquishment of a privileged draft status and eventual loss of personal liberty. For underclassmen at least, although no draft at all would have been preferable, their immediate interest still lay in seeking to retain a protected status. The 2S constituted a limited privilege.

Thus preemptive resistance created a mixed constituency for a movement bent on organizing male college students. The protest provided a realistic alternative for one group but a costly venture for another. However, in line with the ideological perspective of the movement, the student deferment could still be seen as a hardship. For instance, it was reasoned that as students realized that their own immunity resulted in a greater probability of injury and death for other registrants, they would be afflicted with deep psychological distress. This interpretation received articulation and credibility in a lengthy article by a psychiatrist who administered the campus psychiatric services at the University of Wisconsin (Halleck, 1968). Drawing on his own counseling experience, he observed: "I have become convinced that a substantial number of male students who accept the 2-S deferment pay an enormous psychological price for this privilege. Nor surprisingly, they are plagued with guilt, an unremitting guilt which dominates every aspect of their existence. Although this guilt is often denied or rationalized, it is a significant factor among the causes of unrest on our campuses, and it contributes to a deep sense of personal despair in the lives of many students." This article, published in February 1968, was promptly circulated within the Resistance. It was reprinted within a month in the Boston Resistance newsletter (11).

It could also be argued that Selective Service channeling was a major burden for students. There were significant personal costs as students struggled for good grades to avoid reclassification, sought exempt occupations upon graduation, and in other ways let their relationship with the local board color numerous private decisions. A rationale developed around this issue as well, expressed here in the words of another Resistance activist:

> Channelled college students only begin to throw off their oppression when they translate the social issues of the draft, the war it feeds and the garrison society it sustains, into a personal problem. To return their draft cards and take the attendant risks may be the only way that the channelled can "seize control of their own lives," and initiate a process of political resistance to the source of *their* oppression (Zimmerman, 1967, 34).

Nevertheless, an important cleavage remained between student registrants facing induction and those less directly affected by the draft. Although the early Resistance ideology stressed assisting the former, the preemptive strike inherently included the latter. Through an extension of the class logic, deferred students were included among those directly pressed by conscription, since they should be prone to respond to the Resistance on a similar basis. However, there remained a clear difference in the degree of discomfort experienced by the two groups.

VIEW FROM THE ORGANIZED

How did the Resistance enroll new members? Were registrants drawn on the basis of immediate concern with their own draft problems, or were they attracted by identification with the broader political objectives of the protest? If immediate draft problems were paramount, the belief shared by Resistance organizers that an antidraft program was an effective way to organize students around their own self-interest would be confirmed. However, if political identification with the general political aims of the Resistance were more important in drawing people to the movement, it would be indicated that the Resistance was reaching students much the same way as had earlier campus movements (before they began to view college students as an oppressed sector of the society). The evidence suggests that both recruitment processes were important.

Draft Situation

The Resistance attracted men in both draft-threatened and relatively immune situations. During the 1967–1968 period, approximately *one in ten* Selective Service registrants was classified as available for military service (Table 4.1).

Table 4.1   Selective Service Classification of All Registrants and Two Sets of Boston Area Draft Resisters, 1967–1968

		Boston Area Resisters (%)	
Draft Classification	Selective Service Registrants, June 1967 (%)	New England Resistance, January 1968	Sample, 1967–1968
Eligible for induction	9	14	21
Deferred or exempt			
Student (1S, 2S)	14	36	52
Divinity student or			
minister (4D)	1	14	11
Other *	74	30	16
Unclassified	2	6	0
N		(222)	(63)

SOURCE. Selective Service registrant figures are from U.S. Selective Service System (1968a, 20); the distribution remained relatively unchanged through mid-1968. The New England Resistance data are based on analysis by that organization of the classifications of its full membership as of early January 1968 (of the total of 250 resisters, information was unavailable on 25 and 3 were unregistered; *New England Resistance Newsletter*, January 19, 1968).
* Mental, physical, occupational, fatherhood, hardship, veteran, and sole-surviving-son deferments.

Of the 63 noncooperators we interviewed and for whom information was available on preresistance classification, *one in five* had been liable for a call-up before resisting. Similarly, *one in seven* resisters affiliated with the New England Resistance as of January 1968 held a 1A classification prior to resisting (nearly all had joined during the two public card returns on October 16 and November 16).

The resisters we interviewed were asked to reflect on the importance of various considerations in their decision to resist. Twelve factors were listed (described more fully in a moment); ten related to political and moral issues, but two concerned draft pressures specifically. Only six of the more than 90 resisters answering ascribed any importance to one of the two draft-related factors—a call for induction. However, half of the total number asserted that a decision to avoid the armed services at all costs (the second draft pressure factor) was an element in their decision to resist. This avoidance commitment, coupled with dealings with the local draft board indicating that eventual induction was likely, quite frequently contributed to the decision to join the Resistance as a preemptive move. One person, for instance, graduated from college in the spring of 1967. On commencement day he was notified that he had been reclassified from 2S to 1A, and a week after taking his preinduction physical he returned his card at the October 16 ceremonies in Boston.

The effects of channeling and guilt over a privileged draft status also appear in the resisters' recollections. One young man had worried about his military obligations for months, but receipt of a 1A classification notice precipitated an attempt to obtain classification as a conscientious objector. He learned from a draft counseling center that some people were returning their draft cards to the Justice Department rather than file for a CO, but he initially rejected that option and proceeded to work on the lengthy Selective Service CO forms. However, he concluded that they could not be completed: "In my semiconscious mind I was thinking that the Selective Service System was snooping into my private beliefs in asking about that CO stuff, and I also knew I was just lucky to be educated enough to

be able to fill out a form." Four months after receiving the
1A notice, he resolved the acute uncertainty by mailing his
draft card back to the local board and joining the Resistance.

Another person had resolved to accept neither a 2S nor
military service when he stumbled on a Resistance announcement:

> I was walking down the street two days before the
> 16th [of October] and saw a leaflet. It said to call if you
> were thinking of turning in a card and instead I just
> stopped by their office. I had thought about not taking
> a 2S deferment and if drafted thought I would refuse.
> I had already decided against the 2S, since my brother
> didn't have a 2S and he was being drafted. Over the
> summer I had begun to think about all this quite seri-
> ously and when I saw the flyer I thought that since I
> would be called for induction eventually and would
> ultimately refuse, I might as well do it with this group.

Table 4.1 also reveals that a large fraction of the resisters
were not threatened by conscription in any immediate
way. Some of those on student deferments (from 36 to 52
percent of the total) were under incipient pressures as they
foresaw the loss of protection upon graduation (12). But
many were just beginning college or had several years remaining in deferred graduate studies. Furthermore, divinity students, who composed more than one-tenth of the
Boston area resisters, were virtually permanently exempt.
Entry into the ministry ensured continuation of the 4D deferment, and there was no discussion of lifting the exemption. Those on mental and physical deferments (1Y or 4F),
occupational deferment (2A), or fatherhood and hardship
deferment (3A) could anticipate few if any threats to their
secure status. Consequently, at least one-third to one-half
of the noncooperators in the Boston area were not compelled by circumstance to resist. The Resistance was reach-

ing people on the twin bases of specific grievance and general political appeal.

Politics: To Give Moral Witness or to Organize

A movement projects many images, and people are attracted to it through identification with various objectives of the organization. The Resistance was at once an antidraft, antiwar, and radical protest movement. The theme that appealed to virtually all those who joined was its militant attack on the war. During our interviews, the resisters were asked to reflect on their decision to enter the movement. Putting an end to the Asian war was the overriding consideration irrespective of draft status: "I looked upon the war as a crisis, something that just had to be stopped before you could get into other things." Another reported:

> Although I had been in some sit-ins during the civil rights days, I was hardly political and was strongly dedictated to privatism. It was really the war that woke me up. I knew about the [David] Miller, [David] O'Brien [one of the 1966 resisters who received extensive publicity] and Sheep's Meadow events [draft card burnings in Central Park, April 15, 1967], but I didn't visualize myself doing it. It took a real depression about the war which was rapidly becoming an obsessional thing. I couldn't sleep well and nightmares about the war were frequent when I could sleep. . . . I have a metaphysical bent which can isolate acts through my imagination. If you take the fact of one child or soldier dying 12,000 miles away, it seemed that the distance was arbitrary and it was as if it were happening in my backyard to those I loved. The war became personalized through an extrapolation of the perception of senseless death, steel, and bullets. LBJ

> could rain death down on innocent millions. The
> enormity of the crime was terrible. . . . I felt a total
> disaffection with America, it had betrayed me, and I
> could think of no other solution except resistance.

The dominance of feelings against the war in the decision to join the Resistance was apparent when the resisters were asked to compare the relative significance of the war and other considerations. The question required that the resisters reconstruct their original rationale for acting against the draft (13). A distinction was drawn between the purpose of draft resistance at the individual and collective levels—what did the resister hope to gain through his individual action and what expectations did he have for the movement of resisters? At both levels, stopping the Asian war was the most pressing concern: for nearly nine out of ten resisters it was of high importance in their decision, and it was the only dimension to which all respondents attributed at least some influence (Table 4.2).

Although antipathy toward the U.S. engagement in Indochina unified the Resistance membership, less consensus could be expected on others issues because of the movement's membership standards. A draft registrant who committed an overt act of resistance was *ipso facto* a full member of the movement. His ethnicity, occupation, or family background could not serve as a basis for exclusion, since the use of any such criteria would directly contradict the movement's aim of creating a strike of all draft registrants. It was assumed that the rhetoric of the Resistance would discourage prowar resisters from joining, but otherwise no particular political allegiance was prerequisite. Moreover, degrees of formal membership were not distinguished, and once a person resisted he was eligible for full participation (14). Thus the single-step entry and action criterion (rather than a screening on the basis of beliefs or social characteristics) opened the movement to people who held a great variety of political outlooks.

*Table 4.2   Political Considerations in the Decision
to Resist the Draft*

Consideration	Respondents Rating Highly Important * (%)
A. Individual Aims †	
Demonstrate your opposition to the Vietnam War	88
Moral witness as an expression of personal convictions	71
Cut your connections with the military system	61
Organize other people through your own example	60
Attempt to impede the draft system	59
Protest against the nature of the draft system	57
Create publicity for antidraft organizations or the antiwar movement	48
Put yourself outside the system to increase political effectiveness	33
Cut your connection with the whole system	19
Act in accordance with certain religious beliefs	17
B. Resistance Movement Goals ‡	
Help end U.S. involvement in Vietnam	86
Awaken the conscience of America	59
Impede and change the draft system	52
Build a movement for restructuring America	40

* The factors were rated on a five-point scale ranging from "no importance" to "prime importance." "Highly important" in this table includes the two highest points.

† The question: "How important were each of the following considerations in your own decision to resist, at the time you took the step?" The base N for the 10 items ranges from 93 to 95.

‡ The question: "There follows a list of some of the major political goals that some people have mentioned as important for the Resistance movement. How important did you consider each of these at the time of your original resistance?" The base N ranges from 87 to 88.

The specific substance of the action criterion also ensured that the movement would appeal to registrants with a range of political viewpoints. Collective noncooperation could be seen as a way of forcing a change in war policies through a direct threat to the draft system. But it could also be viewed as a symbolic form of expression, potentially capable of arousing public sentiment against the government's foreign policy. In more individual terms, draft resistance could be identified as a means for ending one's own complicity with policies and institutions viewed as abhorrent. The movement stressed the strike aspect, but the other rationales were not explicitly rejected. Thus the Resistance movement could serve different purposes for different people. To the degree that these reasons for resisting derived from more general belief systems, people representing a variety of political outlooks could be expected to be drawn to the protest.

A diversity in views on the utility of noncooperation was apparent among the Boston resisters we interviewed. Some defined noncooperation as a means of expressing dissociation from military institutions; others saw it as a way of publicly dramatizing the strength of their convictions against the war, and still others emphasized the strike element. Illustratively, one person identified dissociation from the draft as the central theme in his decision:

> The idea of cutting myself off from the Selective Service System was precisely because of what that service was doing for the war in calling [people] up for combat and for what it was doing to the poor and for how it was affecting peoples' lives. If I was not going to cooperate with evil I could no longer cooperate with the system, and hence the turning in of the card. There was also the realization that the local draft board was in a very real sense a microcosm of what this country was doing on a world scale—planning men's lives for global murder. I just couldn't cooperate with that.

. . . So it was some kind of moral witness to say *no* to society and to all the atrocities being done in my name.

Another resister reasoned that thousands of young men returning their draft cards and accepting imprisonment would precipitate a domestic crisis in the United States:

> My principal rationale for doing it was that I had a hope that the Selective Service and courts could be stopped, although this was not a very realistic hope even at the time. I did expect, however, that a lot of people would commit themselves and sacrifice their immediate self-interest to force the government out of the war. I had thought that several thousand middle-class kids resisting the draft would be enough to move a lot of people to really work to end the war. . . . I really believed that a bunch of straight middle-class people going to jail might effect change in this country.

The liberal public was viewed as an intermediate constituency between the movement and the federal government. It was theorized that the movement's daring action would help galvanize liberal groups into more active challenges of Vietnam policy.

The strike rationale, of course, was expressed by most of the initial organizers, but it also appeared in the thinking of many who entered later. In the words of one: "The main thing in my decision [to resist] was a desire to build a mass movement to change the system, and this had to come through people dissociating themselves. I wanted to build a nonviolent society and I had to take the first step in order to encourage other people to do the same first step." Thus there were considerable differences in the perspectives on individual resistance and the movement's objectives, and these discrepancies suggested that the Resistance was reaching a politically varied constituency.

During the interviews we also asked the resisters to describe their general political outlook and activities during the period just before they began to think about resisting. These preresistance political perspectives covered a broad range. A number of veteran members of the New Left entered the Resistance after it was launched. Another set of registrants had been ideologically sympathetic to the American left but had not yet translated their identification into active participation in a radical organization. One person saw the turn-in as a "commitment to get off the fence. My problem of fence sitting was not that the issues were too complicated. I was liberal politically but radical in thought, and I didn't yet connect my viewpoint with my life. . . . I identified with the Movement intellectually, but I was not *in* the Movement before October 1967."

The war and the draft were instrumental in moving radical proclivities to the point of action, and the Resistance appeared to offer a particularly effective protest vehicle. Another resister described the turmoil he shared with his friends as college graduation approached in 1967:

> During the spring of my senior year a group of people came down from Stanford to discuss the possibilities of resistance. My friends were increasingly political in this period; it was a very politically aware group, and everybody had been talking about this whole concept of resistance even before these other people spoke on our campus. We had all been moving to the left because of the war, the draft, uncertainty about what to do after graduation, new ideas coming out of Berkeley, and people we knew in the Bay area. There was no personal crisis which caused this, but just a tremendous sense of apocalypse—it just didn't seem that the United States could last for more than two or three years. But we were all worried about how we could integrate your thoughts with your actions, and resistance seemed like a possibility.

On weighing the political gains against the personal consequences of noncooperation, this individual initially rejected the movement; at the time, he saw little merit in volunteering for "martyrdom." Within a year, however, his draft card was among those collected on one of the special Resistance occasions.

We have seen that a sizable block entered the movement with fairly well-developed radical views, but another group brought with them a much more moderate outlook. These were primarily students who had had little involvement in student or antiwar organizations but for whom the events in Vietnam had become deeply distressing. Conventional liberal views of American institutions were predominant, and there was little notion of how to instigate social change. A sense of moral obligation to act had grown with each escalation of the war, and yet existing political alternatives seemed to be futile. The Resistance appeared to offer the first credible means of attack. One resister had been involved in the Vietnam Summer organizing project in 1967 when he learned of the plans for October 16:

> I never got into antiwar stuff with both feet. I had done a lot of work but I didn't see anything people could really do. There had been nothing dramatic enough to reach the government, and this is why the idea of the Resistance struck me. People were planning on a mass scale to sever their ties with the Selective Service and this would really put on the pressure. And people were placing themselves on the line, so this was the best thing I had heard of so far. . . . As soon as I learned of it I began talking to people right away, and it was not long until I had talked myself into resisting. I would have to be involved in the movement. I was done talking, and it was time for meaningful action.

The search for a viable protest form is apparent in the recollections of another person who eventually became a leader of the Boston movement:

In the summer of 1967 I got interested in the war for
the first time. I was enrolled in an anthropology
course at Harvard's summer school, and one person in
there was a friend of PL [Progressive Labor Party]
and we talked a lot. The anthropology course was terrible and we started talking about relevant things like
riots. Also, at the time I was reading Malcolm X's au-
tobiography, and if one thing turned me onto politics
it was this. It turned me on viscerally. Then I went to
the Socialist Scholars' Conference in New York and
this was really boring, but on the way back I had a
ride with a guy from CADRE [Chicago Area Draft
Resisters]. I was bitching about this conference and
asked what I could do that was meaningful. He said
you can turn your draft card in. I decided there on
the spot. I'm very impulsive. I settled on an act of real
noncooperation, I was going to have nothing to do
with those bastards. . . . Also, there was a kind of appeal to manliness. . . . You had to have balls to do it.
Now this is seen as foolish but I don't regret it because it helped involve me. I believed it would get me
into a really big thing. And so it was an intense feeling
against the war and a desire to involve myself in something big that caused me to act. But even this ma-
chismo had latent political content. I had been pushed
around for 20 years and I felt windblown. So my reactions were very gut level and impulsive against this.

As expected, the recruits' preresistance political ideology and their specific views on the aims of draft resistance
were closely related. Radicals tended to enter the Resistance with the expectation that their act would contribute
to the building of insurgent protest. For instance, among
the individual considerations in the decision to resist listed
in Table 4.2, radicals were prone to emphasize the movement organizing items (e.g., "organize other people through
your own example"). Besides ending the war, the collective goal of greatest priority was usually the creation
of a "movement for restructuring America." By contrast,

those whose preresitance persuasion had been liberal were more likely to stress the individual dissociation aspect of the act (e.g., "cut your connections with the military system," "moral witness as an expression of personal convictions"). They felt that the major impact of the Resistance should be a stirring of the "American conscience." The divergence in outlook on the movement's goals is shown in Table 4.3.

Table 4.3 *Preresistance Political Perspective and Importance of Resistance Movement Goals*

Resistance Movement Goals (Respondents Rating Highly Important * [%])	Preresistance Political Perspective	
	Moderate–Liberal ($N=49$)	Radical–Revolutionary ($N=37–38$)
Awaken the conscience of America	71	44
Build a movement for restructuring America	40	66

* "Highly important" is defined as in Table 4.2.

[The preresistance political perspective came from a question asking for a description of political beliefs for the six-month period preceding the first time noncooperation was considered (15). The structured part of the question requested a self-description using a set of eight terms which were dichotomized here along the liberal–radical line. (16).]

Due to the broad spectrum of the resisters' political experience, there was considerable variation in their immediate reactions to joining the Resistance; emotions reported ranged from indifference and nonchalance to exhilaration and intense anxiety. For the veteran radical activist, political confrontation and the threat of arrest had been experienced previously. By contrast, for those attracted from outside radical cricles, resisting the draft was typically a much more momentous step. More than half the resisters interviewed described the period just after joining the movement in positive terms ranging from pride to euphoria; one-tenth reported adverse reactions such as apprehension, and one-sixth indicated that both elements had been present. However, preresistance liberals were twice as likely as radicals to report feelings of anxiety, and they were also somewhat more prone to recall positive reactions (60 versus 49 percent). Radicals were three times as likely to recall a general sense of indifference. The blend of liberation and fear experienced by many of those fresh to militant actions is illustrated in the reactions of a person who was introduced to radical politics by the act of resisting:

> There was a kind of extreme relief and unburdening to get rid of my card. . . . Before that, I felt very trapped and very angry because I was trapped. I was trapped by the War and the fact that I couldn't do anything about the War except in a self-destructive way. The next day I just felt so innocent and exhilarated and involved and committed to something. I was getting out of myself and joining up with other people. . . . I had made this moral statement and put myself on the line.

ORGANIZATIONAL CONSEQUENCES

A protest program can have a decisive influence on the social organization of a movement. For instance, if a strategy depends on the coordinated actions of the entire membership (as in a boycott or a sit-in), the movement organization would be apt to elaborate complex means of maintaining internal discipline. On the other hand, if the strategy requires only passive cooperation on the part of the rank and file (such as payment of dues), simpler disciplinary measures can be expected (17). In the case of the Resistance, an exceptionally close connection should appear between its program and organization. The outlines of the preemptive resistance program had been defined before the organization existed (building the organization was a major point of the program). Thus the early Resistance activists did not have to overcome preexisting organizational inertia—they were relatively free to design a structure that would closely conform to the requirements of the new program.

The resulting organizational structure was extremely amorphous. Since the demands of the Resistance were in effect nonnegotiable, no elaborate bargaining apparatus was necessary. There was simply no need for a procedure to select representatives who could meet with the Selective Service, nor for machinery for modifying the movement's demands in light of later developments or government counterproposals. Resistance members individually related to the government through their contact with the local draft board and the Justice Department, but a collective interface was unneeded at either the local or the national level. Furthermore, since the outlines of the Resistance program had been settled before the movement existed, there was not even a requirement for a framework in which to debate and resolve major policy questions on the strike strategy. Resistance chapters were to encourage as many registrants as possible to start noncooperation, and the details of recruiting could be left in local hands without detrimental effects for the national movement.

As a consequence, a formalized national Resistance organization did not evolve after the movement's creation. Several national conferences were held, a national newsletter was published, and days for collective resistance were specified on a countrywide basis. But there were no national officers, no central office, and no formal conventions. The national coordination that did appear provided information rather than direction to the local chapters. This information primarily involved such topics as the growth rate of the national movement and the activities of various Resistance groups.

A similar amorphousness existed in the local Boston organization, the New England Resistance. Official positions were not established, decision-making bodies were not formed, and an ethos of direct participation by all members prevailed (though in practice this gave control to the most active participants; 20 to 30 relatively full-time workers staffed the organization at its peak).

Most of the movement's daily routine was predetermined by its overall aim of instigating a draft strike. Consolidation of noncooperation acts into collective ceremonies was encouraged by the element of personal risk, the movement's dependency on the media for communicating its existence to the public and potential recruits, and the need for evidence of widespread resistance to trigger the snowballing psychology. The card return events, held every few months until late 1968, became the major focus of Resistance activity, and they introduced a cycle into the movement's work level.

Building for a card return required considerable planning as well as canvassing of the Boston region. Leaflets and posters were written, produced, and distributed, endorsements were solicited from other antiwar and student organizations, and arrangements were made for speakers, marshals, and permits. In Boston this work generally proved to be fruitful, and attendance at several of the rallies numbered in the thousands (it was estimated that approximately 5000 were present for the October 1967 event and that 10,000 attended an April 1968 rally and card return). However, between these peak occasions, the focus of activity was less well defined. The lack of local targets and issues related to the strike discouraged formulation of subsidiary short-term programs. Therefore, it was difficult to integrate many of the newcomers into the organization's daily life. A Resistance party and an orientation meeting welcomed the new resisters, but many would drift away when they found that there was little to be done in the days immediately following the Resistance event.

Some became involved in draft unions on several major campuses in the Boston region, and these bodies were loosely affiliated with the New England Resistance. Other resisters found work with another major off-campus anti-draft organization, the Boston Draft Resistance Group (BDRG). This group grew out of a campaign to collect We Won't Go pledges on several campuses in the spring of 1967 and thus predated the Resistance. BDRG was more oriented toward the foundation of draft unions and the encouragement of reactive resistance, especially among noncollege youth. Although a sizable fraction of its full-time staff of one to two dozen became noncooperators along with the New England Resistance, BDRG remained ambivalent about preemptive resistance. BDRG's position was more in line with the viewpoint on draft resistance that was then prevalent in SDS. Like the New England Resistance, most of the leadership had been active with SDS and other radical student organizations such as Vietnam Summer, and most were college students or ex-students. BDRG placed heavy emphasis on politically oriented draft counseling, demonstrations at induction centers and army bases, and contacting draft registrants assembled at local draft boards for transportation to induction centers. These activities were aimed at encouraging people to consider resisting the draft, but only when under the immediate threat of conscription (18).

After October 16 national Resistance card returns were again held in December 1967 (November in Boston), and April and November 1968 (Boston canceled its November plans). Some chapters continued to stage such events in 1969, but no national days were scheduled. In addition to these four major resistance days, local events often served as a pretext for smaller card returns. During the march on the Pentagon in late October 1968, a large number of cards were burnt. When Dr. Spock and others were arraigned in Boston in early 1968, several dozen new resisters joined the New England Resistance. On relatively minor occasions, such as the meeting of a concerned religious group, several registrants often chose to announce their noncooperation. One estimate of the card returns on the four national resistance days placed the totals at 1200, 415, 1000, and 750, for an overall number near 3300. Another estimate of the Boston returns arrived at figures of 200, 60, and 200 for the three events in October and November 1967 and April 1968. At least 50 more cards were returned at other times, for a tally exceeding 500 (19). Since people also used other means to announce their noncooperation, the figures just cited are a minimal gauge of Resistance membership. Among the men we interviewed, three-quarters had returned or burnt their cards at one of the Resistance rallies. However, direct mailing to the draft board or other government agency had been employed by another 10 percent, and the remainder had used a variety of modes, such as refusing to appear for a preinduction physical examination or destroying the draft card at another type of antiwar event. Conventional wisdom in the New England Resistance set its peak membership at from 500 to 1000 resisting members, and the national estimate eventually reached roughly 4000. However, 4000 noncooperators was not even close to the minimum necessary for a significant disruption of the draft system. This gap between the expected scale of the movement and its actual size after more than a year of intense effort proved to be a fundamental challenge to its existence.

NOTES

1. "Bill Dowling's column," *The Resistance,* October 25, 1967 (early newsletter of the New England Resistance).

2. Campus surveys were conducted shortly after the Berkeley Free Speech Movement in 1964 and the Columbia University strike in 1968. In both cases approximately three-fifths of the students backed the main objectives of the initial demonstration, but only 25 to 34 percent in the University of California's case and 19 percent on the Columbia campus supported the specific tactics employed (Somers, 1965; Gales, 1966; Barton, 1968). A national survey conducted in 1969 also revealed that the grievances articulated by the student left found a receptive response far beyond the activist membership. One in 20 identified himself as an activist, but nearly one in two declared "sympathy with most of the activists' objectives" (although not all their tactics), and only one in ten adamantly opposed the protestors (Columbia Broadcasting System, 1969, 31).

3. "N. C. Resolutions," *New Left Notes,* October 22, 1967.

4. "Movement" was the term often used within the New Left to label itself.

5. "The Resistance Strategy, April 3," leaflet circulated by the New York Resistance, March–April, 1968.

6. "National survey," *The Resistance,* March 15–April 3, 1968, p. 2.

7. "The logic of resistance April 3," *The Resistance,* March 1–15, 1968, p. 3.

8. Leaflet cited in note 5.

9. See, for instance, the studies by Sills (1957), Kornhauser (1962), Festinger, Riecken, and Schachter (1964), Lofland (1966), Gerlach and Hine (1970), and Bolton (1972).

10. From a statement circulated by the Harvard Draft Project, Harvard University, February 1968.

11.   *The Resistance*, March 15–April 3, 1968, p. 15.

12.   The campus roots of the Resistance are apparent in the composition of its membership. Approximately 60 percent of the 97 resisters we interviewed were pursuing university studies at the time of the interview (in part built into the sampling design). They were evenly divided between undergraduate and graduate programs. Of those not enrolled, almost half had completed at least a bachelor's degree and nearly all had attended college (most majored in the humanities or social sciences). A similar composition is revealed in an analysis of the school or work situation of members of the New England Resistance as of mid-1968. This organization found that half its ranks were enrolled in college, one-sixth were classed as working in professional white collar occupations, and another sixth were engaged in full-time political work (no information was available on the remaining fraction; *Journal of the New England Resistance*, October 1968). Since most young, full-time political activists in the Boston region were former students, at least three-quarters and perhaps nearly all members of the New England Resistance had attended college.

The upper-middle-class family background characteristic of white student activists in the mid-1960s is also found among the resisters interviewed (for summaries of the considerable literature, see Horn and Knott, 1971; Mankoff and Flacks, 1971; Lipset 1972). More than half of the resisters' fathers and one-third of their mothers had completed college; nearly one-third of the fathers had received some postgraduate training. Approximately 60 percent of the resisters' fathers were business executives or professionals (sales, service, crafts, manual labor, technical, and military occupations equally divided the remainder).

13.   Most of those interviewed had initiated noncooperation at least one year prior to the interview, and this introduced the usual problems of selective distortion of retrospective information. However, the significance of the step tended to minimize recall difficulties, and the resisters were generally able to point out how their thinking on draft resistance had evolved from the time of the original decision.

14.   A minor informal distinction in membership status did exist. Some women, men beyond draft age, and a few registrants who had not actually resisted did become active with the movement. As a rule, membership for the nonresisters was dependent on

heavy contribution to Resistance political work. However, as could be expected in a movement defined around people who had taken a risky action against the state, those who did not or could not share in the action held a marginal status (for a discussion of the subordinate position of women in the Resistance and reactions to it, see Thorne, 1972).

15. One-third of the resisters report that they had contemplated resisting for a month or less before taking the step, another third had been debating the move for times ranging between one and four months, and the remainder had been considering it for up to several years. Since more than 80 percent had resisted within 18 months of the interview, most were being asked to assess their political outlook for a period less than 30 months previous. Again, this retrospective probing is problematic because of selective recall and distortion, and the results should be cautiously interpreted.

16. The eight labels were: conservative or moderate, liberal, radical, revolutionary, anarchist, communalist, apolitical, and cynic. Since virtually all respondents selected some combination of the first four terms, these alone are used here. This set of labels was originally developed for use in conjunction with a friendship evaluation procedure, which is described in Chapter 6. The terms were selected on the basis of their general currency in student political circles at the time of the interviewing.

17. For an extended discussion of this and related issues in the social organization of political protest movements, see Schwartz (1971, Ch. 4).

18. For a lengthy discussion of the internal culture and organization of the New England Resistance and Boston Draft Resistance Group, see Thorne (1971).

19. The national estimates are by Ferber and Lynd (1971, 222–223) and the Boston figures are by Thorne (1971).

FIVE

I was personally and politically very slothful, and I thought the only way to shake out of it was to put myself in danger. . . . I was afraid I would cynically sit out the whole war unless I brought things down on myself.

Boston draft resister.

POLITICAL INCORPORATION

Once a protest movement is formed, a number of standard organizational problems must be attacked. These range from specification of an internal discipline code to formulation of a budgeting procedure. Of special concern to most protest organizations is establishment of a program for dealing with the recruitment, socialization, and performance of members. Membership issues—especially retaining people who have been recruited—are of paramount importance because mobilization of the discontented is one of the few political resources available to protest movements. Reliance on numbers of people reached an extreme degree in the Resistance. Successful disruption of the draft was entirely contingent on a massive expansion of the Resistance ranks.

The immediate membership problem following recruitment concerns incorporation of the newcomers into the movement organization. Incorporation entails bringing the new recruits' beliefs and commitments into line with the movement's aims, creating a sense of identity with the social world of the protest, and assigning newcomers to appropriate roles in the organization.

Incorporation is apt to be especially problematic, however, since major social and political gaps frequently develop between a protest movement and its base constituency. For instance, if the conditions that spawned the movement are deep-rooted and if a solution requires transformation in major institutions or the entire society, a comprehensive, change-oriented ideology usually emerges. However, such a critical analysis of the society is likely to be alien to the everyday experience and traditional beliefs of many whom the movement would like to recruit. Certain movement actions can also alienate the base constituency. The use of programs regarded as illegitimate in the prevailing culture often provokes hostility, even among those who will be benefited. Tactics sometimes backfire, producing a negative effect on the movement's constituency, as when a planned action brings on a punitive response, applied indiscriminantly against movement members and the uninvolved alike. Still other factors reduce the social ties between the protest organization and the discontent population. The frequent use of solidarity as a major incentive for maintaining membership tends to break preexisting networks between members and the outside world. Internal commitments are strengthened to the extent that competing external involvements are minimized, and the result is that outside friendships disintegrate.

Various means exist for bridging the ideological, action, and interpersonal gaps that often develop between the protest movement and its recruitment base. One traditional method is to recruit through a "front" organization whose carefully limited purpose helps obscure political differences. In another method, the programs chosen for implementation focus on issues of concern to a cross section of the constituent population. The Resistance utilized the latter technique. It concentrated on an issue of widespread vexation—conscription—which cut across political lines. And it used a membership-defining tactic—noncooperation—which was sufficiently ambiguous to appeal to a spectrum of opinion from moderate liberal to far left. The result, as we have seen, was an influx of members with highly divergent views on the act of resistance, the purpose of the Resistance movement, and the major problems confronting America. The new members' prior connections with radical student organizations and related movements ranged from none to extensive ties, acquired through years of activism.

A movement that successfully overcomes the gulf with its base and attracts a diverse set of members must next attempt to integrate a highly varied group of newcomers. One approach is to accept only those who are already socially and ideologically close to the protest organization. This can be done by making entry dependent on personal nomination by several movement members or by requiring evidence of prior commitment to the movement's aims. An alternative is to open the organization to all who choose to join, establishing an extensive initiation period for new members. A third possibility is simply to allow "natural" social processes in the protest context to produce the incorporation.

The Resistance could not use preentry screening because it would have been contrary to the principle of mobilizing all draft registrants. Extended postentry initiation was also inhibited by the characteristic amorphousness of the movement and its relative infancy throughout its existence (it lasted less than two years). Consequently, the Resistance was primarily dependent on the direct socialization of the new resisters by the protest experience.

From half to three-quarters of the new members shared neither social ties nor political ideology with the Resistance organizers or with the radical student movement. The sudden influx of these people and their fragile ties with the movement created a potentially volatile situation (1). Their full incorporation into the Resistance was essential not only for sustaining the radical protest against the draft, but also for building the radical left in the United States, another central purpose of the Resistance. Yet without a formalized incorporation procedure there was little guarantee that incorporation would be achieved. If socialization did not happen quickly, the Resistance emphasis on direct democracy and its weak authority structure would render the original leadership vulnerable to challenges from the unincorporated newcomers, which could deradicalize the movement (2). However, the original organizers were quite confident that resisting the draft and immersion in the movement would be sufficient to convert the new recruits before they could dampen the basic thrust of the movement.

We next explore the political and social changes that did accompany involvement in this movement. The ideological aspect is taken up in this chapter, and the interpersonal element is considered in the next.

RADICALIZATION

Since the Resistance attracted draft registrants from diversified political backgrounds, incorporation was likely to result in varying degrees of change among the new resisters. Impact should be minimal for those already involved in the radical student movement, since the Resistance shared many assumptions and connections with the student left. On the other hand, those joining the Resistance from a more liberal and less activist background should undergo more extensive changes in their politics. There was considerable disparity between their liberal outlook and the radical aims of the protest. We start with the experience of the seasoned leftists and then turn to that of the moderate resisters.

Two dimensions of individual political change are distinguished. One is the change in a person's cognitive and evaluational map of the American political arena. Included here are shifts in the overall analysis of the existing social order, the image of a more ideal society, and beliefs dealing with the occurrence of social change. The second dimension is behavioral and concerns changes in the level and type of political activities in which a person is engaged.

Veteran Leftists

The radicals generally passed through the Resistance involvement with little change in basic political beliefs. Their major concerns continued to include ending U.S. imperialism, creating a socialized economy, and working for social democracy and economic equality. The creation of mass movements among the society's most powerless groups was still viewed as the only realistic strategy for change. Basic assumptions remained unaltered, but many reported an enrichment of their understanding of American life and protest politics. One noncooperator made this comparison between his preresistance views and those he acquired a year after joining the movement:

> I thought I was a radical during the [preresistance period] but I didn't really know what that meant. I considered myself to be a socialist but I wasn't even very acquainted with Marx. I felt close to [a community organizing project] in SDS but I certainly had little

affinity to urban guerrilla warfare. There was no question that I wanted to do some organizing and some work in the Movement but the imagery I wanted was that of the civil rights movement which I never was really a part of.

At the present I'm basically the same except that I know a lot more now. I've read Marx and I agree with the analysis of Baran and Sweezy [Paul A. Baran and Paul M. Sweezy, *Monopoly Capital*] at least at the economic level. . . . I have never shied away from violence if necessary but it doesn't play a big role in my thinking. But I think revolutionary change is necessary and . . . this was true even during [the preresistance period] although at that time I had a tendency to pay more of a lip service to a revolutionary position. . . . I still see the importance of working against specific injustices and organizing around them, but [it is important] to be always talking about the other injustices.

Another resister offered this overview of the evolution of his thinking:

As a senior in high school I was completely apolitical but latently a conservative or reactionary. I argued for Nixon, thought capitalism and individualism were the most important things in the world, and felt it was a good country for Nietzsche supermen. But this began to change by my sophomore year of college as I got involved in civil rights stuff. It came as a shock the way black people were treated. But you know, it was the Vietnam War that really pushed me to the left, so that by the spring of 1967 I had a high level of consciousness. However, the theoretical framework was not very good, I didn't know if imperialism was a valid concept, and I had a lot of militancy without much thought. I was a fuzzy radical.

When I turned my card in [April 1968] I had a very romantic feeling about the Movement. It was a revolutionary romanticism without much thinking through on what really changes a society. The difference between now and then is the difference between

being an idealistic socialist and being a Marxist. . . .
Last year I felt much less certain about the way words
relate to reality and there was something of an anti-in-
tellectual bias. Now I feel you have to have a concrete
analysis of society in order to change things. . . . Now
I have an intellectual framework from which to work.
My analysis of American foreign policy and domestic
life is much sharper.

Although involvement in the Resistance for preradicalized recruits primarily deepened their understanding of
American politics without transforming it, there were significant changes within this framework. The movement
confirmed the commitment of some resisters to such principles as nonviolence and anarchism, whereas it weakened
the beliefs held by others. For instance, the following
speaker had been politically active as early as 1966, mainly
with radical pacifist organizations. He registered with the
draft in 1966 and would have become a noncooperator
soon thereafter except for fear of the personal consequences. He finally returned his draft card at a Resistance
rally in early 1968:

> I was very active [in 1966] and at the time I described
> myself as an "internationalist," a Thoreauvian, and
> definitely a pacifist. Now I still believe in nonviolence
> but also realize that although it is the most creative
> way to respond, it is also the most difficult. And I also
> believe in the black movement's action, whether vio-
> lent or nonviolent.
>
> In 1966 I was an anarchist without knowing it—
> now I know it. I'm not a Marxist and have never
> really been into that much. In [1966] my roots were
> in solid American things like Thoreau, and when I
> turned in my card I had visions of Garrison and the
> abolitionists. It was really all-American. And my anar-
> chist interests were always in the American variety,
> like the Haymarket anarchists. . . . Now I recognize
> my anarchism, I'm for anarchosyndicalism and I am

really a Wobblie [member of the Industrial Workers
of the World]. I dig their theory now. I've come into
personal contact with the community of resisters and
this way of life, and this has been essential for my understanding of anarchism.

Yet for another youth the Resistance experience eroded
a long-standing commitment to pacifism. He had been active with SNCC in the south and had spent his junior year
of college in India (1965–1966) studying the Gandhian
movement and nonviolence. On returning to the United
States he had become active in antiwar activities, and in the
summer of 1967 he had joined the small group of activists
in Boston who were planning the October beginning of
the Resistance. Eighteen months later his tactical thinking
had evolved substantially:

Now pacifism is no longer a primary interest. I don't
see that pacifism is necessarily good for social change,
it's just a stage that people go through. I now see violence as sometimes necessary, especially for self-de-
fense. . . . We are now in a prerevolutionary period
and I would not oppose revolutionary violence later
on when that stage is reached.

For a few, the Resistance experience increased the value
placed on "cultural liberation" and reduced acceptance of
traditional Marxist tenets, as one movement member suggests:

My politics has always been left inasmuch as my parents are leftwing. My father is a trade unionist, a
semi-Marxist, and has always been active politically.
On my mother's side it's a matter of third-generation
radicalism, Communist party variety. When I resisted
I became a semihero among my mother's relatives and
friends of the family. But my radicalism has been very
different from theirs. For my father it was a matter of

economics and security under socialism, with absolutely no aesthetic component. . . . [In early 1967] I
was somewhat anarchical in direction and read Kro-
potkin and Paul Goodman. [Now] I suppose I'm basically the same as in 1967 although I have more knowledge and more concern for the human side of
radicalism. I really detest [Progressive Labor], which I
might not have before. I had kind of a Marxist approach but now something more of a Marcusian view,
with students and other marginal groups being critical.
I also see possibilities for a different kind of
revolution—a revolution in the quality of life.

In the realm of changes in commitment and involvement, the results were more mixed. At the time of the interviewing many were still active with the Resistance or
had moved into other radical student groups, particularly
SDS. However, a fraction had become extremely gloomy
over the prospects for creating the change they saw as
needed in the United States. Their political outlook remained essentially unchanged, but they had lost confidence
that a means of creating social change could be found.
Identification with the Resistance weakened, and some
withdrew from active involvement of any type. The loss
of hopefulness is apparent in the reflections of one person
interviewed:

[Before resisting] my consciousness was quite high. I
was strongly opposed to the Vietnam War, a pacifist
and a socialist, and way back I participated in protests
against [the House Un-American Activities Commit-
tee] and the Vietnam War, and I had been active with
SNCC. The major shifts since then have only been in
my assessment of the practical value of radical
politics—I'm more pessimistic about change and
consequently less inclined to participate. So I still have
the same goals, I'm still for a socialist state through
pacifist means, but the cynicism is much greater.

Antiwar Liberals

Those who brought a liberal point of view into the Resistance movement typically underwent a much greater transformation in political perspective. Within a year or two most had come to embrace some variety of radical political thought, and a significant fraction even drifted into revolutionary politics. The changes were similar to what Keniston has labeled a "radical reinterpretation" of the American social order (1968, 129–131). These resisters made a fundamental break with certain dominant assumptions concerning the structure of the society. Prior to involvement in the Resistance, there was a tendency to view social problems as unrelated and temporary departures from American ideals; this was accompanied by the belief that traditional democratic processes would in time solve the problems. After a year of Resistance experience, however, many had adopted a power elite or ruling class analysis of American politics in place of a pluralist viewpoint. Pressing domestic problems and the Vietnam War were understood to be rooted in antidemocratic and privately controlled economic and political systems. A graduate student who became one of the early resisters offered this assessment of his changing political outlook:

> I was considerably more politically aware of the world around me [by the 1967 spring], I knew much more about Near Eastern politics, but what I didn't know was what the U.S. was doing in Vietnam and Latin America. What I did know was mainly from the *New York Times* and I thought James Reston was a radical commentator. Nothing was sharply focused. I was opposed to the war and the draft, but there was nothing too militant in my attitudes. . . . The U.S. government was essentially benign, the Vietnam War an aberration, and so I talked about the Vietnam conflict as a separate issue in that it did not match up to U.S.

ideals. I believed these ideals to be valued and wide-spread. Events were largely isolated—Vietnam, the atomic bombing of Japan, our refusal of support for Hungary—these were not connected, not yet part of a string of events. . . .

King's assassination [in April 1968] was a radicalizing influence. People had been telling me I wasn't radical enough, and there were some disputes with people in radical organizations. I was at a meeting of the New England Resistance when word on King's death came through. And then notions in economic theory started making sense, and I was beginning to believe that America had as a working basis the suppression of the poor. So I began to think America was malevolent, not benign. It was in the American government's interest to be in Vietnam, and it was in her interest to assert her presence around the world. And it was in her interest to keep people unemployed, and certain people unemployed, namely, the poor who don't say much and don't vote. But then to change the distribution of things would be to change the economic system, and this is revolution.

Another person joined the Resistance in mid-spring 1968, but within a year he had become a full-time SDS activist, identifying his views as close to those of the Progressive Labor party:

I was liberal during my last year in high school. I liked [New York mayor, John V.] Lindsay and Bobby Kennedy, although I detested Johnson and was fairly convinced that he had killed [President] Kennedy. . . . [In the fall of 1967, senior year in college] I was in a sense very apolitical. I had come back to school with a cosmology of moral relativism . . . which meant nonaction because it was difficult to pick sides. But during the fall I gradually came to the view that action is important, and also that the Vietnam War was not a mistake [that the country had blundered into]—I knew about Guatemala etc. etc. etc. at that time. I was ambivalent about McCarthy, although I

thought he would get us out of the war. I also believed that the working class was racist and fascist, a
real danger to this country; shades of Lipset. This all
propelled me to act in a very moral way [in turning
the draft card in].

Now I'm very pro-working class. I don't think they
are bought off, nor that it's impossible to build a mass
movement. Change in this country can only take place
through a mass movement of workers and students
who combine to make a revolution.

Radicalization was not always in the direction of a traditional leftist analysis. For some there was an undercurrent
of counterculture in the new politics, with an emphasis on
establishing a liberated life style and new solidarist communities as prerequisites to creating an effective political
movement. For a few, the countercultural elements became
even more important than the movement. It was felt that
efforts should be spent instead on developing self-enclosed
communities based on new principles of cooperation and
intense personal bonds. It was argued that such counter-
communities, which could play the role of exemplifying
the form of social organization possible for the entire society, should be more effective in convincing people than
the usual protest movement process. The strategy combined elements of political attack and social withdrawal, as
expressed in the words of one resister:

I have committed my act with an awareness of a desire to create a community where I can live a new life
style [and] develop a society of brotherhood and love.
. . . Resisting for me was almost apolitical because I
was going to change things through a new life style,
an alternative life style, by making this revolutionary
apolitical community. For example, restructuring myself and the people in this community would ultimately lead to a restructuring of America. Our goal is
brotherhood, peace, and love, and everything else is

combined in this. Ending the draft and war is inherent
in creating this life style.

With respect to the dimension of political action, the
dominant tendency among those coming from a liberal
background was increased commitment to activism. This
included the self-conscious adoption of an identity as a
"radical" or "revolutionary" and growing interest in other
insurgent movements in the United States. A few preresistance liberals reverted to an apolitical state after a period
with the Resistance, and within a year of joining they had
lost all interest in protest and change. For most, however,
the act of resisting constituted a conscious decision to
begin participating in leftist politics (except when it was
precipitated more directly by the threat of induction). "I
thought it would involve me in a really important thing. I
had a real feeling against the war and a great desire to involve myself in something," recalled one person. Some rec-
ognized at the time of noncooperation that the act represented a symbolic "bridge burning" and that taking the
step would inexorably generate deeper involvement in political activities. As an individual's political perspective
drifted leftward after joining the movement, his rationale
justifying membership in the Resistance was also reformulated. The resisters increasingly came to view their own
action in terms akin to those of the original organizers.
The sense of moral witness and the belief that it was im-
perative to do something militant against the war were replaced by colder calculations of strategy and attempts to
assess the contribution of one's own actions to collective
protest. In some cases this line of logic ended in the rejection, for tactical reasons, of the original step of noncooperation. One resister explained:

> I plan to get a deferment. It was exceedingly impor-
> tant for me to commit the act on [October] 16th,

since the commitments after that were easier to make.
. . . It took the act to solidify the commitment and to
galvanize my thinking. It has led to a rapid development in my thinking on American society and my role
to effect change in it. Now I do not want to be in a
position of facing jail or leaving the country, and the
taking of a deferment represents a political decision as
to where I can be effective. . . .

I'm a socialist and part of my politics involves confronting authority. But in confrontation you have to
make some sort of assessment of the tactical limitations
of your strength. I'll commit myself to a given line of
action if it's going to be effective. Tactical defeats or
retreats can be good because you can assess your
strength. So in line with this, it's natural for political
reasons to decide the draft is important at one point of
time but now to see it as just one of many repressive
institutions which all have to be attacked. So taking a
deferment now is a logical step, [since] prison means
I'm virtually isolated for three years.

Another aspect of becoming involved in protest politics
is learning about the historical tradition of insurgent movements in the United States and the composition of the pres-
ent-day protest scene. For those without previous connections, the Resistance provided the first introduction to the
inner byways and culture of the radical left. In time, many
of these resisters acquired an insider's sense for the political
morphology of dissenting groups in America. Here is the
account of one person who arrived in the Boston area
shortly before the demonstration of October 16 and who
joined the Resistance on that date:

There was no New Left in my home state so when I
came here I tried to find out about things. . . . I made
contact with SDS people at [one of the universities]
and I already had some idea what they were thinking,
since the year before I had read a lot about the left
and wrote papers on it. I was really interested in [an

SDS community organizing project] and I was moving
to the point where I wanted to jump in, although I
was still careerist and a graduate student in orientation. . . . So I either had to get in or remain an outside observer—but then I sort of overshot it.

Now I'm definitely further to the left in analysis,
and a lot more things make sense. I can talk to people
about the history of the left and I can begin to piece
together what has happened in this country and what
it's all about. I'm not that widely read but I can work
with left groups in America and I'm able to determine
what their politics mean and why certain positions are
advanced. And with this experience it's easier to tie
what I have read together. Working with [the Resis-
tance] for two years really helped. The left is no
longer a great mysterious unknown or just a bunch of
sects.

Thus the experience of joining the Resistance had little
effect on the political philosophy of the radicals who became members, although it did enhance their understanding of American politics. For the preresistance liberals,
however, the experience had many elements of conversion.
Their paradigm for viewing political events was fundamentally reformulated. Within a relatively short period,
most had abandoned their starting views in favor of a far-
reaching leftist critique of the society. This transformation
is apparent when comparison is made between the political
labels the resisters used for their outlook during the period
just before considering noncooperation and those used for
the period immediately prior to the interview (see Table
5.1; note 16, Ch. 4, describes the labels used). More than
two-thirds of the radicals reported no change one to two
years later, but less than one-sixth of the preresistance liberals retained their original politics. A sizable fraction of
the liberals even moved to embrace what they saw as a
"revolutionary" analysis. The overall pattern suggests that
social processes were present which served to incorporate

Table 5.1   *Preresistance Versus Preinterview*
Political Perspective

Preinterview Perspective	Preresistance Perspective (%)	
	Liberal	Radical
Liberal	15	0
Radical	46	69
Revolutionary	38	31
N	(52)	(36)

politically those resisters who did not initially share the movement's basic ideology.

Such political changes could be expected to affect related personal values in the resisters' lives. Becoming highly politicized should reduce interest in nonpolitical concerns, and becoming a radical should throw prior career plans into serious question. A number of resisters reported such ramifications, particularly resisters who had been relatively apolitical before joining the movement. "This was a period of complete chaos," observed one person who had been marginally active before starting noncooperation. "You change your outlook on life, you become a new person. This was really rapid change, and really traumatic. It was like a cardhouse that fell apart. You start rebuilding but look carefully at the values as you do. A lot of the values you had before [noncooperation] you keep, but now they are felt more strongly and there is a greater sense of living the way you really feel, and there is a more authentic sense of values."

For some, the experience led to a consuming concern with radical protest and an abandonment of other long-standing interests. At the time of the interview, one in six of the noncooperators identified himself as a full-time political activist. This represented triple the number that had been regular organizers before resisting. Academic and vocational concerns seriously suffered in some cases. One resister had been studying for a career in the creative arts: "It gradually dawned on me in the few months immediately following [return of the draft card] that I really wanted to work full-time in the Movement. I always had revolutionary ideas but never did anything about them, and I discovered that you could go into politics as a full-time vocation." Others did not discard previous interests, and they made attempts to integrate the new priorities with old ones. A number of the undergraduates remained in school but placed less stress on the intellectual and occupational reasons for being there and more on the political opportunities in campus organizing. Many graduate students became interested in work with leftist counterassociations, which were springing up in several of the scholarly professions. Four resisters in one graduate department played a major role in forming a radical caucus in their discipline. This broadening of identity is apparent in the reflections of one doctoral student in physics:

> Before resisting I had realized that a Ph.D. didn't mean everything but I couldn't conceive of anything else but teaching college. But the step was liberating [and] all of a sudden you realize you will do goofy things. Up till then you didn't want to get arrested so you could get a good teaching job, but once this severance is undertaken you are no longer strongly identified with teaching alone. I could now do other things besides teaching college, like teaching high school, driving a cab, digging ditches. Teaching would still be my first choice but I no longer have to fight to preserve that choice. The middle-class success patterns are no longer that important, since I can now get intrinsic satisfaction in other realms like politics, and this is very important to me now. But it's bad to work full-time in the Movement, and people should earn money on the outside. Paid people in the Movement

create bureaucracy and professionalism, which creates
strange pressures. So I still would like to teach college,
but this is not as essential as it used to be.

THE INCORPORATION PROCESS

The Resistance had no formalized procedures for politically socializing its newcomers. Consequently, transformations in beliefs and values accompanying involvement
could only stem from processes intrinsic in the structure of
the movement. From the interviews, we identified three
factors that combined to exert a major influence on the resisters' political outlook: (1) a membership criterion that
put the participants in direct conflict with the government,
(2) a membership criterion that resulted in strong initial
commitments to the movement, and (3) a movement milieu
that helped place the personal conflict in a broader in-
terpretive framework.

The movement had set out to recruit people on the basis
of offering them help in solving their own problems with
the military draft. However, the actual effect was to
worsen the problems of those who joined. The privilege of
a deferment was lost, and an open conflict with the government was substituted. The typical result of returning a
draft card was reclassification to a draft-eligible status by
the Selective Service. This status was usually a special "delinquent" category, which facilitated a quick call for the
registrant's induction into the armed forces. The resister
refused induction, and usually after some investigation the
Justice Department moved to indict the person for violation of Selective Service law. The Justice Department was
extremely slow to initiate prosecution in some cases, but
this did not reduce the resister's tension, since eventual indictment was expected.

At the time of the interview, 32 percent of the resisters were still classified in a deferred status by their local board. However, 20 percent were classified as eligible for induction although they had not yet appeared for induction. Eleven percent had already refused induction but had not yet been indicted, and another 21 percent had been or were being prosecuted by the government (the remaining 14 percent were uncertain of their draft status or were in still other situations). Noncooperation therefore placed a major proportion of the movement membership in a highly antagonistic relationship with the state. Few movements impose such a drastic change in personal security on those who join. Illegal, underground, and guerrilla movements carry similar consequences for the individuals who enter, but usually such organizations also provide for the personal safety of their members, or at least they keep their membership lists secret.

The resisters' conflict with the government typically influenced their relationships with other institutions as well. Some acquaintances in the school or work place reacted hostilely on learning of the illegal action. For example, several graduate students report a significant cooling of the relation with their academic advisor, and one divinity student nearly lost his position with a local church when he announced in a sermon that he had become a draft resister. As one noncooperator noted, there was a conflict logic that carried the fight against conscription into other spheres: "Breaking the bonds of our fear of the [Selective Service] has sensitized us to the other repressive institutions in the society."

Thus becoming a draft resister introduced a person to an experience that was crucial to the formation of a radical consciousness. For the first time many personally felt "oppressed" by the government and other dominant institutions in the society. There was a clear connection between government action and one's adverse circumstances, and other institutions appeared to support the government's position. One person who joined the Resistance in October 1967 and participated in the march on the Pentagon a few days later offered this account of his changing perceptions:

> Turning my card in and going to the Pentagon set off a chain of events. Together they meant I was no longer a moral protester with an elite background. When I turned my card in I felt like an official member of the Movement, I had to be at all the Movement functions, and my life should be with the Movement. Then I went to the Pentagon—it was my first confrontation—and up to that time I saw the police as protecting me. Boy, was I surprised. All these people were clubbed, the paper did a real job of [misreporting] it, and the balloon had burst. The world had turned against *me*. I had known about the power elite of C. Wright Mills, but then you suddenly realize that repression is the mode and that change within the system will not be allowed. This was the first time I personally felt identified with the repressed class. Until then I had been a member of the elite, going to Harvard and all that, and sympathetic to the repressed. But this identification [with the repressed] was brought home and it confirmed a true radical consciousness in that I was fighting for myself in a socially relevent way.

Soon after joining the Resistance and demonstrating at the Pentagon, the respondent took part in a student blockade intended to prevent a representative of the Dow Chemical Company from recruiting employees on campus. Disciplinary probation resulted (which forced him off the school's tennis team), and the college administration came to be viewed as protecting the same war interests as the government.

The action that created the type of open conflict just illustrated between the resister and the government also facilitated involvement in the movement's activities. A rapid expansion of the protest would minimize one's personal risk and increase the chance that the individual act would be contributing to a movement that was a real threat to the draft and war. Building the Resistance was a matter of self-interest and collective interest alike. In addition, certain psychological by-products of the noncooperation act served to further reinforce involvement. The step was both costly and seemingly irreversible, and the value of having become a resister could be enhanced by, for example, increasing one's regard for the intrinsic attractions of membership in an organization for which noncooperation was the prerequisite (3). In a revealing if bizarre instance, one person disposed of his draft card at a Resistance rally but did not decide to become involved in the movement until several days later, when he learned of the legal consequences of the act. In the words of another:

> [Resisting] occurred at the right time, when you were getting involved, and this sealed your involvement. You already had lost everything. On becoming a revolutionary you have to be dead, you have to be willing to make sacrifices. It was a step of total commitment, and after the act you have to work hard to justify it and its consequences. If you are going to jail, you have to make a lot of noise on the way.

Some resisters were later presented with unexpected opportunities to reverse their stand when local boards offered to reissue the destroyed or relinquished card and to restore the original deferment in return for cessation of noncooperation. A few accepted the invitation. However, most did not, and their interest in the movement was reintensified with each reopening of the decision. Ambivalence aroused over the continuing high costs of the action was reduced by renewed commitment to the cause. The anguish of receiving an offer of safe exit is recounted by one noncooperator who was heavily involved in Resistance organizing:

> I felt it was the Second Coming. At the time this was
> the most important decision of my life. . . . It was an
> appropriate personal and political step, and the ques-
> tion was just whether or not I would do it. It could
> really mess up my life. As a resister, industries could
> screw me if the antiwar protest didn't swell. My fu-
> ture life, jobs, income, and how people would react to
> me were all up for question. So it was a pretty hard
> step to take. It could put me in a concentration camp
> or jail and I would then have a sentence on my rec-
> ord. And conditions in jail could be really bad, they
> could really destroy me. . . . Everytime I got a letter
> [from the local board] asking if I wanted my card
> back I had to go through this October 16 thing all
> over again. I had to make the decision again, and I
> couldn't sleep every time I got these letters.

Other psychological consequences of resisting eased the road to involvement in the protest. Once the initial step of noncooperation had been taken, there was less hesitancy about participating in further quasi-illegal activities of the movement (e.g., urging others to resist the draft; staging "sanctuaries" for draft fugitives and soldiers who had de-serted) (4). In addition, returning the cards in groups led to a type of initiation ceremony. The turn-in occasion in Boston included speeches, prayers, processions, witnesses, and media cameras. The first Boston return was held in a historic Boston church, and several ministers and a priest accepted draft cards from members of their respective faiths (a professor of philosophy collected cards from the nonreligious). "The act of turning in the card created the solidarity, it served as initation rites for a fraternity of radicals, and having turned in our cards was like passing from neophytes to brothers in a symbolic way," was one resister's reaction.

The foregoing positive effects of resisting the draft could not in themselves fully radicalize the Resistance members who had joined with liberal sentiments. However, they did establish conditions favorable to such a development. The resisters shared a new conflict relationship with the government, as well as various incentives to involve themselves in the protest organization. Their subsequent experience within the movement added two other decisive elements. These were opportunities offered by the protest organization for contact between radicals and nonradicals and for direct participation by all members in running a protest program. Work with the Resistance primarily consisted of activities oriented around encouraging more people to resist the draft; however, some new resisters found this work uninviting and there were periods in which there was little work at all.

For those who were not veteran leftists, the period was marked by great turmoil in reaching a new understanding of American politics. Vietnam War policies contradicted their conventional liberal images of a benign government, and the image suffered further when the government took punitive actions against recalcitrant conscripts. However, the connections fundamental to a leftist interpretation of the role of the state in a capitalist society were not transparent in this situation. Nevertheless, such connections were understood by a minority of the new resisters who had been previously active in other radical organizations. The Resistance contained a substantial number of "deployable personnel" (Selznick, 1952), people who were already thoroughly committed to leftist radicalism.

Education and persuasion of the liberal newcomers by these veteran leftists was facilitated by the political mixture of the Resistance membership, which resulted from its success in reaching a varied constituency. The Resistance maintained no formal novitiate status, and the new recruits were immediately exposed to the full operation of the organization. Moreover, a rapid influx of newcomers holding a variety of political viewpoints prevented the inner culture of the movement from acquiring an intimidating ambience. Liberal resisters encountered many people whose political outlooks were as uncertain as their own. The movement's initial ideological heterogeneity undercut any appearance of indoctrination or party line. This attractive aspect was recalled by one resister:

> At the time [of resisting] I was very suspicious of SDS. I didn't know much about them, but their literature I did not like. I felt much more at home in the Resistance at that time because I didn't feel like I had to know much about imperialism. SDS knew the left rhetoric, but in the Resistance they were more like me and I felt much more comfortable.

As previously noted, the other element adding further content to a radical world view was direct participation in formulation and execution of Resistance programs. A major leftist tenet is the view that significant social change can be effectively achieved only through the application of collective pressure by those suffering because of the existing social arrangements. Although this idea was part of the original foundation of the Resistance, those coming from liberal and apolitical backgrounds were generally unaware or unconvinced of the position. Direct experience in organizing Resistance actions helped make this operating principle seem both comprehensible and valid. The impact of participation is reflected in the remarks of one person:

> It was a really big thing for me because up to that time I had been a radical liberal, but this was largely an environmental thing, since all of my friends had the same position. But during [an association with the Resistance] a lot of things became a lot clearer. Now I'm much more radicalized and less apolitical because of the Resistance experience. It came through participating in discussions, going to rallies, finding out what

was going on in other parts of the country, and just sort of interrelating with these people.

Another noncooperator emphasized the contact with radical resisters who came into the movement:

> It was the major force behind my political awareness. Any political thoughts I have now I owe to the Resistance. There's no question that I got my political education there, and it stands out as my dominant experience in the past two years. . . . I had ·no radical perspective back before resisting, and it began with the Pentagon [demonstration in October, 1967] and meeting people in the Resistance.

The broader movement context of the Resistance also had an impact on the resisters' political thought. Formation of the Resistance did not end its special relationship with other radical student organizations. In the Boston area, the New England Resistance, Boston Draft Resistance Group, SDS, and other campus organizations jointly sponsored events and generally followed one another's activities. Some resisters worked with several of these organizations simultaneously, and the active leftists who joined the Resistance continued to be well informed of trends in political thought in other organizations. For those new to radical politics, involvement in the Resistance opened new networks of access into the surrounding protest milieu. In 1968 the major campus organization in this milieu, SDS, was becoming increasingly militant, more interested in traditional Marxist ideas, and more concerned with reaching the American blue collar working class. In addition, SDS had never formally endorsed a preemptive resistance program, and its opposition was hardening in light of the failure of the Resistance to achieve a threatening scale. These attitudes filtered into the Resistance, and some members began to turn against the preemptive strategy on the

grounds that it lacked sufficient appeal to working-class registrants, as well as the potential for fundamentally challenging the social order. The reaction of an SDS activist
who had joined the Resistance is illustrative. For half a
year he was heavily involved in helping to build the Resistance, but he subsequently became disillusioned:

> Turning in my card was a moral and quasi-political
> act with no understanding of strategy. My pacifism,
> opposition to the war, and frustration over any other
> tactic to end it [went into the decision]. I just wanted
> to stop the killing.
>
> I really believed [draft resistance] would work. We
> thought 20,000 people might do it and just end the
> war. It did raise the cost of the war and got people
> into the Movement, and so it was good despite its
> middle-class base and appeal and failure to reach
> working-class kids. By the second or third card return
> it was becoming apparent that it wasn't working.
> Practice showed that the theory was full of shit. I
> turned against the Resistance because it didn't work
> and also because it had bad tendencies, and these were
> becoming clearer in time. Since it didn't work all these
> other criticisms became much more decisive.
>
> Now I think pacifism is unrealistic. Today I have a
> much more developed analysis and a much more seri-
> ous, long-range commitment. I know a lot more about
> theory, like Marx and Lenin, and I am a thoroughgo-
> ing Marxist. I support the [Vietnam National Libera-
> tion Front] and would say I'm a revolutionary social-
> ist, working for the revolution in America. And now I
> think you can't build a revolution with middle-class
> kids. But [the Resistance] was good then because SDS
> was losing its base and becoming sectarian. The Resis-
> tance filled the void and served a very useful role. But
> you can't build a revolutionary movement around the
> draft. Moral witness won't do—you have to appeal
> to people's rational economic self-interest.

By the time of the interview, this resister had become a
full-time SDS organizer.

A similar outcome was reached in another case. This person, by contrast, had been virtually unconcerned with political issues before joining the Resistance. He became a noncooperator in spring 1968. By the following fall he was already fairly active with SDS on his campus, to the extent of planning and participating in one of their major sit-in actions. Several months later, still within a year of his original act of noncooperation, he became heavily involved in the Worker–Student Alliance of SDS (which regarded the industrial working class as the only potentially revolutionary sector of American society). His view of draft resistance had changed considerably by then:

> I don't think it's possible to accomplish anything through moral witness, which is simply an appeal to the conscience of the ruling class. Furthermore, it expresses a very elitist attitude. You put yourself above other people, and this is clearly counterproductive in terms of building a mass movement. Essentially my feeling is that it is an incredibly self-indulgent action; it's silly, since you put yourself in jail for five years and you are going to have little effectiveness in prison. The assumption behind this kind of thinking is that the Vietnam War is just an aberration and that the people who run this country are decent but just made some unfortunate mistakes. This is inaccurate, to say the least.
>
> The Resistance was a very bad mistake. It had terrible politics to begin with [and] an elitist conception of itself. It was self-indulgent, self-righteous, and altogether incredibly appalling. A lot of people in it feel liberated, they have a groovy life style, [and] subjectively they think of themselves as radical. But they really are liberals or anarchists.

One consequence of the spread of such political doubts about the validity of preemptive resistance was the drifting into SDS programs of a substantial fraction of the resisters, after a stretch of activity with the Resistance. During the half-year period before those who were interviewed began to consider noncooperation, 13 percent were lightly involved in SDS activities (this included attendance at SDS demonstrations and occasional organizing activities—up to 10 to 20 hours per week) and another 7 percent were heavily engaged in SDS (from 10 to 20 hours per week to full-time work). In the period just before the interviews, these proportions had risen to 18 and 19 percent, respectively.

It is apparent that natural social processes did lead to an effective ideological incorporation of the movement's diverse membership. Although largely unintended, the use of preemptive resistance as an organizational strategy served as a major facilitator for the conversion. Since the resistance strategy made membership in the organization prerequisite on the commission of an illegal act, it ensured that all members would be inclined to involve themselves in the life of the movement. It also put them in open conflict with some of the society's major institutions. But this personal experience was insufficient to spontaneously generate a full leftist critique of the American social order. It remained for participation in the protest movement to place hostility toward the government in a broader perspective and to add the anticapitalist analysis.

This suggests that protest programs that direct demands at the government rather than at economic institutions can nonetheless help spread radical criticism of the economic order. The crucial element for such a protest is a focus on an issue that is attractive to both seasoned leftist activists and people who are not already committed to radical change. When both types of members are recruited into the same movement organization, the setting is conducive to changing the newcomers' nascent radical beliefs into the vision shared by the veterans, especially when this vision helps interpret the newcomers' personal experience outside the movement. Leftist organizers and political organizations in other settings have been found to play similar roles in shaping discontent into a comprehensive socialist critique of the society (e.g., Lipset, 1968; Petras and Zeitlin, 1967).

NOTES

1. A social organization faces tensions in accepting the new members when it actively recruits from a constituency representing divergent values and with which it has few social ties. Such tension is particularly evident when regularized means are not available for the socialization of the neophytes. Wilson (1967), for instance, has stressed the existence of problems associated with the evangelism of "conversionist" religious sects. New converts are seldom carefully screened or trained for entry into the sect, and they can signficantly affect the sect's character when their numbers are substantial.

2. The significance of organizational structure in determining a movement's susceptibility to pressures from the rank and file is apparent in a study of the rise of the black power ideology in two civil rights organizations (Rudwick and Meier, 1970). CORE shifted from an integrationist stance to a black power program in the mid-1960s but the NAACP retained its moderate integrationist orientation. Rudwick and Meier concluded that the degree of bureaucratization of the two movements accounted for much of the difference in response. As black power thinking spread through the ranks of CORE, the organization's system of direct democracy allowed for a new generation of more militant and more separatist-oriented activists to assume control. By contrast, despite some similar grass-roots pressures in the NAACP, a complex hierarchic decision-making structure blocked the rising sentiment there, and control remained in the hands of the traditional leadership.

3. There were elements of dissonance reduction in this process. Experimental evidence on initiation effects indicates that the greater the personal costs in joining an association, the larger the subsequent commitment to it (Aronson and Mills, 1959; Gerard and Mathewson, 1966).

4. This "foot-in-the-door" effect has been substantiated experimentally (Freedman and Fraser, 1966). Also, a type of self-labeling following the act of noncooperation made the liberal resisters more receptive to the movement's radical ideology. The militant character of the act led some to perceive themselves as "radical" although they had not yet acquired a radical world view. "I wanted to radicalize myself by radical action," commented one person.

SIX

*The single most important weapon we have is
our commitment and unity as a group. We must
let them know that harassment or arrest of one
of us will mean a response by all of us.*

Newsletter of the New England Resistance,
1967.

SOLIDARITY AND
ESTRANGEMENT

Political incorporation is only half of the integration of new recruits into a protest organization. Equally important is their social incorporation, which involves the creation of loyalty to the movement and bonds of fellowship with other members. Political incorporation is required if a movement is to retain its original aims, but a movement cannot exercise effective control over its members if it lacks social incorporation.

There are several types of incentives with which an organization can reinforce membership allegiance and ensure compliance with the rules of operation. *Shared principles and interests* involves the overlap between a movement's objectives and the values and social needs of its members. *Individual rewards* consists of the distribution of individually consumable resources such as a salary, the benefits of holding office, or access to low-cost housing. *Solidarity* involves the obligations stemming from a sense of community identity and mutual regard. *Coercion* entails the use or threat of direct force (1). The incentive of shared principles and interests is available to all protest movements, since the overlap between individual and collective aims is the defining basis of a protest organization. Similarly, solidarity can be used by nearly all movements, for it only requires that people be cooperatively working toward common ends. The resources necessary for using coercive or material incentives are rarely available to protest movements, however, and thus protest organizations tend to be particularly reliant on social solidarity and overlapping interests for maintaining internal order and cohesion.

The Resistance could draw on the incentives of shared principles and solidarity, but it had no means of coercing compliance, and individual rewards were at a minimum. Financial resources were scarce, and less tangible rewards, such as leadership status, were also limited by the movement's unwillingness to move toward bureaucracy and elitism. If anything, the Resistance was decidedly deficient in individual material incentives, since the personal consequences of joining the movement were costly. Thus, along with shared principles, solidarity was the primary means by which the Resistance could control its membership.

The political environment of the Resistance made reliance on solidarity especially useful. Most protest movements challenge vested and well-organized interests, and such challenges are often labeled as exceeding the legitimate bounds of political dissent. As a result, attacks are frequently made on not only the policies advocated but on the very existence of the protest organization. The creation of a tight-knit solidary organization can be a particularly effective means for coping with this kind of environment. Morale and personal security are enhanced when a strong sense of mutual obligation and trust exists among the members (2). The Resistance was unusually susceptible to assaults by its opponent—the government—since it was founded around urging draft registrants to defy federal authority and all members had taken an illegal action. Unlike some protest movements, the Resistance could not withdraw or go underground without undercutting its effort to expand. In this dangerous and exposed situation, solidarity was a very important factor in sustaining commitment.

An emphasis on solidarity within a movement leads to a reciprocal effect on its members' relations with people outside the organization. Esprit de corps is strongest when competing outside loyalites are extinguished (see Kanter, 1968). Consequently, the generation of camaraderie among the members should be accompanied by estrangement from nonmembers. Thus the process of effective social incorporation into the Resistance implies a dual transformation in the social worlds of the new resisters. While new friendships were being forged in the Resistance, contacts with those who did not also become draft resisters should be withering. The process would be one of interpersonal conversion paralleling that of ideological conversion.

Explicit movement policies can facilitate the social incorporation of new members. Internal solidarity is bolstered by instituting ritual occasions, integrating family life into the movement, and creating intimate discussion groups. External ties can be undermined through imposition of strictures against association with nonmembers and insistence that members invest their spare time in the movement. However, again because of the infancy and weak authority structure of the Resistance, formalized arrangements and rules of this type could not be developed soon enough to accommodate the sudden influx of new resisters. The Resistance was forced to rely on natural processes for social as well as political incorporation.

This chapter explores the interpersonal transformations associated with involvement in the Resistance, as well as processes that led to these changes. We begin with a consideration of movement solidarity in its several phases and then turn to the social networks of movement members.

THE RESISTANCE COMMUNITY

A community of draft resisters existed for a year in greater Boston. Although membership was in flux, the association that was formed after the first card collection in October 1967 demonstrated a brief period of relative stability, going into serious decline only in late 1968. Noncooperators and others working actively with the movement were included in the formal fold. In time, performing antiwar work with the Resistance became the de facto definition of membership, although the belief persisted that the organization still represented all resisters, including those who were no longer active with the movement. A shared culture emerged which included a status system, internal gossip, insignias of collective identity (e.g., the uniquely styled omega symbol, its national logo), and communal activities such as parties, weekly dinners, and the founding of several communes of Resistance members.

Many of the resisters we interviewed reported an intense identification with all fellow resisters during the height of the movement. Resisters took the community's collective opinion into account in forming their own views on political matters, and they felt an obligation to participate in the movement's program. The lapel-displayed omega button was popular, and unacquainted members would often strike up conversation in non-Resistance settings such as a classroom, a party, or a streetcorner. In speaking of the early days some mentioned an instinctive affinity for anyone in the Resistance, whether a personal acquaintance or unknown. One person recalled:

> For awhile the Resistance was conceived of as an iden-
> tity, and for me this peaked about a month or so after
> I turned in the card. In meeting people who turned
> out to be resisters a sense of solidarity was felt. There
> was a period when wearing the omega pin signified
> that the person had resisted, and people were sensitive
> to wearing this if they were not actually resisters.

The diffuse identification with the community of draft resisters generally followed immediately after the step of noncooperation. "The day I did it I accepted myself as part of the movement. . . . I felt very close to my friends who had resisted, the Resistance, and the Movement in general," said one person. But there was also a rhythm to the esprit de corps. It peaked in the periods during which a major card return was planned, as the movement's purpose was given its most concrete expression.

Solidarity was also linked to the movement's successes and to counterattacks by the government. A euphoria of accomplishment gave the first wave of resisters their initial unity. Spirit sagged when the showing at the second card return (November, 1967) was weaker than expected. But the specter of collective prosecution raised by the conspiracy indictments of Benjamin Spock and others, and the surprisingly large rallies during the 1968 spring, revitalized community spirit. The solidarity often extended well beyond Resistance boundaries. Some report an increased sense of common purpose with other radical organizations, ranging from the Industrial Workers of the World to SNCC and the student movement. Within the movement itself, there was a generational component to the solidarity, and those who joined at the same Resistance rally were particularly close.

The community spirit was not shared by all. A few had principled objections to cooperating in any group effort, and others found the movement's atmosphere unattractive.

Some of those already active in leftist politics retained preexisting allegiance with other organizations. Thus one person contributed his full energies to the Resistance for half a year but the association remained utilitarian:

> I had a close working relation with the people active in the office of the New England Resistance and I identified myself as someone working with the Resistance, but there was no personal immersion. I didn't develop any close friendships with people in the Resistance, so the ties to the group were mainly ideological rather than emotional.

The communal atmosphere began to wane in mid-1968 in Boston and by the end of the year it had virtually disappeared, although several dozen people continued to staff the local organization. The omega button ceased to be an automatic bridge between strangers, meetings and events drew dwindling numbers of resisters and newcomers, and draft resistance as an obsessive topic of conversation yielded to new concerns. These circumstances, accompanied by some bitter quarrels and faction fights, produced consternation and distress for those still drawing sustenance from the feeling of solidarity. Some fatalistically viewed it as unfortunate but predictable, and a few looked on with either indifference or satisfaction. For many, however, the passing marked the end of a brief but highly meaningful involvement. Recollections of the movement's heyday acquired a nostalgic tone. There was turnover in active membership throughout the movement's short history, but the departures greatly outnumbered the new arrivals as the end neared. This precipitated a withdrawal for one active member:

> I'm really glad I [resisted], since I still think it fixed many things in my mind and I met a lot of interesting people. The most important thing was the feeling of

community with the people with whom I did it. So even if it is politically ineffective, the ruling class cannot stop the spontaneous sense of community among people who do things together. . . . All the people I met I had great respect for, and these people took me over the hump in rejecting America. My loyalties are really to people in doing things. By being an outgroup you are an in-group, and they were talking about things at the edge of my awareness.

It died for me when the great people like Henry, Bob, Rick, and Irene did not come back in the fall [of 1968], and when they left for other things I began losing interest. . . . The loss of identity with the Resistance was rather painful, since I really thought that this was the place to do good work. The death date was November 14th [1968, the day of the final nationally coordinated card return]. Two weeks before I had gone to the planning meeting and argued for a turn-in—probably because I wanted more people to come into the community—but everybody else talked against it.

As the movement edged toward its peak, the growth of camaraderie among the draft resisters was marked by a reverse development in their outside loyalties. The campus, work place, and other groups receded in primacy. People in these contexts seemed to be less interesting, and their opinions became less important to the resisters. For example, several graduate students reported that their department and profession seemed to be much less relevant to their lives as they became involved in the Resistance. One person was finishing a doctorate when he joined the movement. By the time of the interview he had become a full-time political organizer:

I began to feel that my interests and those of my friends in graduate school were not on the same paths and were increasingly farther apart. We had chemistry to talk about, but I was becoming less interested in

> sitting around and talking about the most recent
> breakthroughs in the field. . . . Finally, I decided I
> didn't want to stay with graduate school any more, al-
> though I would finish up my degree, and last spring I
> started working full-time with [a radical organiza-
> tion]. I think I felt more liberated since getting out of
> graduate school and going to work with this group
> than in turning in my card. When I returned the card
> I still fully anticipated becoming a chemist, but oppo-
> sition to my political activities from my advisor and
> others made me realize what they wanted out of me if
> I were to lead a professional life.

The factors that led to the political incorporation of
new movement members were largely responsible for their
social incorporation as well. The overlap of collective and
individual interests and the several psychological consequences of resisting all encouraged the new members to
become active in the protest. The noncooperators were
then exposed to experiences within the organization which
helped activate the sense of solidarity. Chief among these
was involvement in a cooperative effort aimed at securing
common gains against a hostile and threatening opposition (3).

In addition, the movement's leadership made a few conscious efforts to draw people together in the organization.
For instance, the Boston area resisters were scattered across
a large metropolitan region, and much of the movement's
work was decentralized. Local clusters of resisters emerged
on several campuses and in several organizations, but the
lack of regular intercluster contact inhibited formation of
an overarching brotherhood. Shortly after the movement's
founding, in an attempt to promote a sense of community,
a weekly dinner for all resisters and supporters was organized. It ran for more than a year and provided a routin-
ized opportunity for both social contact and discussion of

movement issues. Its rationale was outlined by one Resistance leader:

> Resistance continues to be an expression of conscience, but the expression involves the whole person—not just his politics and morality. Consequently, we felt that it is now most crucial that resisters in New England begin to develop a sense of community. We should take an active interest in the many loves we all have. . . . [Resistance] should never become a bureaucracy substituting for the [Selective Service System], but a complex of human concerns, humanly expressed and focused. One concrete proposal was a weekly dinner. . . . Here will be a place to discuss business, but also to get to know each other and to get to like and enjoy one another. . . . [F]or too long we have had a large group of invisible resisters. As repression increases, we will need each other more and more; it shouldn't be necessary though, for half of us to be in jail for the other half to start swinging together (Kugelmass, 1968).

The processes mentioned helped generate solidarity within the movement but did not lead directly to a reduction in relations with the outside world. External estrangement was primarily a product of the dangerous action each draft registrant took on becoming a member of the movement. The movement aimed for a collective payoff that would benefit members and nonmembers alike. Nevertheless, the Resistance could not offer its members any special benefits on joining, and it actually worsened their draft situation. Consequently, the resisters faced an implicitly inequitable exchange relationship with that sector of American society which opposed the war and conscription. In the event of success, the resisters' high personal investments in the movement would lead to equal gains for nonresisters as well as for themselves. Resisting the draft thus constituted a contribution to the welfare of others without a quid pro quo. The exchange inequity was sharpest with nonresisting draft registrants, whose continued cooperation with the Selective Service constituted a tacit contribution to the opposition. The deferred male was in a role analogous to that of the worker who refuses to leave his job during an industrial strike. Nonstriking registrants would share in the movement's collective gains despite their weakening of the action designed to secure those gains. As a result, the resisters tended to react with hostility to those who could have benefited from the resisters' risks but who were unwilling to share in them. This theme emerged in a number of the interviews; a typical comment was: "For awhile I felt closer to people who had turned in their cards and more distant from people who hadn't. It was that simple. I respected those people who had made the gesture, and those who hadn't were cowards."

Noncooperation as a membership criterion also reinforced the sense of community within the movement by placing all members in a common danger. The Resistance milieu offered resisters mutual acceptance, reinforcement, and commiseration in a form that outside groups could not provide. A number of the resisters recall an instinctive huddling upon joining:

> I was scared shitless and quite nervous for two or three days afterward. The only people I would have anything to do with were the people who had also turned their cards in . . . and with them it was a nervous camaraderie. . . . There was a feeling afterward that we had done something very bad and were under the sinister eyes of the government. There was a lot of nervous laughter.

The fellowship of shared danger peaked soon after the initial exposure. However, most resisters remained anxious for many months as the government slowly responded to their noncooperation, and this helped sustain the solidarity over time. A resurgence of security seeking usually accompanied later events, such as receiving induction orders or an indictment (approximately 50 Boston resisters were indicted in 1968). Unlike the initial act of resistance, however, the indictments, and so on, did not have a collective timing. One individual's interest in the movement would be revived by a governmental action relating to him, but others were not being similarly pressed at the same time. The movement's inability to control the government's power to single out Resistance members proved to be a major source of weakness. But for a period, the shared risk was a principal component in the movement's group identity. One person reported that it was a primary factor in his experience:

> [The Resistance] was my group until early summer 1968. I liked them, as meetings went they were not bad, and I felt an instinctive closeness to people in the Resistance. There was a definite sense of community in the spring of 1968, although there was also great confusion over exactly what the group was to be based on. Common fear or jeopardy was not enough. . . . There was a lot of talk about not getting picked off one by one, but this was just not going to happen.
>
> The only thing that made me feel close to other resisters was the common danger. I was ambivalent about the group. My friends were not in it except for one, and he was less attached to it than I. I was older than most people there, and I felt a combination of admiration and pity for the group. . . . The feeling of danger is still with me, but I get bored of talking about it. I've gotten used to the danger. I may need companions when I get my next induction notice, although the companions then will be those I already had before resisting. But for awhile I realized if there weren't people at home it was nice to have a ready made set of friends who accepted you immediately.

Where else did people consider you to be a friend until proven otherwise? It was nice to have these people always available to have a drink, take in a movie, or whatever.

TRANSFORMATIONS IN SOCIAL NETWORKS

Much of the impetus for the social withdrawal into the movement was due to the resisters' changing relations with their immediate friends and acquaintances. Solidarity with the movement and estrangement from the outside world were in large part a projection of the resisters' own experiences with their personal relations. New friendships with fellow resisters were taken to characterize one's relations with all draft resisters; alienation from nonresisting friends came to represent one's relations with all nonmembers. Much of the growth of group solidarity could be attributed to the aggregation of these individual experiences (4). We therefore focus on changes in the resisters' interpersonal relations during their association with the Resistance movement. A qualitative portrait of social conversion at this level is followed by a more quantitative analysis of the resisters' changing friendship networks.

External Estrangement

Underground movements encourage members to conceal their membership as a means of preserving on-going relations with nonmembers. For the Resistance, however, covertness would be counterproductive, since new recruits could not be attracted in sufficient numbers unless the movement's presence were dramatized. Most resisters made no secret of their membership. In any event, the media and companions who attended the Resistance rally at which cards were returned often informed a resister's acquaintances before he had a chance to do so. Otherwise the resister usually made a point to discuss the step and its implications with his associates. A few did not inform even their most intimate companions, but these individuals were typically in very conservative milieus. If movement membership were revealed at all, however, widespread interest in draft resistance and the Resistance movement on many campuses ensured that the information was quickly disseminated (5). Thus, even though more than one-third of those interviewed reported avoiding informing casual contacts about their resistance unless a special opportunity arose, most people acquainted with the resisters eventually became aware of the new member's connection with the movement.

The predominant trend in the resisters' relations with people outside the movement was one of deterioration. This was the result of mutual estrangement between resisters and nonresisters. Three dialectical processes were identifiable: (1) reciprocated antagonism deriving from the personal jeopardy entailed by movement membership, (2) mutual estrangement resulting from radicalization of the resisters, and (3) loss of shared interests as the resisters became involved in politics.

As at the aggregate level, the resisters stood in an asymmetric exchange relationship with their nonresisting acquaintances. Their personal sacrifice was not reciprocated by friends who benefited from the action. The disparity typically became manifest in a sense of moral superiority among the resisters and intimidation and self-doubt on the part of nonresisting companions. The radical acquaintance was castigated for not placing political commitments above immediate self-interest; the nonradical was condemned for avoiding militant action. One resister recalled:

I've become a lot more political in my thought in recent months, and I think I'm not as moralistic as I
used to be. When I first burned my card I used to get
in these terrible arguments with other people who
hadn't taken a step of personal sacrifice. [In resisting],
I wanted my intentions and actions to match up. The
[implication] of being against the war was to actively
oppose the war, and I could see no way of admitting
all these things without turning my card in. For eight
or nine months afterwards I couldn't be comfortable
with people who were against the war but didn't return their card. I became contemptuous of my own
friends.

Another person reported a similar hostility:

When I turned in my card I was quite certain I would
end up in jail. My ambivalence now about the action
is more tactical. My questioning is whether that particular form of direct action is correct. However, I
still feel the best way to express yourself is to put
yourself on the line, as well as being the most psycho-
logically satisfying way. But I was a little too self-satis-
fied [just after the return] in my feelings about people
who didn't take that route. I was very belligerent and
would denounce people. It may have been a defense.
Since then I have come to better understand people
who are opposed to the war but aren't willing to resist.

Some of the sharpest disputes flared with friends whose
failure to act could not be excused on the basis of fundamental political differences with the Resistance. One friendship ended over a tactical dispute on the efficacy of draft
resistance:

I think I intimidated some friends at the time, and in
fact this did dissolve one friendship. [My friend] reacted very strongly when I resisted, and I got the
sense that he too would have liked to have done it but

couldn't, so jumped on me for acting so hastily. We were roommates then and we split up in January, and it was exactly over this issue of whether to resist. We shared our politics and had long arguments over the Resistance, and he finally did convince me of the inefficacy of resisting and the need to develop a broader commitment. But I sensed that he felt guilty about not having gone through with it.

A few people we interviewed became resisters several months after friends had taken that step, and the interim period was one of acute distress. One person joined the Resistance six months after his roommate:

A major factor [in deciding to resist] was the idea that many of my friends had done so. It was an act of conscience but also a moral duty. The fact that these people had stuck their necks out and I remained in the safety of a 2S left a definite sense of guilt, especially seeing the way my roommate was being knocked around [by the FBI]. But the year before I had been preparing to go to West Point, so it took me awhile to work things through for myself.

Tensions from unshared risks appeared mainly in relations with those close to the resisters in political outlook. The second source of tension affecting ties outside the movement—mutual ideological antagonism—primarily touched relations with politically divergent associates. For resisters who had been active in other radical organizations before joining the Resistance, such differences tended to be relatively small. Splits occurred over political tactics rather than principles, and consequently most of the veteran leftists rarely experienced tension of this type, "I get very little hostility—maybe because I had already sifted out my friends before," commented a former SDS activist. However, resisters from liberal backgrounds tended to develop major differences of opinion with their friends after involvement in the movement. Politicization often brought to the fore latent disparities in outlook between the liberal resisters and their more moderate friends: "I would say it sensitized me to their insensitivities, and this has not abated. I am no longer as close to them and see them much less now." Radicalization led to an increased intolerance for conservative views:

> The months immediately after I turned in my card were a very unusual time. To know a man I wanted to know his politics. I was contemptuous of people who had not taken a political commitment, so if a person had turned in his card he was almost by definition politically acceptable. At times I overreacted and adopted a hard line, usually with people who held assumptions different from mine, like the position that the U.S. government is benign. I would really react strongly when I heard this. . . . In the middle of the Resistance stuff I was willing to argue with practically anybody at any time. I had the greatest conflict with people who did not share my political commitments. They were more threatening than those people who were of similar politics but had not resisted. It was threatening because I saw myself as a missionary, and when confronted with people of a different political persuasion I was quite uncomfortable.

Alienation from conservative friends was generally most acute in the several months following the step of noncooperation. Some of these friends eventually moved leftward themselves, often aided by the resister's proselytizing, and estrangement lessened. But relations with those who did not change either cooled or were redefined to exclude politics. Even before entering the Resistance, one person had attempted to eliminate such tensions by segregating his friendship sets:

> I have a personal life and a political life, and I don't mix the two. I have friends for fairly different reasons,

and their politics extend to both ends of the spectrum. With my more patriotic friends I just don't discuss politics, so I never discussed the Resistance nor told them about my own resisting. I figure, the hell with arguments that won't convince anybody of anything.

Resisting had special implications for the relationship with girlfriends because of the prospect of forced separation; even with incarceration on the horizon, however, some female companions were fully supportive of the decision to join the Resistance. In other cases, the action led to a breaking of the relationship, including an engagement in several instances. The stress usually related to the increasing differences in political outlook and commitment—the women remaining unchanged and the resisters rapidly moving leftward—and intimate relationships were particularly sensitive to such changes. One person had been aware of a widening split with his fiancée before resisting, and joining the Resistance precipitated a final break:

We had talked about politics before [the turn-in] and we felt that we could accept different politics, but as it turned out we couldn't accept each other's views. I knew beforehand that the Resistance would be a fairly significant step in my life and that I was saying something about a new life style. But my fiancée's view was that you cannot reject a citizen's obligation and role. Resisting threw everything into a state of flux. We had planned to marry a year after the turn-in, but these plans were canceled about two months after I resisted. We carried on a dialogue for a year, but eventually the whole thing was broken off. We both had no idea at the time that this would lead to a separation.

In another case, ideological conflict was less responsible than differing levels of commitment to radical action:

A girlfriend was living with me at the time and our relationship gradually deteriorated because of what I was doing and because of the restructuring of my life and the new life style. It wasn't that we had opposite political views but she just did not have an active political view, and this ultimately led to a different life style. For example, she objected to the amount of time I felt I had to put into Resistance activities, . . . and she used to ask me if I wasn't bugged by the fact that our apartment didn't look that great and that I didn't have an interest in fixing it up. It was difficult to get her to understand that even though I liked nice things I could live like we were, since to live differently would have meant a sacrifice in political activities.

The third factor leading to dissolution of ties outside the movement world was the loss of shared interests. Prolonged engagement in the Resistance often produced a redefinition of a person's concerns, especially among the preresistance liberals. Radical politics became an obsessive interest at the cost of some long-standing interests. Relations with old friends suffered less from hostility than from lack of mutual concerns. Resisters found they had less and less in common with their old companions:

The strain was mainly with those who were apolitical. It wasn't felt so much immediately, but over the year I became more aware of it. Before I would always go to parties with these friends, but now it's less interesting and there are other things to do. The conversations are more like grooming behavior now. You talk back and forth at each other without any real communication. Before I could get involved in this small talk, but now it just takes too much time.

For noncooperators who had lacked radical involvements prior to the Resistance, the elements facilitating severance of outside connections varied in significance over time. Immediately after joining the movement, tensions were sharpest with those who shared the resisters' politics but not the risks of resisting. Political differences gained in importance as the resisters became radicalized. Finally, once a more secure anchoring in the Resistance had been formed, lack of shared concerns with nonmembers became more salient. At this point some resisters consciously undertook to regenerate outside connections, feeling that extreme withdrawal would debilitate the movement's effectiveness in recruiting. With the new radical identity consolidated, external contacts were less threatening and more desirable (for their instrumental value). Cultivating friendships with the unconverted was viewed as a means of encouraging interest in the radical left. For one activist this principle meant that his life was "depersonalized to a degree since resisting. Friendships may develop, but they are only incidental to my political role." Another person, who had become heavily involved in SDS activities by the time of the interview, altered his friendships in a similar way:

> My friends are defined in political terms and not in the bourgeois terms which this study seems to be implying. I will make friends with people for political purposes, and a sense of comfort or discomfort is not that critical or even important. I won't break off a friendship if someone is not of my political persuasion because I feel that friendships are not to be determined by personal pleasure considerations. I will keep a contact even if discomforting if I think the person can be talked to. Of course most of my closest friends are those people who are active in politics, especially SDS. But even with them I don't always live in comfort, since at times in political discussion there can be sharp personal criticism. Many of [my preresistance friends] have also gotten active and have come into SDS. What we shared a couple of years ago was mainly drama and similar such interests; now it's politics. Some of them have not changed, and one or two I don't see any more.

Internal Solidarity

As preexisting networks with nonresisters were being weakened, new acquaintance nets were expanding through the inner world of the Resistance. These ties developed for reasons similar to those which led to the growth of movement solidarity discussed previously. Yet although the movement's esprit de corps consisted of roughly equivalent degrees of affinity among all those composing the movement, these internal friendship networks allowed for a much more complex solidarity structure.

We know from the snowball sampling that the resisters did not randomly form friendships with other movement members. In the snowball interview procedure, noncooperators were asked to name several resisting friends who were then interviewed in the following wave, and this cycle was repeated through eight stages. If the friendship links were randomly arrayed, a large number of resisters should be reached in the eight stages, since there would be few overlapping choices. On the other hand, the presence of cliques should inhibit the spread of the snowballing net, since there would be considerable inbreeding among the choices, and a smaller proportion should be reached in the eight stages.

Let us assume for sake of comparison that the Boston Resistance community totaled nearly 1000 noncooperators. The nine interviews used to start the snowball chains therefore covered approximately 1 percent of the population. Using a similar starting fraction, Fararo and Sunshine (1964, 39) estimated the proportion that would be accumulated in a similar snowballing through a population in which the friendship choices were made at random. In the Resistance snowballing, the fractions of the full population reached in the third, sixth, and eighth stages were 5, 8, and 8 percent, respectively. By contrast, in the random net the fractions reached in the same three stages were 6, 37, and 65 percent (6). A model assuming that the largest cliques present are only three-person groups can account for much of this discrepancy (see Foster, Rapoport, and Orwant, 1963). But it is apparent that the friendship structure that emerged in the Resistance community was far from random.

If not random, how were the friendship networks structured in the Resistance? The movement itself made little attempt to influence the resisters' opportunities for contact with other resisters. However, two additional factors should have helped shape the friendship patterns. One was related to the degree of participation in the protest organization: those most active with the movement should have had ample opportunity to meet, and in fact the leadership of the New England Resistance did constitute one major friendship cluster. The other potential source was the resisters' outside institutional contexts: a preexisting friendship should have carried into the movement if both people became resisters. In addition, even if previously unacquainted, resisters sharing common organizational settings outside the movement, such as a college campus or a political association, would be more likely to develop ties than resisters in different settings. Resisters in common contexts shared more nonpolitical concerns, and the decentralized character of some resistance activity would encourage working contact within these settings.

Preexisting acquaintanceships among people who became noncooperators together not only did carry into the movement but were usually strengthened there. Even casual contacts were transformed into deep loyalties upon discovery of shared status. One person had been only slightly acquainted with several classmates who simulataneously became resisters. He had arrived alone at the church for the Resistance ceremony but was pleasantly shocked to discover several familiar faces in adjoining pews, with draft cards in hand: "After [resisting] Frank and I became very good friends. It created a strong sense of solidarity with Frank and these other people. There was a feeling of trust and confidence. It was almost love and they were like brothers."

Outside institutional lines also channeled friendships among formerly unacquainted resisters. Campuses and graduate departments were particularly significant for students in the movement. Some of the resisters had been acquainted prior to the card return, but most resisters previously had been unknown to one another. However, the preexisting contacts helped the unacquainted to find one another, and this process was further aided by their common involvement in campus resistance chapters and draft unions (whose activities included draft counseling, sponsoring forums and pamphlets on the draft and resistance, rallying support for campus resisters called for induction, and organizing for Boston area Resistance events). In one graduate division, for instance, half a dozen resisters soon found one another and formed a group, meeting frequently to discuss ethical and political implications of draft resistance, Resistance programs, and private consequences of being a noncooperator. One person joined the Resistance several months after the others and entered the small group when it was well formed:

> When I turned in my card I knew none of these people but I very quickly got to know them all well and two or three really closely. Initial contact with a few turned into an intense friendship with all within a few weeks. When I turned in my card I felt that I was being welcomed into the best group I had ever been welcomed into. There was real warmth and tenderness in this group, and complete equality. Leadership at that time was of no concern. Solidarity was very strong, there was much mutual respect and concern, and it was all very intense.

Further changes occurred with the passage of time, both in the new friendships formed in the movement and in the reinforced old friendships. The desire for collective security and contact with people sharing similar values and interests underlay many of the new friendships, and as these primacies receded in late 1968, so also did many of the companionships. A person who was heavily involved in Resistance organizing for several months, although politically passive both before and after this spurt of activity, noted: "My close friends at school remained my close friends. I acquired a new set of friends, the other resisters at school, but these only lasted as long as I stayed with the Resistance."

Some of those who moved on to other radical organizations dropped most of their Resistance contacts, but many of the ties established in the movement outlived the movement. Other shared interests were discovered, and in time the relationships deepened, as one resister recalled:

> At first the only people I had anything to do with were the ones who turned in their cards [at the same collective return]. . . . People I had never known before, I soon became good friends with, although some of my new friends I had known casually before. We talked a lot about the Resistance but this was just a vehicle for getting together. Then we found that we had other common activities, traits, and other things. One person I discovered was into painting and I was too, so we became close friends. Three people who I'm now very close to I met through the Resistance.

Changed and Exchanged Friends

A more quantitative look at the extent of social incorporation of resisters into the movement comes from an evaluation of their changing friendship networks during the period. A person's most meaningful and significant linkages into the social world are his closest companions, and any social conversion associated with joining the Resistance should be manifest in these primary relations.

During the interview each resister was asked to list his "close friends." This list was to include his primary companions over the half year just prior to the interview, and the list could be of any length. Another list of friends was requested for the half-year period just before the person began to consider becoming a noncooperator. Information was then requested about each of the friends listed, including the length of friendship, the friends' political views and activities, their work or academic situation, whether they were also noncooperators, their life style, religious affiliation, similarity of cultural interests and social awareness to those of the resister, and the degree of friendship among the friends themselves (7).

There was substantial continuity in two skeletal elements of the friendship sets between the two periods—namely, the number of friends and the extent of friendship among the resister's friends (8). However, the turnover in friendship was high within this relatively fixed framework. Slightly more than 200 individuals appeared on both lists, but they were only 30 percent of the preresistance total (671) and 24 percent of the more recent list (851). This high flux was not solely related to joining the Resistance. Two-thirds of the friendships listed during both periods were only one or two years old.

As resisters became involved in the movement, a significant change occurred in the type of people the members considered to be their close companions. The substantial variation in the number of friends listed by the resisters requires that *friendship sets* rather than *friends* be taken as the unit of analysis; these sets are compared for the periods before and after entry into the Resistance in Table 6.1. There was a decided shift to the left among the friendship

Table 6:1   Political Characteristics of the Resisters' Friendship Sets

Characteristic	Period ($N=93-96$)		
	Prere-sistance	Prein-terview	Interperiod Difference
Resistance			
Proportion noncooperators	.03	.20	+.17
Political action			
Proportion active in one or			
more political organizations *	.30	.49	+.19
Political perspective			
Radicalism †	.42	.62	+.20
Proportion apolitical ‡	.24	.23	−.01
Social awareness			
Degree of similarity §	.41	.52	+.11

* Included are draft resistance groups, peace and religious action groups, SDS, community and high school organizing groups, civil rights organizations, and other leftist groups.
† The resisters characterized their friends using the set of labels described in note 16, Chapter 4. The same four terms singled out in that note are used here, with "conservative or moderate" scored as zero, "liberal" as .33, "radical" as .67, and "revolutionary" as 1.0.
‡ Identification as either "apolitical" or "cynical."
§ The question: "However you define your own social awareness, in political, humanistic, religious, or other terms, would you describe each friend as having a level of social awareness very similar, moderately similar, or dissimilar to your own?" The three responses are scored 1.0, .5, and zero, respectively.

sets. In the more recent period, one out of every five of the resister's friends had also cut his ties with the Selective Service (up from 3 percent), half the friends were engaged in a political organization (a two-thirds increase), the number of friends classed as radical was up by half, and the resister considered his friends to have a social awareness more similar to his own. With respect to the nonpolitical dimensions (not shown in the table), the newer friends were more involved in counterculture life styles, were less likely to hold visible religious sentiments, and were less likely to be in the same type of school or work situation as the resister.

However, the shifting character of the resisters' social world did not stem entirely from entry into new movement networks. A significant fraction (30 percent) of the preresistance friends were retained throughout this period and they, like the resisters themselves, were undergoing considerable radicalization (Table 6.2). A substantial proportion of those remaining close to the resisters also became noncooperators, and many adopted radical politics.

Table 6.2   Political Characteristics of Resisters' Carryover Friends

	Period ($N = 199$–204)		
Characteristics	Preresistance	Preinterview	Interperiod Difference
Resistance Noncooperator	3.0%	17.2%	+ 14.2%

Political action
    Active in one or more
        political organizations
	27.5	40.2	+ 12.7

Political perspective
    Radical
    Apolitical
	22.1
	21.1
		45.6
		25.5
			+ 23.5
			+ 4.4

Social awareness
    "Very similar" to
        resisters
	52.0	45.1	− 6.9

As in the case of the resisters, friends who were already radical during the preresistance period changed little (four of five retained their same political outlook); but those who had been liberal shifted considerably (fewer than half kept the same position), and the change was almost invariably one of radicalization.

The changes described indicate that the process of incorporation did not involve a complete break in social circles. A segment of the original friendship network was preserved during the transition period. We would expect the retained friendships to be with people who were already more politicized and radical, since there was likely to be less estrangement in these relations. On the other hand, since the new friendships were being forged primarily in the Resistance and allied radical organizations, the carryover companions should tend to be somewhat more conservative than the new friends. An empirical check on this process is complicated by the varying carryover fraction; moreover, a few people (3) retained all their preresistance friends and a substantial number (29) carried over none of their friends. Consequently, analysis is limited to the 64 resisters who maintained some but not all of their friendships between the two periods. The mean value for the carryover and noncarryover friends is calculated separately within each set, the carryover mean is subtracted from the noncarryover mean, and the differences are averaged across the 64 resisters (with all dimensions standardized on a range of 0–1).

The differences are presented in Table 6.3. A positive figure indicates that, on the average, noncarryover friends had a higher mean on a dimension than their retained counterparts. The differences are small, but it is evident that the retained friends were more similar in social awareness, more active, and further to the left than those dropped (however, they were not more likely to have resisted). During the preinterview period the retained friends were less radical than the new friends, even though the carryover friends were changing extensively themselves.

Table 6.3   Political Characteristics of Carryover and Noncarryover Friends

| Characteristic | Period * (N=61-64) | | Total Set Interperiod Difference (from Table 6.1) |
	Prere- sistance	Prein- terview	
Resistance Proportion noncooperators	+.01	+.01	+.17
Political action Proportion active in one or more political organizations	−.03	+.04	+.19
Political perspective Radicalism	−.01	+.09	+.20
Social awareness Degree of similarity	−.08	+.09	+.11

* Based on the 64 resisters whose friendship sets had some but not complete carryover of friends between the two periods. Within each friendship set, the average proportion or position on each of the dimensions is calculated separately for the carryover and non-carryover friends. The figures represent the difference between the noncarryover and carryover means, averaged across the resisters' sets. A positive value indicates that the noncarryover friends had a higher value or proportion on a dimension than their carryover counterparts.

This suggests that the transformative process was relatively continuous and that old friendships gradually gave way to new, more radical contacts (9). However, many noncooperators reported a sharp disjunction in their lives, both politically and socially, upon joining the Resistance. Indirect evidence indicates that the social conversion did involve such a discontinuity. Information was collected on the length of duration of the relations with each of the more recent friends. More than four-fifths of the noncooperators had entered the movement from one to two years before the time of the interview. Consequently, friendships that were one to two years old tended to be those formed near and shortly after the act of resistance.

Political characteristics of the recent friends as a function of length of friendship are given in Table 6.4 (data on friends rather than friendship sets are presented, but the percentages are nearly identical in either mode of calculation). The companionships formed just after joining the Resistance were more politicized than either long-standing or very young friendships. A person befriended during this period was twice as likely to have been a resister than a friend from before or after the period. He was less likely to be apolitical and more prone to be involved in a political organization. There was also a substantial jump in the radical perspective of all friends met since entering the Resistance, and this pattern was even stronger on the social consciousness dimension. The change in the friendship set

Table 6.4 Political Characteristics of Preinterview Friends and Length of Friendship

Characteristic	Length of Friendship		
	More than 2 years	1–2 years	Less than 1 year
Resistance			
Noncooperator	16%	29%	13%
Political action			
Active in one or more political organizations	40	60	50
Political perspective			
Radical	47	69	63
Apolitical	29	15	21
Social awareness			
Very similar	47	67	68
Moderately similar	37	26	28
Dissimilar	15	6	6
N	(282)	(314)	(247)

characteristics was not gradual, and it appears that involvement in this protest movement did entail a political break with the resister's existing world.

New resisters were socially integrated into the Resistance through processes similar to those accounting for their political incorporation. These processes were not consciously engineered by the movement organization. Rather, they were intrinsic in the situation of the protest movement itself. For example, joining the Resistance placed the members in open conflict with the established order, and this circumstance directly facilitated both acceptance of a radical analysis of the society and the formation of friendships within the movement. Thus we might speculate that under propitious circumstances a protest movement will consolidate "spontaneously." With time and experience, leadership is prone to capitalize on the natural processes that reinforce the movement's existence and to counteract those which are destructive. The Resistance never achieved sufficient maturity and organizational strength to allow for conscious consideration of such plans although it probably would have, had it survived infancy.

The Resistance experience also indicates that the presence of a dangerous situation shared by all movement members is particularly effective for seeing a protest organization through the earliest stage of development. This feature alone accounted for a number of consequences that were "functional" for the ideological and interpersonal consolidation of the movement. Effectiveness notwithstanding, however, it is rare for a movement to find a membership criterion that can attract new recruits by offering them substantial personal danger.

NOTES

1. Discussions of compliance mechanisms can be found in Clark and Wilson (1961), Etzioni (1968), and Kanter (1968).

2. Siegel (1970) has argued that several such adaptions are used by organizations in coping with threatening environments.

3. See Coser (1956) and Coleman (1957) for an analysis of the relation between intergroup conflict and intragroup solidarity.

4. A number of studies have revealed that a social environment's influence on those in the environment is primarily mediated through networks of interpersonal relations (e.g., Katz and Lazarsfeld, 1955; Campbell and Alexander, 1965; Coleman, Katz, and Menzel, 1966; Woefel and Haller, 1971).

5. The previously mentioned Harris poll of college seniors in the spring of 1968 found that more than one in four felt that their respect for a person would increase on learning that he had refused induction out of opposition to the Vietnam War (see p. 120).

6. The average number of friendship choices per person in the Resistance community was 2.3; a figure of 2.0 was used in the random choice net calculations.

7. These dimensions were selected after preliminary observations indicated that they were both salient and discriminating in defining friendship among the resisters. There was some random error and surely some systematic bias in reporting the friendship information. Laumann (1969) found that misreporting was minimal among an urban male population when the attributes under assessment were relatively visible, such as age or occupation. When the characteristics were attitudinal, such as political party preference, a respondent tended to bring the friend's attributes into greater congruence with his own. Newcomb (1961) found a similar tendency.

8. The mean number of individuals identified as friends for the early period was seven, and for the later period, nearly nine. The ranges were zero to 14 and zero to 17, respectively; the standard deviation for both list lengths was 2.7. On the average, approximately one-third of the potential friendship bonds among the friends were formed during both periods. Stability in size and degree of friendship among the friends is reflected in the interperiod correlations of .53 and .43 for these two elements.

9. For a general analysis of the tendency for friendships to be retained and to form among people sharing common values, see Lazarsfeld and Merton (1954).

SEVEN

While most anti-war protest only involves peo-ple in repudiation of a particular policy . . . or aspect . . . of the U.S. government, draft resis-tance is the sort of program that puts people into battle with the government itself. Anti-draft organizing moves from protest activity to activity that takes on more and more of the characteristics of a seditious resistance move-ment.

Newsletter of Students for a Democratic
Society, 1967

The Resistance begins on October 16. It will not stop until the war is over.

New England Resistance leaflet, 1967.

THE DILEMMAS OF
ANTICONSCRIPTION PROTEST

In the autumn of 1969 the New York chapter of the Resistance published its own "eulogy": "The death whimper was so nearly inaudible that no one is really sure when it occurred. So New York Resistance, once numbered among the mightiest of the mightiest, now lies in an unmarked grave on the movement's own Boot Hill. Who shall follow into such ignominy? The decaying caucus of New England Resistance? The still flourishing Philadelphia branch? San Francisco? LA? . . . The New York Resistance, perhaps because it was too slow to change, became forsaken and died young, but it lived long enough to insure it will not be forgotten. Rest in peace, my friend." (Suffet, 1969).

The "decaying" New England Resistance could not follow the New York Resistance into the movement graveyard, for it was already there. The New England Resistance officially affiliated as a chapter of SDS just before the SDS convention in June 1969. Its active membership had already declined to several dozen, and by summer's end it folded. The Boston Draft Resistance Group closed its doors shortly thereafter, following months of decline in membership and morale. The Wisconsin Draft Resistance Union ceased to exist near the same time, and San Francisco organizations dissolved before Christmas.

There were exceptions, but they proved to be insufficient to reverse the general decline. The Philadelphia Resistance staged a classic card return ceremony in May 1969 (185 cards collected), and it attempted to renew national waves of card returns during the 1970 spring (prior to the spread of the Indochina conflict into Cambodia). Paralleling the diffusion of student unrest onto nonelite campuses during the end of the decade, the resistance strategy was also finding fresh organizational expression at new colleges. In November 1968, the national Resistance card return failed to materialize in Boston, but membership in the Michigan State University Resistance doubled (with three new turn-ins), and half a dozen cards were destroyed at the University of Oregon. By late spring 1969, Resistance activities were gaining momentum at the University of Montana and the Colorado School of Mines. During the national antiwar moratorium in October 1969, the Notre Dame University Resistance was founded, as six young men took a symbolic step of noncooperation at a "Resistance Mass" attended by 2000 students and faculty. The Northern Virginia Resistance hosted the destruction of five draft cards in November and was actively engaged in a campaign to close several local draft boards.

The most significant resurgence followed the U.S.-sponsored military invasion of Cambodia in May 1970. An entirely new preemptive resistance organization was formed, the Union for National Draft Opposition (UNDO). It was organized and staffed by people fresh to draft resistance; few of the Resistance veterans participated. UNDO assembled approximately 10,000 draft cards within several weeks, but the organization did not survive the crisis atmosphere induced by the Cambodian invasion and the deaths of protesting students on several campuses (1).

For a movement which successfully recruited, radicalized, and socially incorporated several thousand young men willing to face lengthy imprisonment, the Resistance had a surprisingly short lifespan. This chapter is devoted to exploring some of the weaknesses of anticonscription protest that led to the early failure of the Resistance. Several types of explanations for the collapse of a protest movement are distinguishable, each touching on a different aspect of the protest matrix. One form of explanation refers to the social conditions responsible for the formation of the movement. If the conditions underlying the discontent are substantially altered, or if new means for effective political expression become available, there is less reason for people to resort to protest politics. Another type of explanation focuses on the movement's opposition. Concessions, cooptation, and direct or indirect repression by the opponent all can undermine the movement's existence. A third type of explanation directs attention at the internal structure and policies of the organization. Frequently identified problems include excessive militancy, inflexible leadership, overreliance on unstable coalitions, oligarchic tendencies, sectarian quarrels, and weak internal coordination (2).

The New England Resistance was affected by such serious internal weaknesses as a bitter faction fight and a poorly formalized organizational structure that often left daily decision making in the hands of a small core of active members. Policy shortcomings included failure to fashion a program capable of absorbing the energies of new members. These developments added to the progressive demoralization of the organization in the latter half of 1968, as related by one of the founding members:

The Resistance superstructure is dissolving and re-forming as new groups. People go into one group, get politicized, and move on, since organizations fail to change with their thinking. It is hard to stay with one group for more than six months. A lot of people have moved on to other groups—some into SDS, others into campus organizing, and some into artistic and cultural scenes. Last spring [1968] was the high point for the New England Resistance. Many programs were active, like high school organizing, the newspaper, support groups, speakers, etc. A whole variety of programs developed in the spring, but one by one they seemed to end during the summer. There has been a great deal of disillusionment with working in the Resistance office. We had a lot of personality clashes, factions, and feuds, and people were at each other's throats. People then began to drop out. A feeling of disorientation spread. . . . Awareness had developed remarkably far, but then developing programs to fit the new critiques was difficult. There was also a great division over the role of the central office vis-à-vis the other 500 resisters in the New England area. During the fall and spring of 1967–1968 we had good contact with the 500, but after that the loss was great. I left about June 1968. I had been working on the newspaper, but there was a clash with the rest of the office over the degree of control the office should have over the newspaper. We kind of split off and formed [another journal] and a whole new group took over the Resistance newspaper, but they too have now stopped publishing.

Although such problems did undercut the movement's solidarity, many of the difficulties appeared only after the Resistance had encountered clear signs that its basic program of snowballing noncooperation was yielding a growth rate far short of expectations. Many of the organizational problems were in large part symptomatic of more fundamental issues plaguing the Resistance. To examine these, we begin with a second look at trends in the immediate precipitants of the Resistance—the radical student movement and the Vietnam draft. Attention is then turned to several aspects of the relationship of the movement to its opponent, the government.

STUDENT PROTEST AND VIETNAM CONSCRIPTION

Campus unrest showed no sign of abatement at the time of the dissolution of the national Resistance movement. During the 1968–1969 academic year, the year the Resistance collapsed, nearly one in four colleges experienced a disruptive or violent protest episode. The rate was considerably higher for universities, and 43 percent of the public institutions and 71 percent of the private universities had at least one major protest incident. Data from the 1970–1971 academic year reveal a comparable level of protest, although there was a shift of activity from elite institutions to less selective and smaller colleges (3). The number of students identifying as "doves" increased from 35 percent in the spring of 1967 to 69 percent in the fall of 1969. Students characterizing themselves as "radical or far left" grew from 4 percent in the early months of 1968 to 8 percent a year later and 11 percent by spring 1970 (however, the proportion dipped to 7 percent in the fall of 1970) (4).

The Vietnam War and its costs also remained high through 1968 and 1969. American troop presence in Vietnam was 50,000 stronger at the end of 1968 than 1967, and there were more draftees in the war zone in mid-1969 than in mid-1967 (see Figure 3.1). In 1968 and 1969 U.S. casualties in Vietnam exceeded those of 1967 (14,600 were killed in action and 46,800 hospitalized in 1968). The absolute and relative number of former college students entering the service was also on the increase, and their representation in the Vietnam theater was growing at an even faster pace (Figures 3.2 and 3.3).

Campus opinion and individual acts of draft resistance evidenced parallel developments. Among graduating seniors in the spring of 1968, 29 percent indicated that their respect for a person would increase if he refused military induction because of opposition to the Vietnam war. A year later, 48 percent of the college seniors shared this viewpoint, and by May 1970 the proportion had reached 57 percent. Of the seniors graduating from large schools (more than 10,000 students), 70 percent supported draft resisters (Table 3.7). Selective Service complaints of draft law violations rose from nearly 20,000 in fiscal 1967 to 27,000 in fiscal 1969. A similar trend was visible in the number of cases prosecuted by the Justice Department (Figure 3.4).

Public opposition to the war and draft continued to grow through 1970. Poll data show that backing for the Nixon administration's war policies and the existing conscription system were in constant decline through the end of the decade. One study of the number of participants in antiwar demonstrations through 1968 found that 1968 ranked with 1967; 0.33 million protesters had joined various rallies in the first eight months of 1968 (Tanter, 1969). Other surveys revealed a steady growth in public alienation from and distrust of the government. In 1966, for example, 28 percent of a national sample agreed with a Harris question, "The people running this country don't really care what happens to people like yourself." By 1968 the result was 36 percent agreeing, and the trend continued to 41 percent in 1971 and 50 percent in 1972 (5).

There were some countertrends. Overall draft levels tapered off somewhat, dropping from 340,000 in fiscal 1968 to 265,000 a year later and 207,000 in fiscal 1970. Despite the lifting of graduate deferments, the number of college students inducted in 1968–1969 did not approach the dire predictions that had circulated on campus the previous year. The early successes of Eugene McCarthy in the presidential primaries and the decision of the Johnson administration to suspend the bombing of North Vietnam helped create a temporary air of optimism in antiwar circles (6). Nevertheless, the predominant pattern was one of continuation and even some intensification of campus discontent over the war and draft through 1968 and 1969.

Perhaps the Resistance disintegrated amidst the circumstances just outlined because sharp changes in the conditions rather than their absolute level were primarily responsible for the movement's existence. Historically, sudden imposition of military conscription has occasionally served to catalyze festering discontent into open rebellion (7). If this sequence were descriptive of the Resistance, however, other manifestations of student malaise, such as campus protest and individual draft avoidance, should have shown a parallel decline after 1968. In fact they remained strong well past 1968, and yet the Resistance never revived nor reappeared as a significant national movement (the Union for National Draft Opposition in 1970 was little more than a spontaneous eruption; it had no permanent organizational life). Consequently it is doubtful if the lack of further sharp intensifications of the conditions facing student registrants could have accounted for the downfall of the Resistance.

However, an important change was occurring in the radical student movement, and it was to have significant effect on Resistance confidence in its own program. Even though no existing organization embraced a preemptive resistance strategy in 1967, the idea had aroused widespread interest in the loosely aligned set of New Left organizations and dissenting campus subculture. SDS had adopted an aggressive antidraft program late in 1966 and had extensively debated the potential of draft resistance for mobilizing students. In 1967 *New Left Notes* ran numerous articles on resistance, and the SDS National Council endorsed a resolution offering support to those who joined the Resistance. Thus the direction of the Resistance in the early days was ambivalently accepted by the major leftist student organization. Refusing induction became acceptable conduct in many student circles, and it was backed by a number of dissident groups. (8).

SDS continued antidraft programs through much of 1968, stressing such projects as campus counseling and organizing community and high school draft unions. But the 1968–1969 academic year was to prove a watershed for SDS. Its general political emphasis once again shifted off-campus. The position advocated by the Progressive Labor party (PLP) and its close affiliate in SDS, the Worker–Student Alliance (WSA), was becoming increasingly important. Conventions were racked by divisions between this wing, which stressed the primary revolutionary role of the blue collar working class, and the rest of the organization, in which various themes, including "new working class" analysis, remained dominant. The lines had been drawn the year before, but it was only in fall of 1968 and spring of 1969 that the PLP–WSA faction achieved sufficient strength to ensure debate of its position. At a tumultuous national convention in June 1969, SDS splintered over this division, but a new emphasis on working class politics was spreading throughout the radical student movement.

As the criteria utilized by the radical student movement for judging a program increasingly dealt with the program's capacity to reach poor and working-class Americans, the Resistance came under both internal and external criticism for its apparent failure under the new standards.

One of the early organizers of the Resistance dropped out of the movement even before its founding in October 1967, anticipating an evaluation of the movement that was to spread a year later: "Our primary mistake . . . was in building a movement that hoped to stir one more wave of middle-class liberal sentiment against the war and American militarism. . . . We must recognize that the job of revolutionaries is to organize those who can make revolutionary change—black, poor white, and working class people" (Hamilton, 1967). Similarly, a year and a half later a member of the SDS Worker–Student Alliance condemned his former organization, the New England Resistance, for antagonizing working youth: "[B]urning or turning in one's draft card takes on a decided anti-working class character if done as a public ceremony. Working people are deeply alienated by these tactics—indeed, the image of the draft-card burner has been used to discredit the whole movement" (Putnam, 1969, 351) (9).

Had the Resistance been insulated from this broader movement culture, denigration of the strategy of resistance would have been less demoralizing. There were barriers that protected the movement's faith against attacks by the press, government, and friends. However, the close links of the Resistance to radical campus circles made unfavorable judgments from this quarter particularly disheartening. The broader movement context constituted what Von Eschen, Kirk, and Pinard (1971) have labeled "the organizational substructure of disorderly politics." This infrastructure can play an important role in legitimizing and backing a specific movement campaign, but it can also undercut an organization if the organization falls out of favor with the dissident infrastructure. This happened to the Resistance. A sustaining culture had been replaced by a hostile movement context in 1968–1969.

THE STATE AS PROTEST TARGET

Mobilization of draft registrants to withhold their services from the state defined the existence of the Resistance, but the relationship of registrants to the Selective Service made it exceptionally difficult to organize them to take this action. Effective mobilization of a discontented group is affected by such factors as the visibility of the structural origins of the problem, the unity of the affected population, the availability of a well-defined target for protest action, and the possibility that real gains will result from movement activity (10). The source of the problems facing draft registrants was clear, but other factors were less conducive to achieving mobilization.

Registrants were sharply divided by a classification system that excused some young men from compulsory service while obliging others. Radical student organizations engaged in antidraft work made various attempts to close the gap between students and nonstudents created by the deferment system. In 1966 SDS gave serious consideration to a plan urging students to boycott the revived Selective Service College Qualification Test. Some of the Resistance organizers justified their own noncooperation in terms of eliminating barriers between themselves and registrants who faced induction. One of the central figures of the New England Resistance recalled that "at the time it was impossible to talk with any credibility or sincerity to people from a safe position. . . . I wanted to work with [people affected by the draft] and turning in my card was a way of identifying myself with them." Another resister saw noncooperation as a prerequisite to effective political work: "[I]t was difficult to tell people to do things when I had not done something myself. This was the reason for resisting, and it enabled me to become an organizer. It was a platform to speak from."

Although noncooperation narrowed the gap between resisters and those pressed by conscription, it increased the distance from those remaining on deferment, as was evident in the estrangement that developed between resisters and their nonresisting student friends. There was no easy way for a single movement to relate to both types of registrants at the same time. Gains in recruitment in one milieu were at the sacrifice of effectiveness in the other.

This problem was partially resolved by orientation of the Resistance toward a more uniformly classified population—college students. (Other organizations, such as the Boston Draft Resistance Group, focused on nonstudent youth, but they had little success in politicizing the draft problems of young working-class men.) The campus context facilitated communication, given the presence there of a natural community of many student registrants. However, there was no local target at which the Resistance could direct its activities.

The radical student movement had mounted programs protesting against military training (ROTC) and recruitment, the ranking of students for the draft, and war-related research on campus, and the strength of these attacks on governmental authority lay in the existence of an intermediate target. The college administration appeared to be responsible for policies that served the government's prosecution of the Vietnam War, and these policies ran counter to the academic and political interests of students. Students at an institution shared the same opponent on such issues, and the administration was proximate, whereas the Defense Department was not. The college administration could change policies that were objectionable to students in exchange for suspension of protest activities that were objectionable to the administration. However, since noncooperation did not directly involve college policies, conflict escalation on campus could not serve as a means of generating student support for the Resistance and its demands.

Furthermore, although most college students were united by possession of the 2S deferment and fears of losing it, registrants on a campus were still fractionalized by the decentralized operation of the Selective Service System. During the Vietnam War there was a notoriously wide diversity in local draft board policies. For instance, one study performed in 1966 revealed that some local boards were drafting no college students, whereas others regularly made students eligible for induction while still in their studies (National Advisory Commission on Selective Service, 1967, 95) (11). Resisters we interviewed report post-noncooperation experiences ranging from prompt call for induction to receipt of a new card and quiet neglect.

Sentencing practices of the federal judiciary evidenced a similar variability. During the period from fiscal 1965 to 1968, courts in the Second Federal Circuit sentenced convicted Selective Service violators to a period of probation three times as often as the First Circuit. The Sixth Circuit meted out the maximum sentence of five years in a quarter of its cases, and the First Circuit never imposed the full sentence length. Considerable sentencing variation existed even within districts, and one summary of court practices on the imprisonment of draft violators concluded that "the result of such differences in sentencing is that from a defendant's viewpoint the law appears as if it were a game of Russian roulette" (*Columbia Journal of Law and Social Problems*, 1969, 180).

The only unifying target for student registrants was the national conscription system, and the Resistance focused its action at this level. Draft cards were collected from Resistance chapters around the nation after the October 1967 rallies, and the cards were delivered by a single delegation directly to the Justice Department in Washington. The

Director of the Selective Service System became a much vilified figure in the movement's culture, and Resistance rhetoric repeatedly referred to national rather than local draft issues. An early Resistance flyer made clear the direct attack on national power: "We have chosen to openly defy the draft and confront the government and its war directly" (12). However, the remoteness of the national target prevented the Resistance from waging campaigns that could yield limited but concrete gains against the draft system. Thus the ability of the Resistance to mobilize registrants was circumscribed, since it could not directly demonstrate that the form of protest selected would undermine the draft's power and solve registrants' draft problems. The Resistance was without one of the standard techniques for attracting recruits to a protest movement.

Another common technique for building a movement's strength is to provide to those who join a form of individual or group gain that is not readily available to nonmembers. As we have seen, however, despite its hoped-for payoff—namely, the abolition of conscription—in the short run the Resistance offered members neither individual nor collective gains against the draft. Draft counseling was used by the movement as a means of building support; but any assistance offered the counselee was eliminated if he joined the Resistance, since his draft situation could only be worsened.

FAILURE OF ORGANIZATIONAL TRANSFORMATION

The relation of draft registrants to the national conscription system created major barriers to recruiting Resistance members. Through early 1968 expectations were still optimistic that large numbers could be reached, but by mid-year it was evident that the Resistance would not exceed a membership of several thousand. The movement's impact on the draft and on the war, its ability to protect its members, and its contribution to the radical left all depended on a Resistance of massive proportions. In its failure to reach the necessary level of strength, the Resistance served as outright refutation of the theory behind preemptive resistance. One member rendered his postmortem on the movement in these terms:

> Now the Resistance doesn't seem to be as politically significant as before. It hasn't worked, so you have to assume the original idea was just not very feasible. I don't think anyone knew if it were effective or not last spring [1968]. It was obvious to all by election time. It really didn't stop the draft system, and draft resistance doesn't deal with anything really political. The system is a lot stronger than people realized. It takes more than 10 to 15 thousand students. It's not so much that people didn't have faith in the [Resistance] as they didn't know how strong the system was.

It was also clear that noncooperation appealed to few working-class youth, and the Resistance came under external attack from the radical left for this shortcoming.

Once its defining basis has proved to be invalid, the Resistance organization was clearly in trouble. Several options were open to members. They could leave radical politics altogether (passive exit), transfer allegiance to other radical organizations (active exit), or work for a change of program within the movement (voice) (13). Survival of the Resistance was contingent on most people choosing voice. New England Resistance members chose all three courses. One in four of those interviewed had abandoned all political activities by early 1969. Some reported that the prospects of lengthy incarceration had dampened their enthusiasm for politics, others became more interested in counterculture, and still others were suffering from general exhaustion (14). Active exit was the path taken by more than half. Two in five resisters reported some involvement in SDS activities by early 1969 (half of these were heavily engaged).

Other resisters chose to exercise voice within the organization. In mid-1968 the New England Resistance not only added the issue of racism to its program but even asserted a prerevolutionary identity. "The Resistance . . . declares its commitment not to a two-issue program [on racism and imperialism] but to the building of a revolutionary movement. . . . We now seek to engage in other programs as well as draft resistance which reveal the illegitimacy of the authority over us and build a spirit of unified struggle" (15). The Resistance would broaden its base from students to the "working class" and "other members of the middle class." New strategies for change were formulated. In May 1968 the New England Resistance experimented with "sanctuary," the symbolic harboring of military and draft fugitives. The 1968 summer program included plans for a "free school," an attempt to form an association with black organizations, work with some counter-cultural groups being harassed by local authorities, and radical research projects.

In the fall of 1968 the New England Resistance held a "general membership" meeting to further define new programmatic and organizational directions. Consensus prevailed among the 75 in attendance that the Resistance must go beyond an association of draft resisters, but little agreement existed on what the direction should be. One major position paper called for turning the organization into an alliance of people struggling for control over whatever institution most affected their lives, whether the draft, the school, or the work place. Another urged that the Resistance engage in a variety of antidraft and antimilitary activities that would include not only noncooperation but also high school organizing, sanctuaries, and work with enlisted men in the military services.

Debate on these and other proposals continued through the year, and similar reorientations of program were undertaken in Resistance chapters in Palo Alto, Madison, and elsewhere. New York Resistance made an attempt: "At the second national Resistance conference [March 1969], it became clear to us that if the Resistance was to survive as an organization, we would have to make the transition from a single-issue, single-tactic orientation to a multi-issue one. We agreed that we have to work around the questions of imperialism and corporate power, racism, women's oppression, and alternative ways of living. . . . [But] New York simply couldn't make it" (Albert et al., 1969). Despite attempts to reformulate organizational goals, local chapters were unable to retain their membership. New England Resistance rolls plummeted, and by the spring of 1969 it was reduced to a shell of several dozen activists.

The failure of movement diversification to stem the exit of most resisters was a predictable outcome of the movement's initial principles of membership. The single-action criterion ensured diversity in the political philosophy of those joining. Socialization within the movement narrowed the range of views to a very general radical criticism of the American social order. However, within this shared outlook there was still great variation, and pacifism, anarchism, and multiple interpretations of socialism were represented. These differences had divergent implications for the appropriate movement objectives and structure if it were to be expanded beyond instigating draft resistance. Thus, even given the many political changes the resisters underwent in the movement, their shared commitment to noncooperation could not be readily extended to other strategies. No single new program would appeal to a movement membership originally united by a political action rather than political beliefs.

ANTICONSCRIPTION PROTEST MOVEMENTS

The settings and evolution of the American Resistance, the Australian Draft Resisters' Union, the French Young Resistance, and the British No-Conscription Fellowship suggest that anticonscription protest movements are likely to develop as follows:

1. *Preexisting Discontent.* Political discontent, including an element of antigovernment hostility, exists in a sector of the society, usually students or labor.

2. *Conscription for an Unpopular War.* Compulsory military service for a war considered to be unjust by the discontented sector is imposed on the sector. Since induction requires active contribution to the war effort, those opposed to the war must choose between providing their services or taking some form of illegal action (noncooperation with the draft law, exile, induction refusal, desertion).

3. *Preexisting Protest Organizations.* Preexisting dissenting organizations based in the discontented sector initiate campaigns against the draft and the war when conscription becomes a major concern, but they are incapable of adopting a policy of outright resistance. Antidraft agitation by these organizations furnishes information on the relative merits of various strategies and generates an atmosphere conducive to the formation of a separate resistance organization. These preexisting organizations also supply initial leadership for the new movement.

4. *New Movement of Draft Resisters.* A new movement organization is formed around the cleavage between recal-

citrant registrants and the government, and it logically follows that the organization is opened to all young men who are prepared to resist. Political screening of recruits is likely to be minimal, and since draft resistance can be justified from a variety of political and social standpoints, the membership of the movement will be diverse. The entrance criterion is unlikely to be absolute because the organization's need for hard-working organizers can lead to a stretching of membership standards to include nonresisting individuals who heavily contribute their energies.

5. *Strategic Options.* Several strategic alternatives are available to the new movement. The movement can concentrate on threatened, reactive, or preemptive resistance. It can stress the gains achievable through a strike of draft registrants, or it can emphasize the gains of stirring public opinion through its symbolic action, or it can work for both.

The characters of the movement's opponent and of its base constituency influence the alternatives pursued. The NCF had no choice but to use threatened resistance at the time of its formation in 1914–1915, since the British government had not yet introduced conscription. A resistance movement will turn to reactive or preemptive resistance once the government begins inducting troops. The recruitment constituency affects the decision to emphasize the concrete or the symbolic consequences of the collective action in the reactive or preemptive phase. If there is promise of widespread draft avoidance, the movement is likely to capitalize on the trend, attempting to carry it to the point of real threat. On the other hand, if the movement perceives that its recruitment potential is limited, it will be prone to settle for the symbolic impact. In 1967–1968 the Resistance was encouraged by a number of signs that the draft's authority was under widespread attack, whereas for the NCF, the patriotic fervor just after British entry into the war in 1914–1915, created a greater sense of isolation. As a result the Resistance chose to stress the concrete antidraft strike but the NCF settled on a program aimed at securing essentially symbolic gains against conscription.

6. *Consolidation of the Movement.* A movement organization based on collective defiance of governmental authority inherently possesses a variety of natural processes that help to consolidate the movement. Once launched, solidarity will emerge among the members, and political changes will bring membership beliefs into greater congruence with the radical principles underlying the movement's attack. In time the organization will implement policies to strengthen these tendencies. The Resistance had little opportunity to work through this pattern because of its short lifetime; but the NCF, during its five years of existence, developed an elaborate organizational structure to ensure effective decision making, solidarity, and operation in the face of extensive suppression by the government (e.g., NCF local branches established associations for families of men in the movement).

7. *Barriers to Survival.* The draft resistance movement will not survive a major challenge to its original program. The Resistance floundered once political practice had shown that the theory of the snowballing strike would not work. The NCF collapsed when the critical war-induced need for draft-eligible men ended. The political diversity created by the inclusive membership criterion blocks attempts to move the organization in new political directions. Thus the failure of the Resistance was neither the product of changes in the social conditions that sparked its formation nor the result of leadership or organizational errors. Rather, it was the consequence of severe problems inherent in efforts to organize citizens for a direct assault on state power. The preemptive resistance program was

shown to be invalid, and the movement has no other basis for unity.

The Resistance experience indicates that the appearance of a protest movement is the product of a complex set of historical circumstances. Chief elements include a conflict between a class of people and a major institution (e.g., the relation of student draft registrants to military conscription during the Vietnam era) and the presence of preexisting protest movements rooted in the protesting sector and concerned with its discontent (e.g., radical campus organizations).

Such factors decisively affect not only the timing of the new protest episode but even its political ideology, its change strategy, and its social organization. The Resistance belief that college students could be mobilized for radical action was derived from the experience of other protest organizations such as Students for a Democratic Society, and the strategy of impeding the war effort by disrupting conscription was heavily influenced by the structure of the draft system and its declining authority. With respect to social organization, we have seen that the amorphousness of the Resistance organization was partly related to the inherently decentralized task of encouraging people to go on a draft strike.

Although many fundamental attributes of a protest movement are precast in the movement's social context, the controversial role of protest movements often tends to obscure such connections. The movement itself is prone to picture its members as spontaneously rising up against intolerable social conditions. Prior planning is depicted as incidental to the birth of the movement.

On the other hand, the institution challenged by the protest is likely to minimize the element of popular discontent and to stress the organizing role of the leadership.

Charges are often made that the protest has little popular base and is due mainly to agitation by outsiders. Each side stands to gain if its portrayal prevails. In 1968 the federal government indicted five persons for conspiring to instigate draft resistance, implicitly claiming that the rank and file of the movement had been misled into destroying or returning their cards. In response to receipt of one of the indictments, an architect of the New England Reistance chose by contrast to accent the spontaneous action of distressed young men: "How did this resistance so suddenly get started? Who was behind it? No one. . . . A few mimeographed sheets, magazine statements, and press conferences were all—once the idea was articulated the response came of itself" (Ferber, 1968). But whatever the images portrayed, it is clear that both deep-lying discontent and concerted organizing precede formation of a protest organization (16).

Once the protest organization is constituted, the collective experience of the membership ensures a degree of consolidation of the movement. The overlap of individual and group interests, the joint activities directed against a common enemy, and the personally experienced conflict with the opposition all add to the growth of internal solidarity and a common political outlook. These elements give rise to organizational traits some analysts have labeled as "functional." Bittner (1963), for instance, argues that the establishment of "rigid boundaries" around a movement is an organizational solution that is functional for sustaining a radical social doctrine. In at least the early stages of a movement, these functional elements tend not to be fashioned intentionally. Rather, they are a predictable outcome of a situation in which people jointly struggle against a hostile opposition. If the movement survives infancy, natural tendencies are often reinforced by design, but even then the organization will continue to benefit from unintended processes. Almond's (1954) study of several western communist parties revealed that social segregation from the nonparty world was encouraged both by restrictions on associations outside the movement and by the propensity for members to feel that in any case the company of others in the fold was more comfortable and interesting.

If the radical protest successfully recruits from a broad constituency, the consolidation of the movement will entail political changes that approach conversion for some members. However, the experience of many resisters indicates that there is another and equally significant side to conversion when it occurs in the context of a social movement. The concept of conversion is usually stated in terms of a sudden and drastic change in values, beliefs, and personal identity (17). But if metamorphosis in world view is the most visible and dramatic aspect of conversion, changes in interpersonal relations can be equally salient in redefining a person's existence and behavior. For some people, involvement in the Resistance entailed not only a radical transformation in their understanding of American society but also an extensive break in the type of social circles in which they traveled. The conversion was both ideological and interpersonal.

Even with formation of a community spirit and shared outlook within a movement, however, the protest organization still may fail to survive more than a momentary outburst of fervor and activity. Whatever the changes in the underlying social conditions or the errors of the leadership, contradictions in the definition of the movement can ensure a quick collapse. A movement founded around creation of a rapid and massive mobilization of a group requires an effective means for drawing people into the protest process. But such means may not be readily available for organizing certain types of groups. The chosen tactic of direct assault on governmental authority left the

Resistance without prospects for local campaigns that could yield small but nonetheless tangible victories. In the absence of localized struggles, winning people to the organization necessarily came to be more contingent on creating a faith in the distant goals of the movement, and failure to inspire such long-term commitment was a major cause of the inability of the Resistance to expand its ranks beyond a few thousand resisters. Defeat of the major Resistance program was fatal, since the movement was incapable of redefining its reason for existence.

When the target is the federal government, the consequent lack of a local battleground may well be a crucial barrier to protest organizing. The growth of the American government and its acquisition of new roles has enhanced the potential for antagonism between it and certain sectors of the society. A traditional source of conflict results from governmental exercise of social control on behalf of dominant institutions under challenge, as when the police or the military are used to quell black uprisings in the cities, student protest on campus, and labor strikes in factories. But this conflict has been supplemented by other sources of tension, as in military conscription of reluctant citizens, maintenance of an inequitable tax system, conduct of an unpopular and costly foreign war, and the use of relief programs to control rather than to aid poor recipients (as argued by Piven and Cloward, 1971). A case has even been made for viewing the American government as a major economic exploiter of the country's youth (Rowntree and Rowntree, 1968).

However, not all the major lines of sensitive cleavage can be readily politicized, since an essential ingredient for mobilizing people through a process of conflict escalation is absent in some cases. This ingredient is the reproduction of the state–citizen relations in intermediary institutions in which people are heavily involved, such as the school, the work place, or the residential community. For instance, important supporting instruments for prosecution of the Vietnam War (e.g., ROTC, the conduct of war-related research) were directly manifest in some college institutions. But when the tactic of noncooperation is selected for opposing conscription and the war, the protest action will have no local targets to which limited demands and demonstrations might be aimed. Kornhauser's (1959) familiar thesis that intermediary institutions serve to integrate people into the society's mainstream—and thereby lessen their susceptibility to mass oppositional movements—is reversed in part here. If the social interests of the state and the subordinate sector are harmonious, the intermediary institutions can be stabilizing. But when the intermediary institutions reproduce antagonistic relations between the state and citizen, their effect may be the opposite of stabilizing. That is, the linking institution becomes a forum for resolution of the broader political disputes.

In their early days, despite fundamental organizing problems, anticonscription movements are typically optimistic about their prospects. In 1967 Resistance advocates could realistically entertain hopes that the burgeoning antidraft sentiment among young people might be turned into an outright strike by a great number of registrants. Major difficulties in achieving a strike were not easily foreseen, although they were confronted in practice. In any event, imposition of the draft on young men fundamentally opposed to serving in a war allows them little leeway in choosing a form of protest. If induction is imminent, the registrant faces the alternatives of acquiescence, exile, or resistance, and each has its disadvantages. But resistance may be least undesirable, and since noncooperation undertaken collectively obviously yields greater dividends than the same act done individually, a reasonable course is to join with those who must make a similar choice.

In 1967–1968 it appeared that many college students would soon have to choose acquiescence, exile, or resistance, and the Resistance movement counted among its ranks a significant fraction for whom noncooperation was a logical response to an impending draft call. The same pattern can be seen in the history of the No-Conscription Fellowship. In reflecting on the NCF experience, the man who served as chairman throughout its existence offered this justification for his own action: "We could not help ourselves. By reason of sex and age we chanced to find ourselves confronted by certain demands on the part of the State, and were compelled to consider our reply with a degree of anxiety and care that may seem unnecessary to those who have not actually been potential conscripts. Since we could not avoid it, we were bound to make the best use we could of the situation that was forced upon us" (Allen, 1922, 15).

Seldom, then, are the difficulties inherent in building a lasting anticonscription protest movement based on draft resistance readily foreseen, and in any case these problems may not weigh heavily in the decision to use draft resistance as a protest vehicle.

As the 1973 Vietnam peace accords were signed in Paris, the U.S. Secretary of Defense announced an indefinite suspension of further military induction. For the first time in more than two decades, the country's youth stood free of conscription. Yet a fundamental redirection of America's foreign policy has not accompanied conclusion of the nation's longest armed conflict, and new interventions remain on the horizon as nationalist and revolutionary movements continue to threaten regimes supported by the United States. Should one of these insurgencies lead to a massive dispatch of American troops in an atmosphere of little public backing, and should the expeditionary forces fail to quell the uprising within a few months, the government may again be forced to conscript its soldiers as the only means of ensuring a steady troop supply. Individual acts of resistance are sure to follow.

At least some prospective conscripts committed to resisting are likely to conclude that collective resistance is preferable to private refusal. In this circumstance, even a careful reading of the historical record of the No-Conscription Fellowship and Resistance experiences is unlikely to deter attempts to give organizational coherence to individual actions. The morphology of the new movement would naturally depend on a variety of situational elements, such as the form of the government's manpower levy, the extent and distribution of antiwar hostility among draft-eligible men, and the strength of political organizations capable of articulating an oppositional response to the new draft. A draft system that includes women as registrants or one that randomly selects its conscripts should generate strategies of opposition different from those likely to accompany a system that places a disproportionate burden on the sons of blue collar families. The recent trend for some labor organizations to withhold automatic support of costly military ventures should enhance the prospects for draft resistance among noncollege youth. But whatever the circumstances that serve to provoke the anticonscription movements, can we expect such radical efforts to fare any better than the Resistance during the Vietnam era?

Several strategies might well improve the strength of future draft resistance movements. First, the movement might more effectively mobilize its constituency if some protest demands were addressed to institutions standing between draft registrants and the federal government, such as schools, local communities, corporations, or special interest associations. A group of registrants already would be united by a common institutional setting, the limited goals would be more achievable, and the continuing struggle and bargaining process should provide a meaningful set of daily activities in which to involve members.

Second, close ties between a resistance organization and a more broadly oriented protest movement would provide greater reserve strength for waging an anticonscription campaign. For instance, the broader movement might stage sympathy strikes and demonstrations if the government attempts to repress the strike of draft registrants. An alliance with dissident groups within the armed forces could help dispel the Resistance image of hostility to the enlisted soldier, and joint attacks on military authority from within and without the service could be particularly effective in impeding the prosecution of the war. Also, linkage of the resistance movement to a broader protest organization would facilitate the transfer of resisters into other activities, once noncooperation had exhausted its tactical utility.

Should the United States again resort to the conscription of troops for waging an unpopular foreign war, the initial impetus for an assault on that institution will in all likelihood come from preexisting dissident organizations. The greater the strength and experience of these movements, the more likely is a new draft resistance effort to design optimally effective programs. Without the benefit of this collective wisdom, resisters will have little opportunity to sort out good tactics from poor ones before the war ends or their movement collapses. Thus the best hope for a vigorous draft resistance movement in the future lies in the presence of a strong and broad-based leftist organization which can effectively meet the challenge of a new wartime draft.

NOTES

1. On Michigan State University and the University of Oregon, *The State Journal* (Lansing, Michigan), November 15, 1968, p. 1;

on the University of Montana, *Resist*, May 26, 1969, p. 1; on the Colorado School of Mines, *The Peacemaker* 22, June 28, 1969, p. 1; on Notre Dame University, *The Peacemaker* 22, November 8, 1969, pp. 1–2; on Northern Virginia Resistance, *The Peacemaker* 23, February 7, 1970, p. 1; on the Union for National Draft Opposition, *Resist*, May 30, 1970. The strategic rationale used by UNDO was very similar to that of the Resistance. UNDO reasoned that ending the Indochina War required direct pressure on the government and that the draft provided an effective leverage for applying pressure. One of its leaflets argued: "When enough of us have said No to the Selective Service System, the draft law will become inoperative and the System itself paralyzed. . . . Students must step out from behind their 2-S and mobilize to stop the draft. We must cripple the Selective Service System to end the War now."

2. Often all three types of problem jointly account for a movement's demise, as illustrated in the case of the Townsend movement. The end of the Depression and the passage of the Social Security Act tempered the economic hardships of the country's aged, which had been the chief initial concern of the movement. Tactical errors, such as inept congressional lobbying, reduced the movement's ability to achieve crucial legislative victories. Organizational problems associated with the movement's rigid centralization led to bitter internal quarrels, and the resulting revolts weakened the movement's morale. Politically motivated congressional investigations of the movement's finances further undermined membership confidence in the organization. The effects were manifest in the organization's rolls, which dropped from 750,000 members in 1939 to 22,000 in 1953 (Holtzman, 1963). Similar complexes of themes emerge in the analyses of other political protest movements (e.g., Jackson et al., 1960; Von Eschen, Kirk, and Pinard, 1969; Brill, 1971; Starobin, 1972; for more general treatments, see Zald and Ash, 1966; Lipsky, 1968).

3. Bayer and Astin (1969, 1971); the data came from questionnaires completed by representatives (typically administrators) at nearly 400 colleges and universities. Disruptive or violent protests were incidents that involved physical violence to people or property, interference with the movement of people on campus, or interruption of the institution's normal operations. Peterson's (1970) surveys of campus unrest covered the 1964–1965 and 1967–1968 academic years, and Bayer and Astin's annual surveys

began with the 1968–1969 academic year. However, no single annual survey covered the period of the Resistance movement. One study drew on retrospective information provided by campus presidents for 1967–1970. Using stringent criteria for disruptive protest, this study found that the rate of disruptive protest climbed from 6 percent of the campuses in 1967–1968 to 11 and 14 percent in 1968–1969 and 1969–1970, respectively (the 1970 figure is for the period prior to the Cambodian invasion; Buchanan and Brackett, 1971, 6).

4. From Gallup and Harris surveys of college students, summarized by Lipset (1972, 43, 49).

5. *Boston Globe*, June 19, 1972, p. 16. Responses to other Harris questions on the fairness of the economic order and feelings of powerlessness appeared to evidence similar trends. National survey data collected by the Institute for Social Research (University of Michigan) over the Vietnam War era revealed a parallel pattern. A "trust in government" scale was formed from five related questions (e.g., "How much of the time do you think you can trust the Government in Washington to do what is right?"). In 1964, two-thirds (62 percent) of the national sample placed "high" trust in the government. Confidence increased in 1966, but the 1968 and 1970 surveys revealed marked declines in trust. By 1970 only one-third (35 percent) gave a high rating to the government (Institute for Social Research, 1971).

6. Friedman argued that Eugene McCarthy's campaign for the presidential nomination was fatal for the Resistance, since it created the impression that the war might soon end and because it attracted many "shock troops and followers" away from the Resistance (1971, 156–157). However, few of the Boston resisters we interviewed had been associated with the McCarthy campaign. His candidacy in the presidential primaries did not undermine student protest, and the Resistance was more tied to this world than to electoral politics and the Democratic party.

7. America's introduction of the draft in 1917 sparked the "Green Corn Rebellion." Several hundred destitute Oklahoma sharecroppers, already partially organized by an affiliate of the Industrial Workers of the World, assembled for an armed march on Washington when it became known that conscription was impending (the group consumed green corn in preparation for their attack). Local posses quickly disarmed the rebels and the leaders

were imprisoned (Peterson and Fite, 1968, 40–41). Similarly, the Union's Enrollment Act during the Civil War touched off major rioting in a number of northern cities in 1863, leaving more than 1200 dead (McCague, 1968). The counterrevolution of 1793 in western France, the Vendée, was precipitated when a soldier levy was imposed by an already unpopular government (Tilly, 1967, 308–312).

8. For instance, shortly after the formation of the Resistance, a youth group associated with the Unitarian Universalist Church offered its backing: "The Continental Board of the Student Religious Liberals calls upon all members of Student Religious Liberals, Liberal Religious Youth, and the Unitarian Universalist Association to support and encourage those whose conscience compels them to refuse to cooperate with the Selective Service System" (*The Liberal Context*, November, 1967, p. 4). *Dissent* published a number of articles on draft resistance in early 1968 (January–February issue). In late spring (May–June issue) it printed a statement, signed by a number of people associated with the magazine, which offered support to draft resisters (although questioning the strategic merits of the movement).

9. A survey based on a national sample of American men in 1969 found that white union members were generally hostile to draft card burning. The men were asked whether they considered nine types of behavior as violence. The behaviors ranged from draft card burning to looting, student protest, sit-ins, and police beating of students. The largest difference in opinion between college students and white union members appeared on the issue of draft card burning. Twenty-six percent of the college students felt that it constituted a violent act, 35 percent of the nonstudents with at least a college degree agreed, but 63 percent of the white union members labeled draft card burning as violence (Blumenthal et al., 1972, 76). On the other hand, a study of young white working-class Vietnam veterans in 1972 revealed little sense of vindictiveness toward those who did not serve. Among two subgroups in the study (veterans in drug treatment programs and those affiliated with the Vietnam Veterans Against the War), approximately two in three would urge a brother or close friend to consider draft resistance if he were threatened with induction (Helmer, 1972, 417, 444).

10. For a discussion of some of these factors see Wilson (1961), Lipsky (1968), and Portes (1971).

11. Excerpts from a number of studies of Selective Service administrative practices are reprinted in U.S. Senate Committee of the Judiciary (1969, Appendix IV).

12. "We Refuse to Serve," distributed at the Spring Mobilization to End the War in Vietnam, April 15, 1967, San Francisco (reprinted in Lynd, 1968).

13. "Voice" and "exit" are borrowed from Hirschman (1970). See Weiss (1963) and Hirschman for discussions of the conditions favorable to the different options.

14. The mental exhaustion of the resisters was similar to what Coles (1964) has called protest "weariness."

15. "Multi-Issue," *The Resistance*, n.d. [early fall, 1968].

16. The political considerations underlying the labeling of protest episodes are explored by Grimshaw (1968) for the case of the black inner-city revolts in the late 1960s.

17. For example, Lofland and Stark (1965) write: "All men and human groups have ultimate values, a world view, or a perspective furnishing them a more or less orderly and comprehensible picture of the world. . . . When a person gives up one such perspective or ordered view of the world for another we refer to this process as *conversion*." Also see Shibutani (1961, 862).

REFERENCES

Albert, Marilyn, Ed Fields, Ronnie Lichtman, Mayer Vishner, Lenny Brody, Debby Carter, Jill Boskey, and Bob Kowallik. 1969. "New York Resistance, R.I.P.: Obituary." *Win Magazine* 5 (November 15), 27, 29–30.

Allen, Clifford. 1919. "The faith of the N.C.F." In *The No-Conscription Fellowship: A Souvenir of Its Work During the Years 1914–1919.* London: No-Conscription Fellowship.

———. 1922. "Preface" to *Conscription and Conscience: A History, 1916–1919,* by John W. Graham. London: George Allen & Unwin.

Almond, Gabriel. 1954. *The Appeals of Communism.* Princeton, N.J.: Princeton University Press.

Alsop, Stewart. 1970. "The American class system." *Newsweek,* June 29, p. 80.

Altbach, Philip, and Patti Peterson. 1971. "Before Berkeley: Historical perspectives on American student activism." *The Annals of the American Academy of Political and Social Science* 395 (May), 1–14.

Anderson, Charles H. 1971. *Toward a New Sociology: A Critical View*. Homewood, Ill.: Dorsey.

Aron, Bill. 1970. *Radical Ideology on the University of Chicago Campus*. Chicago: Community and Family Study Center, University of Chicago.

Aronowitz, Stanley. 1971. "Does the United States have a new working class?" In *The Revival of American Socialism*, George Fisher, Editor. New York: Oxford University Press.

Aronson, Elliot, and Judson Mills. 1959. "The effect of severity of initiation on liking for a group." *Journal of Abnormal and Social Psychology* 59, 177–181.

Baran, Paul, and Paul Sweezy. 1966. *Monopoly Capital*. New York: Monthly Review Press.

Barber, Bernard. 1957. *Social Stratification: A Comparative Analysis of Structure and Process*. New York: Harcourt Brace Jovanovich.

Barton, Allen H. 1968. "The Columbia crisis: Campus, Vietnam, and the ghetto." *Public Opinion Quarterly* 32 (Fall), 333–351.

Bayer, Alan E., and Alexander W. Astin. 1969. "Violence and disruption on the U.S. campus, 1968–1969." *Educational Record* 50 (Fall), 337–350.

———. 1971. "Campus unrest, 1970–1971: Was it really all that quiet?" *Educational Record* 52 (Fall), 301–313.

Bayer, Alan E., Alexander W. Astin, and Robert F. Boruch. 1971. "College students' attitudes toward social issues: 1967–70." *Educational Record* 52 (Winter), 52–59.

Bell, Daniel. 1972. "Labor in the post-industrial society." *Dissent* (Winter), 163–189.

Bell, Inge Powell. 1968. *CORE and the Strategy of Nonviolence*. New York: Random House.

Berney, Robert E. 1969. "The incidence of the draft—is it progressive?" *Western Economic Journal* 7 (September), 244–249.

Birnbaum, Norman. 1971. "Late capitalism in the United States." In *The Revival of American Socialism*, George Fisher, Editor. New York: Oxford University Press.

Bittner, Egon. 1963. "Radicalism and the organization of radical movements." *American Sociological Review* 28 (December), 928–940.

Blum, Albert A. 1967. *Drafted or Deferred: Practices Past and Present.* Ann Arbor, Mich.: Bureau of Industrial Relations, Graduate School of Business, University of Michigan.

Blumenthal, Monica, Robert L. Kahn, Frank M. Andrews, and Kendra B. Head. 1972. *Justifying Violence: Attitudes of American Men.* Ann Arbor, Mich.: Institute for Social Research, University of Michigan.

Bolton, Charles D. 1972. "Alienation and action: A study of peace-group members." *American Journal of Sociology* 78 (November), 537–561.

Boulton, David. 1967. *Objection Overruled.* London: MacGibbon & Kee.

Bowles, Samuel. 1972a. "Unequal education and the reproduction of the social division of labor." In *Schooling in a Corporate Society: The Political Economy of Education in America,* Martin Carnoy, Editor. New York: McKay.

———. 1972b. "Contradictions in U.S. higher education." In *The Capitalist System: A Radical Analysis of American Society,* Richard C. Edwards, Michael Reich, and Thomas E. Weisskopf, Editors. Englewood Cliffs, N.J.: Prentice-Hall.

Brill, Harry. 1971. *Why Organizers Fail: The Story of a Rent Strike.* Berkeley: University of California Press.

Brockway, A. Fenner. 1919. "The story of the N.C.F." In *The No-Conscription Fellowship: A Souvenir of Its Work During the Years 1914–1919.* London: No-Conscription Fellowship.

Buchanan, Garth, and Joan Brackett. 1971. *Survey of Campus Incidents as Interpreted by College Presidents, Faculty Chairmen, and Student Body Presidents.* Washington, D.C.: The Urban Institute.

Campbell, Ernest Q., and C. Norman Alexander. 1965. "Structural effects and interpersonal relationships." *American Journal of Sociology* 71 (November), 284–289.

Campbell, Joel T., and Leila S. Cain. 1965. "Public opinion and the outbreak of war." *Journal of Conflict Resolution* 9 (3), 318–329.

Canby, Steven L. 1972. *Military Manpower Procurement: A Policy Analysis.* Lexington, Mass.: Heath.

Civilian Advisory Panel on Military Manpower Procurement. 1967. *Report to the Committee on Armed Services, House of Representatives,* 90th Cong., 1st sess. Washington, D.C.: Government Printing Office.

Clark, Peter B., and James Q. Wilson. 1961. "Incentive system: A theory of organization." *Administrative Science Quarterly* 6 (June), 129–166.

Clayton, James L., and Jerry S. Smith. 1970. "Who pays the ultimate cost of war? A case study of Utah's Vietnam war dead." Unpublished manuscript.

Coleman, James S. 1957. *Community Conflict.* New York: Free Press (Macmillan Company).

Coleman, James S., Elihu Katz, and Herbert Menzel. 1966. *Medical Innovation: A Diffusion Study.* Indianapolis: Bobbs-Merrill.

Coles, Robert. 1964. "Social struggle and weariness." *Psychiatry* 27 (November), 305–315.

Collins, Randall. 1971. "Functional and conflict theories of educational stratification." *American Sociological Review* 36 (December), 1002–1019.

Columbia Broadcasting System. 1969. *Generations Apart.* New York: Columbia Broadcasting System.

Columbia Journal of Law and Social Problems. 1969. "Sentencing Selective Service violators: A judicial wheel of fortune." *Columbia Journal of Law and Social Problems* 5 (August), 164–196.

Converse, Philip E., and Howard Schuman. 1970. " 'Silent majorities' and the Vietnam war." *Scientific American* 222 (June), 17–25.

Cornell, Tom. 1968. "From protest to resistance to jail—a draft resister's story." *New York Times Magazine,* January 19, 22ff.

Coser, Lewis. 1956. *The Functions of Social Conflict.* New York: Free Press (Macmillan Company).

Dahrendorf, Ralf. 1959. *Class and Class Conflict in Industrial Society.* Stanford, Calif.: Stanford University Press.

Dancis, Bruce. 1967. "The logic of resistance." *New Patriot* (Ithaca, N.Y.), November 28.

Davidson, Carl. 1966. "A student syndicalist movement: University reform revisited." *New Left Notes,* September 9.

————. 1967a. "National vice president's report—has SDS gone to pot?" *New Left Notes*, February 3.

————. 1967b. "Praxis makes perfect." *New Left Notes*, March 27.

Davies, James C. 1962. "Toward a theory of revolution." *American Sociological Review* 27 (February), 5–19.

————. 1969. "The J-curve of rising and declining satisfactions as a cause of some great revolutions and a contained rebellion." In *Violence in America: Historical and Comparative Perspectives*, Hugh Davis Graham and Ted Robert Gurr, Editors. New York: Bantam.

————. 1971. *When Men Revolt and Why: A Reader in Political Violence and Revolution*. New York: Free Press (Macmillan Company).

Davis, James W., Jr., and Kenneth M. Dolbeare. 1968. *Little Groups of Neighbors: The Selective Service System*. Chicago: Markham.

Davis, Kingsley, and Wilbert E. Moore. 1945. "Some principles of stratification." *American Sociological Review* 10 (April), 242–249.

Demerath, N. J., III, Gerald Marwell, and Michael T. Aiken. 1971. *Dynamics of Idealism: White Activists in a Black Movement*. San Francisco: Jossey-Bass.

Denitch, Bogdan. 1971. "The New Left and the New Working Class." In *Radical Sociology*, J. David Colfax and Jack L. Roach, Editors. New York: Basic Books.

Duggan, Joseph C. 1946. *The Legislative and Statutory Development of the Federal Concept of Conscription for Military Service*. Washington, D.C.: Catholic University of American Press.

Edwards, Richard C., Michael Reich, and Thomas E. Weisskopf, Editors. 1972. *The Capitalist System: A Radical Analysis of American Society*. Englewood Cliffs, N.J.: Prentice-Hall.

Elias, Thomas. 1970. "Growing problem—southland leading in draft defiance." "Without bribes—wealth proves aid in avoiding draft." *Santa Monica Evening Outlook*. Reprinted in U.S. House Committee on Armed Services, Special Subcommittee on the Draft, *Review of the Administration and Operation of the Draft Law*, Hearings. 91st Cong., 2nd sess. Washington, D.C.: Government Printing Office, pp. 12498–12502.

Emerick, Kenneth Fred. 1972. *War Resisters Canada: The World of the American Military–Political Refugees.* Knox, Pa.: Knox, Pennsylvania, Free Press.

Erskine, Hazel. 1970. "The polls: Is war a mistake?" *Public Opinion Quarterly* 34 (Spring), 134–150.

Etzioni, Amitai. 1968. *The Active Society: A Theory of Societal and Political Processes.* New York: Free Press (Macmillan Company).

Fararo, T. J., and Morris H. Sunshine. 1964. *A Study of a Biased Friendship Net.* Syracuse, N.Y.: Syracuse University Youth Development Center.

Ferber, Michael. 1968. "On being indicted." *New York Review of Books* 10 (April 25), 14–16.

Ferber, Michael, and Staughton Lynd. 1971. *The Resistance.* Boston: Beacon.

Ferriss, Abbott L. 1971. *Indicators of Trends in the Status of American Women.* New York: Russell Sage Foundation.

Festinger, Leon, Henry W. Riecken, and Stanley Schachter. 1964. *When Prophecy Fails.* New York: Harper & Row (Torchbook).

Finn, James, Editor. 1968a. *Protest: Pacifism and Politics, Some Passionate Views on War and Nonviolence.* New York: Random House (Vintage).

———, Editor. 1968b. *A Conflict of Loyalties: The Case for Selective Conscientious Objection.* New York: Pegasus (Western Publishing Company).

Fisher, A. C. 1969. "The cost of the draft and the cost of ending the draft." *American Economic Review* 59 (June), 239–254.

Flacks, Richard. 1971a. "Revolt of the young intelligentsia: Revolutionary class-consciousness in a post-scarcity America." In *The New American Revolution*, Roderick Aya and Norman Miller, Editors. New York: Free Press (Macmillan Company).

———. 1971b. *Youth and Social Change.* Chicago: Markham.

Flyer, Eli S. 1972. "Factors relating to unsuitability discharge and desertion status among army enlisted accessions." Washington, D.C.: Directorate for Manpower Research, Office of the Assistant Secretary of Defense, Manpower and Reserve Affairs, Department of Defense.

Folger, John K., Helen Astin, and Alan E. Bayer. 1970. *Human*

Resources and Higher Education. New York: Russell Sage Foundation.

Fortune Magazine. 1969. "What they believe." In *Youth in Turmoil,* edited by *Fortune Magazine.* New York: Time–Life Books.

Forward, Roy. 1968. "Conscription, 1964–1968." In *Conscription in Australia,* Roy Forward and Bob Reece, Editors. St. Lucia, Queensland, Australia: University of Queensland Press.

Foster, Caxton C., Anatol Rapoport, and Carol J. Orwant. 1963. "A study of a large sociogram II: Elimination of free parameters." *Behavioral Science* 8 (January), 56–65.

Freedman, Jonathan L., and Scott C. Fraser. 1966. "Compliance without pressure: The foot-in-the-door technique." *Journal of Personality and Social Psychology* 4 (2), 195–202.

Friedman, Leon. 1971. *The Wise Minority: An Argument for Draft Resistance and Civil Disobedience.* New York: Dial.

Furst, Randy. 1968. "Draft draws more fire." *The Guardian,* March 23.

Gabriner, Bob, and Barbara Baran. 1969. *The Wisconsin Draft Resistance Union: From Conscience to Class.* Boston: New England Free Press.

Gales, Kathleen E. 1966. "A campus revolution." *British Journal of Sociology* 17, 1–19.

Garcia, Baxter, and Gerald Gray. 1967. "Which side are you on?" A critical analysis of the Resistance." *New Left Notes,* October 9.

Gerard, Harold B., and Grover C. Mathewson. 1966. "The effects of severity of initiation on liking for a group: A replication." *Journal of Experimental Social Psychology* 2 (July), 278–287.

Gerhardt, James M. 1971. *The Draft and Public Policy: Issues in Military Manpower Procurement, 1945–1970.* Columbus, Ohio: Ohio State University Press.

Gerlach, Luther P., and Virginia H. Hine. 1970. *People, Power, Change: Movements of Social Transformation.* Indianapolis: Bobbs-Merrill.

Gilman, Harry J. 1970. "Supply of volunteers to the military services." In *Studies Prepared for the President's Commission on an All-Volunteer Armed Force*, Vol. I. Washington, D.C.: Government Printing Office.

Gintis, Herbert. 1970. "The New Working Class and revolutionary youth." *Socialist Revolution* 1 (May–June), 13–43.

Glass, Andrew J. 1970. "Defense report: Draftees shoulder burden of fighting and dying in Vietnam." *National Journal*, August 15.

Gorz, André. 1965. "Capitalist relations of production and the socially necessary labour force." *International Socialist Journal* 2 (August), 415–429.

———. 1968. *Strategy for Labor: A Radical Proposal*. Martin A. Nicolaus and Victoria Ortiz, Translators. Boston: Beacon.

Gottlieb, Robert, Gerry Tenney, and David Gilbert. 1967. "Toward a theory of social change in America." *New Left Notes*. May 22.

Graham, John W. 1922. *Conscription and Conscience: A History, 1916–1919*. London: George Allen & Unwin.

Grimshaw, Allen D. 1968. "Three views of urban violence: Civil disturbance, racial revolt, class assault." In *Riots and Rebellion: Civil Violence in the Urban Community*, Louis H. Masotti and Don R. Bowen, Editors. Beverly Hills, Calif.: Sage Publications.

Gurr, Ted Robert. 1970. *Why Men Rebel*. Princeton, N.J.: Princeton University Press.

Guyatt, Chris. 1968. "The anti-conscription movement, 1964–1966." In *Conscription in Australia*, Roy Forward and Bob Reece, Editors. St. Lucia, Queensland, Australia: University of Queensland Press.

Halleck, Seymour L. 1968. "A psychiatrist's report: Students and the draft." *The Progressive* 32 (February), 26–30.

Hahn, Harlan. 1970. "Correlates of public sentiment about war: Local referenda on the Vietnam issue." *American Political Science Review* 64 (December), 1186–1198.

Hamel-Green, Michael. 1971. "The making and breaking of conscription in Australia." In *Downdraft: A Draft Resistance Manual*. Melbourne, Australia: Melbourne Draft Resisters' Union.

Hamilton, Richard F. 1968. "A research note on the mass support for 'tough' military initiatives." *American Sociological Review* 33 (June), 439–445.

Hamilton, Steve. 1967. "October 16 . . . a moral witness?" *New Left Notes*, October 2.

Hansen, W. Lee, and Burton A. Weisbrod. 1967. "Economics of the military draft." *Quarterly Journal of Economics* 81 (August), 395–421.

Harris, Louis, and Associates. 1966. "Public opinion and the draft poll." In *Dialogue on the Draft*, June A. Willenz, Editor. Washington, D.C.: American Veterans Committee.

———. 1970. *Codebook: A Survey of the Attitudes of College Seniors*. Chapel Hill, N.C.: Louis Harris Political Data Center, University of North Carolina.

———. 1971a. *A Study of the Problems Facing Vietnam Era Veterans: Their Readjustment to Civilian Life*. New York: Louis Harris and Associates.

———. 1971b. *The Harris Survey Yearbook of Public Opinion, 1970. A Compendium of Current American Attitudes*. New York: Louis Harris and Associates.

Hartnett, Rodney T. 1969. *College and University Trustees: Their Backgrounds, Roles, and Educational Attitudes*. Princeton, N.J.: Educational Testing Service.

Hayes, Denis. 1949. *Conscription Conflict. The Conflict of Ideas in the Struggle for and Against Military Conscription in Britain Between 1901 and 1939*. London: Sheppard.

Helmer, John. 1972. "Bringing the war home: The American soldier in Vietnam and after." Ph.D. dissertation, Department of Sociology, Harvard University.

Hirschman, Albert O. 1970. *Exit, Voice, and Loyalty: Responses to Decline in Firms, Organizations, and States*. Cambridge, Mass.: Harvard University Press.

Holtzman, Abraham. 1963. *The Townsend Movement: A Political Study*. New York: Bookman.

Hopper, Rex D. 1950. "The revolutionary process: A frame of reference for the study of revolutionary movements." *Social Forces* 28 (March), 270–279.

Horn, John L., and Paul D. Knott. 1971. "Activist youth of the 1960's: Summary and prognosis." *Science* 171 (March 12), 977–985.

Horowitz, Irving Louis, and William H. Friedland. 1970. *The Knowledge Factory: Student Power and Academic Politics in America*. Chicago: Aldine.

Howe, Florence. 1966. "We Won't Go conference." *New Left Notes*, December 9.

Inglis, K. S. 1968. "Conscription in peace and war, 1911–1945." In *Conscription in Australia*, Roy Forward and Bob Reece, Editors. St. Lucia, Queensland, Australia: University of Queensland Press.

Institute for Social Research. 1971. "Election time series analysis of attitudes of trust in government." Ann Arbor, Mich.: Center for Political Studies, Institute for Social Research, University of Michigan.

Jackson, Maurice, Eleanora Petersen, James Bull, Sverre Monsen, and Patricia Richmond. 1960. "The failure of an incipient social movement." *Pacific Sociological Review* 3 (Spring), 35–40.

Jacobs, Clyde E., and John F. Gallagher. 1968. *The Selective Service Act: A Case Study of the Governmental Process*. New York: Dodd, Mead.

Jacobs, Paul, and Saul Landau. 1966. *The New Radicals: A Report with Documents*. New York: Random House (Vintage).

Janowitz, Morris. 1971. "Basic education and youth socialization in the armed forces." In *Handbook of Military Institutions*, Roger W. Little, Editor. Beverly Hills, Calif.: Sage Publications.

Jauncey, L. C. 1935. *The Story of Conscription in Australia*. London: George Allen & Unwin.

Johnston, Barry. 1971. "Draft Resisters' Union." In *Downdraft: A Draft Resistance Manual*. Melbourne, Australia: Melbourne Draft Resisters' Union.

Johnston, Jerome, and Jerald G. Bachman. 1970. *Young Men Look at Military Service: A Preliminary Report*. Ann Arbor, Mich.: Survey Research Center, Institute for Social Research, University of Michigan.

Kanter, Rosabeth Moss. 1968. "Commitment and social organization: A study of commitment mechanisms in utopian communities." *American Sociological Review* 33 (August), 499–517.

Karabel, Jerome. 1972. "Community colleges and social stratification." *Harvard Educational Review* 42 (November), 521–562.

Kassing, David B. 1970. "Military experience as a determinant of veterans' earnings." In *Studies Prepared for the President's Commission on an All-Volunteer Armed Force*, Vol. II. Washington, D.C.: Government Printing Office.

Katz, Elihu, and Paul Lazarsfeld. 1955. *Personal Influence: The Part Played by People in the Flow of Mass Communication*. New York: Free Press (Macmillan Company).

Keller, Suzanne, 1963. *Beyond the Ruling Class: Strategic Elites in Modern Society*. New York: Random House.

Keniston, Kenneth. 1968. *Young Radicals: Notes on Committed Youth*. New York: Harcourt Brace Jovanovich.

Kennedy, Thomas Cummins. 1968. "The hound of conscience: A history of the No-Conscription Fellowship, 1914–1919." Ph.D. dissertation, Department of History, University of South Carolina.

Key, V. O., Jr. 1961. *Public Opinion and American Democracy*. New York: Knopf.

Killmer, Richard L., Robert S. Lecky, and Debrah S. Wiley. 1971. *They Can't Go Home Again*. Philadelphia: Pilgrim.

Klassen, Albert D., Jr. 1966. *Military Service in American Life Since World War II: An Overview*. Chicago: National Opinion Research Center.

Knight, Dee, and Jack Colhoun. 1972. "Editorial: Amnesty and the war." *AMEX–Canada* 3 (March–April), 40–43.

Kolko, Gabriel. 1962. *Wealth and Power in America*. New York: Praeger.

Kornhauser, William. 1959. *The Politics of Mass Society*. New York: Free Press (Macmillan Company).

———. 1962. "Social bases of political commitment: A study of liberals and radicals." In *Human Behavior and Social Processes*, Arnold Rose, Editor. Boston: Houghton Mifflin.

Kugelmass, Joel. 1968. "Notes of a meeting." *The New England Resistance*, January 19.

Laumann, Edward O. 1969. "Friends of urban men: An assessment of accuracy in reporting their sociometric attributes, mutual choice, and attitude agreement." *Sociometry* 32 (March), 54–69.

Lauter, Paul, and Florence Howe. 1971. *The Conspiracy of the Young*. New York: World (Meridian).

Lazarsfeld, Paul, and Robert K. Merton. 1954. "Friendship as a social process: A substantive and methodological analysis." In *Freedom and Control in Modern Societies*, Morroe Berger, Theodore Abel, and Charles Page, Editors. New York: Van Nostrand–Reinhold.

Leigh, Duane E., and Robert E. Berney. 1971. "The distribution of hostile casualties on draft-eligible males with differing socioeconomic characteristics." *Social Science Quarterly* 51 (March), 932–940.

Levine, Eric. 1962. *The French Intellectuals and the Algerian War*. New York: Columbia College.

Lindsay, Cotton M. 1968a. "Our national tradition of conscription: The early years." In *Why the Draft? The Case for a Volunteer Army*, James C. Miller III, Editor. Baltimore: Penguin.

———. 1968b. "Our national tradition of conscription: Experience with the draft." In *Why the Draft? The Case for a Volunteer Army*, James C. Miller, III. Baltimore: Penguin.

Lippmann, Walter. 1968. "The draft is difficult to justify." *Washington Post*, March 24.

Lipset, Seymour Martin. 1968. *Agrarian Socialism: The Cooperative Commonwealth Federation in Saskatchewan. A Study in Political Sociology*, revised edition. Garden City, N.Y.: Doubleday (Anchor).

———. 1972. *Rebellion in the University*. Boston: Little, Brown.

Lipsky, Michael. 1968. "Protest as a political resource." *American Political Science Review* 62 (December), 1144–1158.

Lofland, John. 1966. *Doomsday Cult: A Study of Conversion, Proselytization, and Maintenance of Faith*. Englewood Cliffs, N.J.: Prentice-Hall.

———, and Rodney Stark. 1965. "Becoming a world-saver: A theory of conversion to a deviant perspective." *American Sociological Review* 30 (December), 862–875.

Lynd, Alice, Editor. 1968. *We Won't Go: Personal Accounts of War Objectors*. Boston: Beacon.

Lynd, Staughton. 1967a. "Editorial: To stop a war." *Liberation* (April), 4–6.

———. 1967b. "On draft resistance." *New Left Notes*, June 19.

Mallet, Serge. 1965. "Socialism and the New Working Class." *International Socialist Journal* 2 (April), 13–43.

Mankoff, Milton, and Richard Flacks. 1971. "The changing social base of the American student movement." *Annals of the American Academy of Political and Social Science* 395 (May), 54–67.

———. 1972. *The Poverty of Progress: The Political Economy of American Social Problems*. New York: Holt, Rinehart and Winston.

Marmion, Harry A. 1968. *Selective Service: Conflict and Compromise*. New York: Wiley.

Marshall, Kim, and Daniel Pennie. 1968. "A chance to vote on Vietnam." *Harvard Alumni Bulletin*, February 3, 20–23.

Marx, Gary T. 1969. *Protest and Prejudice: A Study of Belief in the Black Community*, revised edition. New York: Harper & Row (Torchbook).

Marx, Gary T., and Michael Useem. 1971. "Majority involvement in minority movements: Civil rights, abolition, untouchability." *Journal of Social Issues* 27 (1), 81–104.

Mayer, Albert J., and Thomas Ford Hoult. 1955. "Social stratification and combat survival." *Social Forces* 34 (December), 155–159.

McCague, James. 1968. *The Second Rebellion: The Story of the New York City Draft Riots of 1863*. New York: Dial.

McGrath, Earl J. 1936. "The control of higher education in America." *Educational Record* 17 (April), 259–272.

Melbourne Draft Resisters' Union, Editor. 1971. *Downdraft: A Draft Resistance Manual*. Melbourne, Australia: Melbourne Draft Resisters' Union.

Merrill, Richard A. 1966. "Deficiencies in the Selective Service System: The Samuel Friedman case." In *Dialogue on the Draft*, June A. Willenz, Editor. Washington, D.C.: American Veterans Committee.

Messinger, Sheldon L. 1955. "Organizational transformation: A case study of a declining social movement." *American Sociological Review* 20 (February), 3–10.

Miles, Michael. 1971. *The Radical Probe: The Logic of the Student Rebellion.* New York: Atheneum.

Miliband, Ralph. 1969. *The State in Capitalist Society.* New York: Basic Books.

Miller, Herman P. 1971. *Rich Man, Poor Man.* New York: Crowell.

Milner, Murray, Jr. 1972. *The Illusion of Equality: The Effect of Education on Opportunity, Inequality, and Social Conflict.* San Francisco: Jossey-Bass.

Mitford, Jessica. 1969. *The Trial of Dr. Spock, The Reverend William Sloane Coffin, Jr., Michael Ferber, Mitchell Goodman, and Marcus Raskin.* New York: Knopf.

Moskos, Charles C., Jr. 1970. *The American Enlisted Man: The Rank and File in Today's Military.* New York: Russell Sage Foundation.

Mueller, John E. 1971. "Trends in popular support for the wars in Korea and Vietnam." *American Political Science Review* 65 (June), 358–375.

Mullins, Nicholas C. 1966. "Social networks among biological scientists." Ph.D. dissertation, Department of Social Relations, Harvard University.

———. 1968. "The distribution of social and cultural properties in informal communication networks." *American Sociological Review* 33 (October), 786–797.

Muntz, Bob. 1971. "Draft resistance." In *Downdraft: A Draft Resistance Manual.* Melbourne, Australia: Melbourne Draft Resisters' Union.

National Advisory Commission on Selective Service. 1967. In *Pursuit of Equity: Who Serves When Not All Serve?* Washington, D.C.: Government Printing Office.

Nearing, Scott. 1917. "Who's who among college trustees." *School and Society* 6 (September), 297–299.

Newcomb, Theodore M. 1961. *The Acquaintance Process.* New York: Holt, Rinehart & Winston.

No-Conscription Fellowship. 1919. *The No-Conscription Fellow-*

ship: A Sourvenir of its Work During the Years 1914–1919.
London: No-Conscription Fellowship.

O'Brien, James. 1969. *A History of the New Left, 1960–1968.*
Boston: New England Free Press.

Oi, Walter Y. 1967. "The economic cost of the draft." *American Economic Review* 57 (May), 39–62.

Oppenheim, Karen. 1966. *Attitudes of Younger American Men Toward Selective Service.* Chicago: National Opinion Research Center.

Oppenheimer, Martin. 1970. "White Collar revisited: The making of a new working class." *Social Policy* 1 (July–August), 27–32.

Owens, Patrick. 1969. "Who they were: A special report on L[ong] I[sland]'s 428 war dead." *Newsday*, August 2.

Parsons, Talcott. 1953. "A revised analytical approach to the theory of social stratification." In *Class, Status and Power*, Reinhard Bendix and Seymour Martin Lipset, Editors. New York: Free Press (Macmillan Company).

————. 1959. "The school class as a social system: Some of its functions in American society." *Harvard Educational Review* 29 (Fall), 297–318.

Peterson, H. C., and Gilbert C. Fite. 1968. *Opponents of War, 1917–1918.* Seattle: University of Washington Press.

Peterson, Richard E. 1970. "The scope of organized student protest." In *Protest! Student Activism in America*, Julian Foster and Durward Long, Editors. New York: Morrow.

Petras, James, and Maurice Zeitlin. 1967. "Miners and agrarian radicalism." *American Sociological Review* 32 (August), 578–586.

Pinard, Maurice, Jerome Kirk, and Donald Von Eschen. 1969. "Process of recruitment in the sit-in movement." *Public Opinion Quarterly* 33 (Fall), 355–369.

Piven, Frances Fox, and Richard A. Cloward. 1971. *Regulating the Poor: The Functions of Public Welfare.* New York: Pantheon Books (Random House).

Portes, Alejandro. 1971. "On the logic of post-factum explanations: The hypothesis of lower-class frustration as the cause of leftist radicalism." *Social Forces* 50 (September), 26–44.

Prasad, Devi, and Tony Smythe. 1968. *Conscription, A World*

Survey: Compulsory Military Service and Resistance to It. London: War Resisters' International.

President's Commission on an All-Volunteer Armed Force. 1970. *Report.* New York: Macmillan Company (Collier Books).

Putnam, Hilary. 1968. "In defense of resistance." *Dissent* 15 (January–February), 16–18.

———. 1969. "From Resistance to Student-Worker Alliance." In *The New Left: A Collection of Essays,* Priscilla Long, Editor. Boston: Porter Sargent.

Rae, John. 1970. *Conscience and Politics: The British Government and the Conscientious Objector to Military Service, 1916–1919.* New York: Oxford University Press.

Rafuse, John L. 1970. "United States' experience with volunteer and conscript forces." In *Studies Prepared for the President's Commission on an All-Volunteer Armed Force,* Vol. II. Washington, D.C.: Government Printing Office.

Reeves, Thomas, and Karl Hess. 1970. *The End of the Draft.* New York: Random House (Vintage).

Reisner, Ralph. 1971. "Selective Service appeal boards and the conscientious objector claimant: Congressional standards and administrative behavior." *Wisconsin Law Review* 1971 (2), 521–546.

Reston, James. 1967. "Washington: Compromise on the military draft." *New York Times,* May 5.

Robson, L. L. 1970. *The First A.I.F.: A Study of Its Recruitment, 1914–1918.* Melbourne, Australia: Melbourne University Press.

Rohr, John A. 1971. *Prophets Without Honor: Public Policy and the Selective Conscientious Objector.* New York: Abingdon.

Rosenbaum, David E. 1968. "Rifles for the men with diplomas." *New York Times,* December 1.

———. 1969. "Thousands of graduate students are called by the army for induction at the end of the academic year." *New York Times,* May 20.

Rosenberg, Milton J., Sidney Verba, and Philip E. Converse. 1970. *Vietnam and the Silent Majority: The Dove's Guide.* New York: Harper & Row.

Ross, Thomas T. 1966. "Note: Reclassification of the sit-in demonstrator: A bezoar stone for the Selective Service." *University of Florida Law Review* 19, 143–163.

Rothenberg, Leslie S. 1968. *The Draft and You: A Handbook on the Selective Service System.* Garden City, N.Y.: Doubleday (Anchor).

Rowntree, John, and Margaret Rowntree. 1968. "Youth as a class." *International Socialist Journal* n. 25 (February), 25–58.

Rudwick, Elliott, and August Meier. 1970. "Organization structure and goal succession: A comparative analysis of the NAACP and CORE, 1964–1968." *Social Science Quarterly* 51 (June), 9–24.

Rushing, William A. 1970. "Class, power, and alienation." *Sociometry* 33 (June), 166–177.

Schlissel, Lilian, Editor. 1968. *Conscience in America: A Documentary History of Conscientious Objection in America, 1757–1967.* New York: Dutton.

Schuman, Howard. 1972. "Two sources of antiwar sentiment in America." *American Journal of Sociology* 78 (November), 513–536.

Schwartz, Michael. 1971. "The Southern Farmers' Alliance: The Organizational Forms of Radical Protest." Ph.D. dissertation, Department of Sociology, Harvard University.

Schwarzschild, Henry. 1972. "Statement," before the U.S. Senate Subcommittee on Administrative Practice and Procedure, March 1. New York: American Civil Liberties Union Foundation.

Selznick, Philip. 1952. *The Organizational Weapon: A Study of Bolshevik Strategy and Tactics.* New York: McGraw-Hill.

Sherman, Howard. 1972. *Radical Political Economy: Capitalism and Socialism from a Marxist–Humanist Perspective.* New York: Basic Books.

Shibutani, Tamotsu. 1961. *Society and Personality: An Interactionist Approach to Social Psychology.* Englewood Cliffs, N.J.: Prentice-Hall.

Shoben, E. Joseph, Jr., Philip Werdell, and Durward Long, 1970. "Radical student organizations." *Protest! Student Activism in America,* Julian Foster and Durward Long, Editors. New York: Morrow.

Siegel, Bernard J. 1970. "Defensive structuring and environmental stress." *American Journal of Sociology* 76 (July), 11–32.

Sjaastad, Larry A., and Ronald W. Hansen. 1970. "The conscription tax: An empirical analysis." In *Studies Prepared for the President's Commission on an All-Volunteer Armed Force*, Vol. II. Washington, D.C.: Government Printing Office.

Smelser, Neil J. 1962. *Theory of Collective Behavior*. New York: Free Press (Macmillan Company).

Smith, Robert B. 1972. "Disaffection, delegitimation, and consequences: Aggregate trends for World War II, Korea and Vietnam." In *Public Opinion and the Military Establishment*, Charles Moskos, Editor. Beverly Hills, Calif.: Sage Publications.

Somers, Robert H. 1965. "The mainsprings of the rebellion: A survey of Berkely students in November 1964." In *The Berkeley Student Revolt: Facts and Interpretations*, Seymour Martin Lipset and Sheldon S. Wolin, Editors. Garden City, N.Y.: Doubleday (Anchor).

Southern Conference Educational Fund. No date. "An enemy of the people: How the draft is used to stop movements for social change." Louisville, Ky.: Southern Conference Educational Fund.

Starobin, Joseph R. 1972. *American Communism in Crisis, 1943–1957*. Cambridge, Mass.: Harvard University Press.

Starr, Paul. 1973. *Troubled Peace: An Epilogue to Vietnam*. Washington, D.C.: Center for the Study of Responsive Law.

Students for a Democratic Society. 1967. *Our Fight is Here: Essays on Draft Resistance*. Chicago: Students for a Democratic Society.

Suffet, Steve. 1969. "New York Resistance, R.I.P.: Eulogy." *Win Magazine* 5 (November 15), 27–29.

Sullivan, John A. 1970. "Qualitative requirements of the armed forces." In *Studies Prepared for the President's Commission on an All-Volunteer Armed Force*, Vol. I. Washington, D.C.: Government Printing Office.

Szymanski, Albert. 1972. "Trends in the American working class." *Socialist Revolution* 10 (July–August), 101–122.

Tanter, Raymond. 1969. "International war and domestic turmoil: Some contemporary evidence." In *Violence in America: His-*

torical and Comparative Perspectives, Hugh Davis Graham and Ted Robert Gurr, Editors. New York: Bantam.

Thorne, Barrie. 1971. "Resisting the draft: An ethnography of the Draft Resistance Movement." Ph.D. dissertation, Department of Sociology, Brandeis University.

————. 1972. "Girls who say yes to guys who say no: Women in the Draft Resistance Movement." Paper delivered at the annual meeting of the American Sociological Association, August.

Tilly, Charles. 1967. *The Vendée: A Sociological Analysis of the Counterrevolution of 1793.* New York: Wiley (Science Editions).

Tobis, Heather. 1967. "Reexamination of the 'We Won't Go' conference." *New Left Notes*, January 13.

Touraine, Alain. 1971a. *The Post-Industrial Society: Tomorrow's Social History. Classes, Conflicts and Culture in the Programmed Society.* Leonard F. X. Mayhew, Translator. New York: Random House.

————. 1971b. *The May Movement: Revolt and Reform.* Leonard F. X. Mayhew, Translator. New York: Random House.

Trow, Martin A. 1957. "Right wing radicalism and political intolerance." Ph.D. dissertation, Department of Sociology, Columbia University.

Trytten, M. H. 1952. *Student Deferment in Selective Service: A Vital Factor in National Security.* Minneapolis: University of Minnesota Press.

Tucker, Robert C. 1967. "The deradicalization of Marxist movements." *American Political Science Review* 61 (June), 343–358.

U.S. Bureau of the Census. 1970. *Statistical Abstracts of the United States: 1970.* Washington, D.C.: Government Printing Office.

————. 1971. *Statistical Abstracts of the United States: 1971.* Washington, D.C.: Government Printing Office.

————. 1972. *Statistical Abstracts of the United States: 1972.* Washington, D.C. Government Printing Office.

U.S. Department of the Army, Office of the Surgeon General, Medical Statistics Agency. 1969. *Supplement to Health of the Army, Results of the Examination of Youths for Military Service, 1968.* Washington, D.C.: Department of the Army.

U.S. Department of Defense. 1969. "Project One Hundred Thousand: Characteristics and performance of 'New Standards' men." Washington, D.C.: Office of the Assistant Secretary of Defense, Manpower and Reserve Affairs, Department of Defense.

———. 1971. *Selected Manpower Statistics*. Washington, D.C.: Department of Defense.

U.S. Department of Justice. 1964. *Annual Report of the Attorney General of the United States, Fiscal Year Ended June 30, 1964*. Washington, D.C.: Government Printing Office.

———. 1968. *Annual Report of the Attorney General of the United States, Fiscal Year 1968*. Washington, D.C.: Government Printing Office.

———. 1969. *Annual Report of the Attorney General of the United States, Fiscal Year 1969*. Washington, D.C.: Government Printing Office.

U.S. Department of Labor. 1971. *Manpower Report of the President, Including a Report of Manpower Requirements, Resources, Utilization, and Training*. Washington, D.C.: Government Printing Office.

U.S. House Committee on Armed Services. 1966. *Review of the Administration and Operation of the Selective Service System*, Hearings, 89th Cong., 2nd sess. Washington, D.C.: Government Printing Office.

———. 1967. *Extension of the Universal Military Training and Service Act*, Hearings, 90th Cong., 1st sess. Washington, D.C.: Government Printing Office.

———. Special Subcommittee on the Draft. 1969. *Hearings on H.R. 14001 and H.R. 14015, To Amend the Military Selective Service System Act of 1967 to Authorize Modifications of the System of Selecting Persons for Induction into the Armed Forces Under this Act*, 91st Cong., 1st sess. Washington, D.C.: Government Printing Office.

———. Special Subcommittee on the Draft. 1970. *Review of the Administration and Operation of the Draft Law*, Hearings, 91st Cong., 2nd sess. Washington, D.C.: Government Printing Office.

———. 1971. *Extension of the Draft and Bills Related to the Voluntary Force Concept and Authorization of Strength Levels*,

Hearings, 92nd Cong., 1st sess. Washington, D.C.: Government Printing Office.

U.S. Selective Service System. 1961. *Outline of Historical Background of Selective Service and Chronology*, revised edition. Washington, D.C.: Government Printing Office.

————. 1967. *Annual Report of the Director of Selective Service for the Fiscal Year 1966*. Washington, D.C.: Government Printing Office.

————. 1968a. *Annual Report of the Director of Selective Service for the Fiscal Year 1967*. Washington, D.C.: Government Printing Office.

————. 1968b. *Semi-Annual Report of the Director of Selective Service for the Period July 1 to December 31, 1967*. Washington, D.C.: Government Printing Office.

————. 1970. *Semi-Annual Report of the Director of Selective Service for the Period January 1 to June 30, 1970*. Washington, D.C.: Government Printing Office.

U.S. Senate Committee of the Judiciary, Subcommittee on Administrative Practice and Procedure. 1969. *Hearings on the Selective Service System: Its Operation, Practices, and Procedures*. 91st Cong., 1st sess. Washington, D.C.: Government Printing Office.

U.S. Senate Committee on Veterans Affairs. 1972. *A Study of the Problems Facing Vietnam Era Veterans on Their Readjustment to Civilian Life*, 92nd Cong., 2nd sess. Washington, D.C.: Government Printing Office.

U.S. Veterans Administration. 1972. Release of April 11. Washington, D.C.: Office of Controller, Veterans Administration.

Useem, Michael. 1970. "Involvement in a radical political movement and patterns of friendship: The draft resistance community." Ph.D. dissertation, Department of Social Relations, Harvard University.

Verba, Sidney, Richard A. Brody, Edwin B. Parker, Norman H. Nie, Nelson Polsby, Paul Ekman, and Gordon S. Black. 1967. "Public opinion and the war in Vietnam." *American Political Science Review* 61 (June), 317–333.

Verlet, Martin. 1967. "A protest of the young." *Liberation* 11 (January), 29–33.

Von Eschen, Donald, Jerome Kirk, and Maurice Pinard. 1969. "The disintegration of the Negro non-violent movement." *Journal of Peace Research* 3, 215–234.

———. 1971. "The organizational substructure of disorderly politics." *Social Forces* 49 (June), 529–544.

Wallerstein, Immanuel, and Paul Starr, Editors. 1971. *The University Crisis Reader*, Vol. I. *The Liberal University Under Attack*. New York: Random House (Vintage).

Walzer, Michael. 1970. *Obligations: Essays on Disobedience, War, and Citizenship*. Cambridge, Mass.: Harvard University Press.

Wamsley, Gary L. 1969. *Selective Service and a Changing America: A Study of Environmental Relationships*. Columbus Ohio: Merrill.

Weiss, Robert Frank. 1963. "Defection from social movements and subsequent recruitment to new movements." *Sociometry* 26, 1–20.

White House Conference on Youth. 1971. *Report of the White House Conference on Youth*. Washington, D.C.: Government Printing Office.

Wicker, Allan W. 1969. "Attitudes versus actions: The relationship of verbal and overt behavioral responses to attitude objects." *Journal of Social Issues* 25 (Autumn), 41–78.

Wicker, Tom. 1967. "In the Nation: Muhammad Ali and dissent." *New York Times*, May 2.

Williams, Roger Neville. 1971. *The New Exiles: American War Resisters in Canada*. New York: Liveright.

Wilson, Bryan R. 1967. "An analysis of sect development." In *Patterns of Sectarianism: Organization and Ideology in Social and Religious Movements*, Bryan R. Wilson, Editor. London: Heinemann Educational Books.

Wilson, James Q. 1961. "Strategy of protest: Problems of Negro civic action." *Journal of Conflict Resolution* 5 (3), 291–303.

Woefel, Joseph, and Archibald O. Haller. 1971. "Significant others, the self-reflexive act and the attitude formation process." *American Sociological Review* 36 (February), 74–87.

Wright, James D. 1972. "Popular misconceptions, public opinion, and the war in Vietnam: Age, class, and trends in support, 1964–1970." Paper delivered at the annual meeting of the Society for the Study of Social Problems, August.

Zald, Mayer N., and Roberta Ash. 1966. "Social movement organizations: Growth, decay, and change." *Social Forces* 44 (March), 327–341.

Zeitlin, Maurice, Editor. 1970a. *American Society, Inc. Studies of the Social Structure and Political Economy of the United States.* Chicago: Markham.

———. 1970b. "A note on death in Vietnam." In *American Society, Inc. Studies of the Social Structure and Political Economy of the United States,* Maurice Zeitlin, Editor. Chicago: Markham.

Zimmerman, David. 1967. "Disruption and the draft." *Liberation* (November), 34–35.

INDEX